Published by Charlotte Square Press,
3960 Clay Street, Denver, Colorado, 80211
ph: (720) 855-8507
ad maiorem Dei gloriam

Printed by Siler Printing, Denver, Colorado

ISBN 0-914449-20-6

PRINTED IN THE UNITED STATES OF AMERICA

Printing (last digit) 10 9 8 7 6 5 4 3 2 1

GETTING TO KNOW
DENVER

five fabulous walking tours

*A unique historical/architectural guide
that rates downtown Denver's top 100
buildings on a comparative 1-10 scale*

Narrative and photography by
Francis J. Pierson

Foreword by Dennis J. Gallagher

CHARLOTTE SQUARE PRESS
Denver, Colorado

Acknowledgements

No work of this scope gets produced without the aid and inspiration of countless individuals, most of whom I remember appreciatively and a few, undoubtedly whom I will forget to mention. Any such slights are purely unintentional. For all of you wonderful people, named and unnamed -many thanks — including my mother a model of endurance, resilience, and determination.

Archdiocese of Denver –
  Roxanne King
  Jennifer Nowak
  Lynn Sharon
Paul & Chris Bormann
Father Tom Carzon, OMV
Colorado Historical Society
David Eitemiller
Dennis Gallagher
Denver Public Library –
  Western History Staff
John Gross
Nadine Karius
Mapsco, Inc.
  Pat Garcia
  Anna Timmons
Dr. Stephen J. Leonard
Tom "Dr. Colorado" Noel
Jean M. O'Brien
Patrick O'Brien
Wes Price
Andy and Alissa Remstad
Deacon Vern Rompot
Sanborn, Ltd.
Rod Spradling
Tom Visocchi

Table of Contents

Part One – history & background

Part Two — walking tours

respectable business began to shun those addresses, Larimer lost its commercial advantage to 16th and 17th Sts. (early wags referred to 17th as "scratch alley"). The whole orientation of downtown shifted, favoring those streets that connected directly to Union Station. From that time on, the thrust of the city's growth was to the southeast, no longer parallel to the tracks but in a perpendicular orientation. Larimer itself, rife with gambling halls, went into a long decline despite its early "Main Street" status. The real wealth headed southeast towards Brown's Bluff (Capitol Hill) and beyond. By the 1890's this new lateral axis was solidly evidenced by buildings such as the Boston, Equitable, Kittredge, and the imposing Brown Palace Hotel, which anchored the opposite end of 17th St. from Union Station.

Conveniently for historians although painful for the optimistic city (second only to San Francisco in the far West), Denver's gilded age ended abruptly in 1893 with the repeal of the Sherman Silver Purchase Act. This bill was passed in response to a national financial panic that hit the Silver State doubly hard. After recovering from that major depression the city matured and entered a more restrained period of development. I refer to this era from 1896 until 1929 simply as the "mercantile period" after the great stores and warehouses that were built downtown. As Denver expanded its trading area, the city developed new industries unrelated to mining, and simultaneously grew more self-conscious about its image.

Much of the flamboyance which typified the railroad city subsided as a more sober style of building predominated. This was the time when the whole country embraced the "City Beautiful" movement, partly inspired by the Chicago World's Columbian Exposition of 1893. This new wave of development, less exuberant than what preceded it, nevertheless enhanced the city and kept many of its finest architects employed, although recessions and serious labor strife plagued this period. The post-war 1920's brought modest economic growth. Unlike New York's "Jazz Era" boom, America's agricultural hinterlands felt the impending Great Depression well before 1929, and it was not until World War II that the city recovered in earnest from that protracted malaise.

The first real building boom, fueled by mining and railroads, lasted from about 1870 until the Panic of 1893. This was the seminal period in which Denver was transformed from a struggling town into a genuine city. We must not underestimate the importance of the railroad to the city's development as the hub of commerce for the Rocky Mountain region. Initially the city was bypassed by the transcontinental railroad in favor of Cheyenne. Undeterred, the city's business community built a spur line to connect with the Union Pacific. Within two months of this gala event the Kansas Pacific pushed into town from the east (Aug. 15, 1870), putting Denver smack at the center of the first truly transcontinental rail line.

Oddly enough, this happened because the Union Pacific, which terminated in Omaha, did not span the Missouri River for another two years. As a result, the only way to travel by train continuously from coast to coast was via the Kansas Pacific, through St. Louis and Denver. The Union Pacific realized Denver's commercial possibilities as new rail lines began to sprout in every direction - to the south, into the mining districts, even to Texas and the Gulf coast.

In 1881 a cutoff was constructed along the South Platte River, meaning that traffic from the east no longer routed through Cheyenne. That same year the Burlington built a parallel line into town, much to the Union Pacific's annoyance. Competition, however ruinous to the railroads, was a boon to the young city. Despite its geographical improbability, Denver developed into the rail hub of a growing inland empire, underpinned by the gold and silver pouring out of the Rockies.

The city developed vigorously over the next 20 years as numerous supply businesses sprang up near the tracks. Equally important, refining plants for the mineral ores shipped down from the mining camps were constructed. The Globe, Argo, Omaha, and Grant smelters, among others, stained the city's sky with billows of inky smoke which translated into hard currency. A boom town mentality infected the city during the 80's as one grandiose scheme after another was proposed. The bonanza attracted architectural talent from afar, enterprising men who were rewarded with hefty commissions from millionaires with names such as Tabor, Evans, Moffat, and Cheesman.

Early photographs from the 1870s depict a rough, raw community tenuously balanced like a tumbleweed on a barren, treeless plain. Its transformation by the 1890s into a permanent, albeit gritty-looking, metropolis is truly incredible. The railroad gave it flesh and sinews and made it thrive. The railroads nurtured the new city, which in turn fed more business back to the railroads as Denver grew and prospered.

Railroads also helped to establish patterns of development in the embryonic metropolis. In Chicago growth tended to string along the rail lines radiating out from the center, but in Denver this was generally not the case. Initially the major stores, hotels, and office blocks stretched out parallel to the rail lines along Larimer and Lawrence. Early residential development spread northeast from the old business center or southeast along 14th St. for the more well-heeled. The first depot was located around 21st St. and Wazee, currently near the right field fence in Coors Field. In 1870 that was considerably removed from the heart of town along lower 15th St. Larimer was the main drag in any event, but by 1881 the various rail interests had jointly constructed a new, consolidated "Union Station" at the head of 17th St. on Wynkoop. The city abandoned a portion of 17th St. to facilitate the magnificent new depot.

This relocation was instrumental in turning the whole commercial geography of the city around. An unsavory element of gambling dens and prostitution had taken root in lower downtown along Larimer, Holladay (Market), and Blake Streets. As more defacements from intervening years. What emerges are designs of consummate skill and subtle intricacy that point arguably to a "Denver Style," a distinctive variant on the "Chicago School," featuring soft Western sandstones (Brown Palace Hotel) or pinkish rhyolites (Trinity Church) that one rarely observes outside of Colorado.

Rookery Bldg. in Chicago's "Loop" (1886) by Burnham & Root. The airy, interior "court" was effectively re-worked in 1905 by Frank Lloyd Wright

Chicago is still the quintessential model for the trans-Appalachian city, and appropriately it was here that both the vertical skyscraper school and horizontal prairie school were born. Denver is to the Great Plains what Chicago is to the Midwestern Prairie, the urban expression of all the energies produced by their respective geographies. Both were destined, if not from inception, then from the advent of the railroad, to animate and dominate vast hinterlands. But landlocked Denver, a mile above the sea, lacked the natural commercial advantages of Chicago. The semi-arid high plains are arable with proper irrigation, but not so fertile as Iowa. Denver is scenically situated where mountains meet the plains just as Chicago sits at the juncture of lake and prairie.

Mountains, unlike lakes, do not facilitate trade, however. Fortunately for the young city, the hills were rich in mineral wealth, stimulating tremendous growth. Mountain ranges also shield Denver from the harsh climatic conditions that the more exposed Midwest must endure. This salubrious climate pulled in successive immigrant waves who liked the place so well they stayed, jobs or none. People came for the crisp air, the mild weather, the panoramas, and the chance to be in on something bigger, and in time bigger things came. Like the mining camps themselves, Denver grew in fits and starts, periodic tides of great building activity alternating with painful slumps. Roughly we might classify these eras of growth as the Victorian – railroad period, the City Beautiful – mercantile period, and the Modern – jet age.

these two watershed events marked the turning point for each of them. From 1871 onward, both were virtually rebuilt from scratch, although Chicago started from a much larger base.

Aristotle remarked that an acropolis was suited for oligarchy or monarchy but that a plain was best suited for democracy. Both Chicago and Denver, which socially and politically exemplify the values of American democracy, are appropriately built upon the Great Plains. Their rugged frontier spirits of "manifest destiny" and "can do" clearly exemplified America's 19th century outlook. In a sense they are textbook expressions of American culture, unfettered by obstacles, traditions, or geography.

A more uniform "American" civilization became politically desirable in the aftermath of the bloody Civil War. In order to downplay the stresses of sectionalism, the American people strove for hegemony, especially in the newer territories. Immigrants posed a challenge to this hegemony and needed to be "Americanized" as thoroughly as possible, but cultural unity in the midst of great ethnic diversity was not always easy to achieve. The American democracy reconciled the paradox most visibly in Chicago, overflowing with waves of foreign immigrants, yet brash and quintessentially American.

It was in Chicago, flooded by new arrivals yet unbound by old traditions, that architects such as Jenny, Adler, Root, Burnham, Sullivan, and Wright created a new, completely American idiom. Europe was still improvising on the Classical Renaissance. Meanwhile, crude but dynamic communities were bursting into full flower on the American prairie. East coast designers, still pursuing the path of revivalism, were initially alarmed by the bold inventiveness of the Chicago men. The ideas of a French architect, Viollet -le-Duc, had a pollinating effect on Chicago designers like John Welborn Root and his mentor Peter B. Wight, who realized that the greatness of the Gothic form lay in its ability to express structure so plainly and beautifully. Not content to limit Gothic expression to stone, however, they applied the form to metal ribbed buildings, making the "Chicago School" famous world-wide. Iron, steel, and the elevator expanded the builder's options: buildings began to soar as they had not soared since the age of gothic cathedrals.

So successful was this new breed of architect / engineer, that collectively they created a whole new building form capable of fluently expressing a building's structure. The Chicago School gained commissions throughout the expanding Midwest, from Cleveland and St. Louis to Kansas City and beyond. Eventually New York and the coastal cities succumbed to the technological advantages of light, steel frames, which made buildings far more profitable. In remote Denver however, the big Chicago firms were pretty well shut out of commissions as a growing fraternity of local architects managed to satisfy demand. The Denver architects demonstrated a surprising independence from the Chicago School although they certainly utilized the technological innovations.

Probably the physical distance between the two cities gave the smaller burg more independence than it might have been otherwise able to assert. Denver was not content to be a mere outpost somewhere in the penumbra of Chicago, but it developed its own vocabulary, parallel to the larger city, capitalizing on its own pool of talent: architects such as Frank E. Edbrooke, Robert Roeschlaub, Aaron Gove, Arthur & William Fisher, and Montana Fallis. The surviving works of Denver's early designers testify eloquently to their creative brilliance, as recent restorations wipe away the grit and cleverly wrapped an ordinary iron spike in white paper, holding it in such a way that the sun's glint made it seem like silver to the milling throng. The decoy was ceremoniously driven home, crowds cheered wildly, and the celebration commenced. Later, Evans quietly redeemed the real silver spike from hock. Denver, a city that was virtually "willed" into existence by determined boosters such as John Evans, William Newton Byers, and David Halliday Moffat, was off and running.

A thousand miles to the east, a much larger and commercially more viable enterprise was teeming with railroads, factories, and warehouses on the shores of Lake Michigan. Chicago had literally exploded during the Civil War (aided by numerous government contracts) to become the largest city west of the Alleghenies. Some 15 months after Denver celebrated the advent of its railroad, the "Windy City" succumbed to a fire started in a wooden barn. Despite popular legend, it has never been conclusively determined whether the fire was a case of bovine arson. No matter, by Oct. 10, 1871, the central third of the sprawling metropolis was reduced to charred ruins.

Like Denver, the city whose motto became "I will" seemed to thrive on adversity. The largest building campaign in the city's history ensued as Chicago sprang up on an even grander scale. Historians rarely note how lucky Chicago was that the fire did not occur two years later in 1873, when the country was gripped in a major depression that would certainly have affected its recovery. As it was, the city employed every spare architect, mason, and carpenter to be found. When the '73 slump came, one of the few places that managed to continue growing was Denver, busily reaping all that mineral wealth. Naturally, many unemployed tradesmen migrated to the Queen City, where work was available. This is an early example of Chicago's feeding Denver with the human capital it needed to continue its development, a dynamic that has consistently enriched the newer city.

Denver Public Library, Western History Collection   X-19468

Denver's business district still follows Larimer in this 1886 prospect – looking up 17th Street from Union Station. The next five years will witness a dramatic urban transformation as business heads up-town, away from Larimer.

In certain respects, Denver and Chicago were similar during the rapid urbanization between 1871 and 1893. While both cities showed great promise before that time, it was the stimulus of the railroad in 1870 and the Great Chicago Fire in 1871 that set them on respective new courses of growth and development. One could argue that

Chapter 1. Denver – Regional Hub

Whoever knows only his own generation remains ever a child.

Denver's existence has little to do with any natural commercial advantages. The Mile High City exists because of the dogged determination of its early promoters who capitalized on the discovery of a few flakes of "free gold" (placer gold) discovered in some local streams. Rumors of gold sparked an initial influx, but ultimately it was the magnificent, healthful setting that made people stay. Even so, it took a few real gold strikes up in the hills and a bit of scrambling to ensure the town's survival.

After a dozen years of "hanging on" through fire, flood, and Indian wars, Denver's destiny was assured when the "David H. Moffat" chugged into town. The "Moffat" was a steam locomotive named for the intrepid banker who helped pioneer the Denver Pacific Railroad. On June 24, 1870, former Governor John Evans, president of the Denver Pacific, was prepared to drive the ceremonial silver spike marking its completion. A last moment twist clouded the script, threatening to de-rail the historic ceremony, however.

The two miners selected to transport the official, engraved spike down from Georgetown apparently worked up a terrible thirst somewhere along the forty-mile route. Having little available cash, the desperate duo pawned their precious cargo, retiring to a nearby saloon for their own private celebration. The two couriers got rip-roaring drunk and passed out even as Governor Evans waited impatiently for that silver staple. Finally, the resourceful Evans decided that the show must proceed, so he

Denver Public Library, Western History Collection   X-25188
Denver's first Union Station looked like this in the early 1880s. Only the end wings survive, minus the Victorian roof-lines

Courtesy, David Eitemiller,
The Voorhies Memorial, 1920, frames the former Arapahoe County Courthouse.

funding to restore historic facades. We've come a long way!

Preservation has become a viable business as cities reap the benefits from tourism, enhanced tax dollars, and a real sense of place for citizens. If preservation also raises the bar for new buildings, requiring more sensitivity to the street, so much the better. New growth and fresh architecture need to remain a large part of the urban equation, otherwise stagnation has already set in.

A real concern in today's developer driven market is the "great blight of dullness," a term coined by the incisive urban critic Jane Jacobs. Step-and-repeat building technologies result in structures that often ignore the street and disdain older architecture. For example, the imposition of "ego statements" or vanilla three-story "McStucco" facades on an older, brick bungalow neighborhood is reprehensible, even if it may be technically legal. Such venal additions too often mar the urban canvas rather than enriching it.

"Context" is as fundamental to good design as "location" is to good real estate. Without proper context buildings create no sense of place. While it may be impossible (and pointless) attempting to legislate good taste, every professional engaged in the building profession should seriously ponder one question: Is my goal to build an empire or a civilization? New buildings need to respect the longstanding urban tradition of cities as the curators of culture. Architecture is too essential to the city's vitality and well being to be treated as a disposable consumer item. The forty year shelf-life that most "big box" retail developments are designed for is unacceptable in the urban sense. What are we going to leave our children, a bunch of depreciated building stock or an urban legacy? We already live in a throw-away sociaty but does that fact predicate disposable cities as well? If so, then the next generation will be unjustly deprived of a history. Preservation, adaptive re-use, and sensitive new development must go hand in hand it the city is to perpetuate the values of an advanced civilization.

A city's history and architecture are inseparable, and to consider one, we must at least have a working knowledge of the other. While the principal actors in our play are Denver's buildings, the canvas scenery and props are necessarily the city itself, and its rich history. I hope, by interweaving those elements into the plot, to create a fresh and interesting perspective which will make exploring architecture that much more enjoyable.

F J P

Photo by J. J. Karius,
May D&F Hyperbolic Paraboloid under construction about 1954. (demolished)

factors, we ought to keep the urban framework ever before our mind. Why did a particular street or neighborhood evolve this way and not that? No one pretends to have all the answers because the city, like society, is a complicated organism of vast dimensions. Nevertheless, individual buildings tend to reflect the urban conditions that produced them.

I truly enjoy the richness of urban history, and buildings are a sort of time capsules from the past. They express both the period fads as well as the values of former generations. Older buildings are also the evidence of localized conditions and traditions, which can be widely divergent. Compare Santa Fe and Boulder, for example, cities similar in size and geography, yet they are physically world's apart, reflecting their different histories. History is often more at risk in the larger cities because their energy level is so great that the past is easily forgotten or neglected, and too often swept away. Social critics like Henry James were complaining about this very phenomenon even in 19th century New York. Without older landmarks, a city loses that sense of continuity that only relics can supply. Even the present moment suffers if it is entirely cut off from the past.

Cities need new buildings and ideas if they want to maintain their vitality in a changing world. I intend to assume a balanced posture. This book is not intended as a souvenir postcard album that ignores the importance of historic buildings, nor is it excessively nostalgic. The preservation movement was galvanized some 30 years ago by several painful losses, locally and nationally, (e.g., the Moffat Mansion on Grant St. or New York's Pennsylvania Station). Today, the State Historical Society provides sense observation, which in practice never limited his own vocabulary. He called a building "an emotional expression." Sullivan was essentially an Expressionist whose forms flowed equally from structural expression as well as function. His richly ornamented buildings do in fact exhibit very functional lines, but never a hint of sterility or banality.

Later designers, under the influence of the mechanical efficiencies which marked the industrial era, tended to obsess over clean, minimalist forms of almost antiseptic sterility, encapsulated in Mies van der Rohe's maxim *less is more*. In Mies' rigorous scheme, form itself became tangential to his primary objective, the expression of structure. In that sense he was closely allied to Sullivan. For each of them, form derived from structure as much as function, despite their very divergent styles and philosophical differences. More than that, they were able to adapt their works to an unprecedented building type – the vertical structure.

Any essay on Denver's architecture must consider the influence of Mies van der Rohe in the United States after 1945. Although Mies never built in Denver, his svelte metal and glass boxes inspired countless imitators across the country, the most successful being the firm of Skidmore, Owings & Merrill (S.O.M.). His less successful imitators are too legion to catalogue, but their naive belief was that basic geometric forms, stripped to the bone by skimpy budgets, could produce satisfying buildings. Mies himself enjoyed prestige and rarely skimped on details, but eventually even he ran up against the limitations imposed by strict functionalism. Mimicking himself eventually became problematic, a common enough hazard when any successful formula is worked out.

The quip that baroque composer Antonio Vivaldi didn't really compose several hundred compositions, but that he composed the same piece several hundred times, could apply to Mies van der Rohe. Eventually he got mired in his elegant crystaline box motif. Compare his 1952 Lake Shore Drive Apartments to the IBM Bldg. (1969) or Federal Center (completed in 1975), all residing in Chicago. One can only refine a cubicle container so far. Minimalist vocabulary becomes extremely limiting by virtue of its very minimalism. Mies bound himself tightly in formalistic cords of abstract purity from which he could not escape.

In the end the most stunning application of Miesian principles came from his understudies, Schipporeit – Heinrich Associates and Graham, Anderson, Probst, White, who collaborated on the Lake Point Tower (1968) in Chicago. Its sculptural sophistication and undulating glass curtain wall pays undying tribute to the master. It falters however by cutting itself off entirely from the city streets, preening in sublime and self-absorbed isolation, poised on its sterile, elevated podium. Lake Point Tower's impressive sculptural purity, when considered in the urban context, is unfortunately reduced to blatant narcissism. Ultimately the question is not whether Mies exhibited genius – he certainly did – but whether minimalist sculpture, imposed non-deferentially upon city streets, produces a vital, enjoyable urban experience. International Style practitioners forgot that, set apart from cities, buildings are isolated events, like remote farmhouses: mere anomalies on the landscape.

Buildings reflect both an urban context and a historical one, and neither should be neglected. Buildings do not stand alone in a confined sphere, like a sculpture in a gallery. An entire host of factors - historical, social, and economic – contributes to a building's construction. While time may preclude any in-depth study of all these provides it context and viability. In order to understand architecture, a firm grasp of cities is essential. A city has two basic dimensions – the physical, which includes all its spatial relationships, and the historical, which is time overlaid on the physical structure. Well-known French aviator/author, Antoine de St. Exupery, likened cities to large ferry-boats that carried human beings from one end of life to the other. A city represents a time line of countless lives and events, most of which transpire in buildings.

What is the city but a matrix, at once indecipherable, complex, layered, ever re-inventing itself? It can be brute, clashing, ugly, and disfigured, but it has a vitality which draws us to it like a moth to flames. The city can be immensely impersonal; it crushes some and elevates others on a whim. It is a living art, like the theater, which revels in its inconsistencies, humorous anecdotes, and cruelties. Architecture is the backdrop for the theater, which is the city. "All streets are theaters," quoth Ronald Blythe, paraphrasing of Shakespeare's, "All the world's a stage." Buildings are stage sets which create impressions and set the mood for the real life drama which is played out upon them. A good building is more than mere accommodation: rather it inspires human activity.

Architecture, like any art, expresses human values symbolically by way of imagery, i.e., an icon which communicates values to the observer. A building's iconic message reaches far more people than a painting ever could for the simple reasons that it is constructed at a very large scale in a public setting where it generally remains for a very long period of time. Architecture is quite different from other mediums of expression because it enjoys a captive audience. Simply put, you can't hide it like a bad painting. Once a building is up the only correctives are a.) demolition, b.) renovation, c.) planting very tall trees to mask it. The architect is more exposed than other artists. His work isn't easily forgotten like a mediocre play. It has staying power, constant exposure, and the potential either to stimulate human intercourse or blunt it.

Louis Sullivan's well known aphorism *form follows function* has too often been interpreted to mean that form somehow implies the pure essence of architecture. Sullivan was not laying down some implacable ordinance, he was making a common

James believed that towers ought to be symbols of grandeur, untainted by speculative profits. William F. "Buffalo Bill" Cody complained about Denver's modest skyline as far back as 1910.

"Every time I see the new massive steel frames of a skyscraper springing into the air, I cannot but think of the time when a view of the foothills could have been obtained...from any point in the city."

In the end resistance waned and the lofty neighbors gained acceptance in the cities, but the fierce debate raised real questions about air and sunlight, transportation, and sensitivity to environment. If skyscrapers represented a new genre in architecture, how should principles of design and urban planning be applied to them?

Architecture implies something more than an envelope to contain private uses. It also engages in a civic dialogue with its surroundings. Skyscrapers, no less than historic and civic buildings, symbolize the very values and aspirations of a modern city. New York without its skyline would not be New York. Take away the density of Manhattan and spread it out over Long Island, suburban style, and you might still have a city of eight million, but it wouldn't have the feel, the intensity, or the dynamic energy of New York as we know it. Its special identity, its public character, if you will, would be irretrievably altered beyond recognition. The human geography of any place impresses itself on our psyches every bit as much as hills and rivers. Buildings project public images in a sense that few other man made things achieve.

What makes a design great? Two things, I believe. First, clarity of vision. The architect, along with the owner, must grasp some vision, over and above strict utility, that is to be expressed conceptually. A Gothic cathedral, for instance, articulates the sublime faith and spiritual aspirations of its builders. Cathedrals assume a particular form precisely because they are the result of a single-minded vision. Without vision, a building becomes a utilitarian warehouse or worse – a muddle of disconnected elements. Notable Finnish architect Eero Saarinen put it this way: "Buildings should have 'guts' and direction, and make statements. Neutral buildings do not stimulate man's imagination."

The second requirement is organization of the idea, which is the acid test of real genius in any field. We may all have moments of inspiration from time to time, but art requires breaking down an idea into its basic parts and re-combining those components stylistically into a rational, efficient, comprehensive statement. It's the difference between merely having a thought and framing it into a flowing, coherent sentence. Compositional balance is the hallmark of all successful art, be it a symphony, a timeless novel, a beautiful painting, or a noble building. "The only architecture that interests me is architecture as a fine art," remarked Mr. Saarinen. 'Clarity of vision' and 'organization of the idea' are the two essential principles which undergird every mature work, regardless of relative periods or styles. Philosophically, the two ideas are basically in tension because "vision" wants to be expressive and unfettered whereas "organization" is the containment of vision within practical, attainable bounds. The successful resolution of that tension is what makes great art, inspiration that is formed and molded into something concrete. The tension remains, but it is brought into balance.

Architecture is the art of form. It is equally the art of context. Buildings are integrated into their natural environment, the city in this case, and both act upon and are acted upon by it . Every building impacts the city to some degree, while the city

Introduction:
Buildings that shape the City

Rounding the hill-crest sprinkled with gingerbread Victorians, one sees a startling vision of Xanadu: a forest of lofty Promethian towers pressing like giant Sequoias upon the bosom of heaven. Skyscrapers huddle tightly, stacked like sheaves, and compressing into a mountain of steel and glass, symbolizing the modern city like no other building type. "Cathedrals of commerce" was a cachet first applied to New York's Woolworth Building though aptly descriptive of skyscrapers in general. Residing atop these lofty titans, the overseers of modern commerce calculate the various fates of mankind, like the ancient deities dwelling upon Mt. Olympus.

In the space of one century, skyscrapers redefined the city, especially at the heart where air space assumed a value proportionate to its underpinning real estate, strategically and economically. The skyscraper ushered in a novel kind of beauty which required a new aesthetic in order to be appreciated. That aesthetic was not immediately grasped by the Victorian sensibilities when tall buildings began to proliferate, however. A century ago most people were skeptical or outright hostile towards the modestly erect (by today's standards) structures that were then beginning to crop up in urban centers. In fact, restrictive height ordinances were passed in cities such as Washington, Boston, St. Louis, and Denver, where nine stories, later raised to twelve, was set as the upper limit. Today, only the nation's capital continues to enforce those early caps.

American novelist Henry James likened New York's skyline to a broken toothed comb with its ugly ragged spines. Although James admired towers, such as Giotto's Renaissance campanile in Florence, he despised the commercial aspect of the perpendicular office buildings marred, in his opinion, by plethoric window apertures.

example to analyze and apply the criteria, judging why a given structure fits into a particular space. He nudges readers to judge, for themselves, the architectural integrity, mass, and scale of those buildings discussed in the book.

Many years ago, Marshall McLuhan, the renowned Media Ecologist, penned an essay entitled, <u>Media, Messages, and Language: The City as Classroom</u>. Mr. Pierson has done just that for us here in Denver. He has given us an historical text, a sort of analytical workbook, in which Denver becomes the classroom. But it hardly feels like work! It is sheer enjoyment to read, or merely thumb over 180 plus fine photos that dramatically capture the city as it was then, and as it is now. These carefully rendered images become visual aids that help us probe into Denver's history and architecture.

The author has arranged the five walking tours according to the ambiance and unique character of downtown's neighborhoods. Appropriately, he starts out with the Lo-Do Tour, proceeding to the next tour, encompassing Auraria and Skyline. The third tour cover's Denver's old and new downtown core. Interestingly, he selects downtown's eastern edge, around Broadway, along with a slice of Henry Brown's Bluff, adjoining Swallow Hill, as tour four. The fifth tour, like the cloak of St. Bridget of Kildare, envelopes Capitol Hill, Civic Center, and the Golden Triangle. I will be anxious to see how these newly ordered tours of our city catch on. For myself, I can hardly wait to walk them all, with this witful guide-book in hand.

So sharpen your pencils, wink your analytical eye, and become the architectural critic you were meant to be. With Denver as our classroom, get ready to fill in your own architectural "values test." And with <u>Getting to Know Denver</u> in hand, then perhaps, as my mother of blessed memory used to pray, "we might be able to find our bearings in this old cow town."

D J G – April 6, 2006

Foreword

By Dennis J. Gallagher

Francis J. (Fran) Pierson has given us an excellent book on Denver that will surely please and delight the reader with its penetrating photos and candid historical perspectives. More importantly it should challenge anyone interested in learning about the history of the city and it's architecture. I know it would have greatly pleased my mother, Nellie Flaherty Gallagher.

My mother was born on 10ᵗʰ Street, "one block up from 9ᵗʰ Street," on what has lately become the Auraria Higher Education Campus. Her father worked as a bartender in Madden's Wet Goods, on Larimer and 11ᵗʰ Street, just east of the Tivoli. Toward the end of her life, having lived most of it in the Highlands Neighborhood of North Denver – from River Drive, W. 26ᵗʰ and 29ᵗʰ Avenues, finally settling at W. 43ʳᵈ & Quitman Street in Berkeley. My mother often told me how she "hated to go downtown. I don't know where I am anymore," she often complained. "I can't seem to get my bearings. The city has torn down all the buildings and landmarks I knew and loved when I was growing up in this cow town."

She once suggested to me that to help her, and others of her generation trying to navigate around the streets of Denver, the city should erect architectural "visual aids" to assist old timers as to where they were. She thought that each block ought to have plywood "corner cutouts" of those historic buildings that once graced the spaces now sprouting "beer can buildings," as Peter Dominic has christened the new, smooth, glassy cloud-scrapers. Only then would she gain her bearings in the wasteland of parking lots and new, tall buildings with "no place for birds to land on window-sills." She spoke lovingly of having lunch at the Denver Dry Tea Room, and fondly recalled working the coat room at the old Auditorium.

Getting to Know Denver is all about restoring our architectural and historical bearings. In my view, readers will enjoy his book because he not only contrasts Denver's architectural styles to those found in other cities, he offers us an analysis of the various local architectural styles as well as their development and regional influence. He hits the mark about how early architects in Denver, specifically, but also the West in general, felt unbound by particular architectural styles and schools. He describes how they developed their own unique styles, which fit Denver's sense of place. His book will help readers get their bearings for both the old and the new in our city.

I think reader's will like the book for another important reason. Pierson creates an "architectural values guide" that encourages the reader to do more than merely absorb the history of particular buildings. He shows us how to apply his "value guide" to buildings selected for analysis in the text. The five walking tours that he has carefully arranged offer ample commentary and analysis. He challenges the readers to use the "value guide" personally, comparing their own assessments of the structures with his own seasoned eye. In my view, Fran is a little more generous to certain buildings than I would be, but that is part of the fun and challenge of this book. *He encourages the reader to become the architectural critic.* He asks readers to develop their own sense of architectural taste, integrity, and imagination. He pushes the reader to follow his

Denver's third and greatest building boom was sparked by its ideal mid-continent location, a prime asset in the unfolding age of jet travel and Cold War fears of missile attack. This post-war boom rose to a crescendo from 1954 to 1984. The West and the South were regions poised for an unprecedented wave of expansion, and Denver rode that wave along with cities such as Dallas and Atlanta. All three grew exponentially despite the fact that they were landlocked. The advent of mass air travel made a major airport more vital economically than the traditional seaport had been to coastal cities. Not surprisingly, these youthful, landlocked cities benefited from fast expanding airports, which transformed them from ho-hum trade centers into international destinations. By the year 2000 the airports in Denver, Dallas, and Atlanta ranked sixth, fourth, and first, respectively, in the United States, and more incredibly eleventh, fifth, and first in the entire world!

Such a prodigious economic stimulus irreversibly changed the face of all three cities, sometimes translating into painful cultural changes. Much of Denver's historical legacy was thoughtlessly swept aside until the mid-80's real estate bust took some pressure off the surviving historic structures. Even then it took the senseless razing of the Neo-Classic Central Bank Bldg. in 1990 for the city to pass a downtown preservation ordinance with real teeth. Since that time the renovation of important structures has pumped millions into the economy and stabilized the downtown core.

THE CONFLUENCE

Denver sits a mile above the sea atop the Colorado Piedmont, which snuggles up against the spiny Rocky Mountains just to the west. The South Platte River pours out of the Rockies, pursuing a northerly course roughly parallel to the Front Range before bending eastward to water Nebraska. The city grew in an unlikely spot where an obscure creek meandering down from the plains intersected the South Platte. This unlikely stream, Cherry Creek, changed the course of history in 1858 when a few flakes of gold were panned from its banks and other nearby streams. Prospectors called the place Cherry Creek Diggin's. There wasn't much mineral wealth in the creek itself, but the shady confluence of waters provided an ideal trading spot and supply point. When richer strikes were made in the hills in the spring of 1859, the seminal communities along Cherry Creek's sandy banks - Auraria and Denver City - began to thrive.

Denver's formal origins represent one of the more Byzantine chain of events in frontier lore, even by the standards of the wild West. Its early founding involved not one, but two successive claim jumpings before things really got started. Back in September of 1858 an optimistic band of "boomers" named the St. Charles Town Company first realized the potential of a new city along the banks of Cherry Creek. The first problem was that the U.S. government clearly recognized this land as property of the Cheyenne and Arapaho Indians. In order to trade in real estate that wasn't rightfully theirs, the organizers drafted a couple of local traders with Indian wives into the new town company. By October, 1858, another party of fortune seekers was platting another town called Auraria, on the opposite bank of Cherry Creek. The same two traders, John Smith and William McGaa, ostensibly representing Native American interests, gladly endorsed this rival town company as well, for a healthy piece of the action. Thus the first claim jumps were at the expense of local tribes.

Pikes Peak gold fever must have been hotter than the Saturday night poker game just then, because in November, a third party of municipal midwives arrived from Leavenworth and immediately jumped the St. Charles Town Company claim. This second act of larceny might be described today as a "hostile takeover." The original St. Charles Town Company had left behind a half-finished cabin as proof of improvement and one of their own, Charles Nichols, to look after the valuable townsite. When William Larimer's boosters arrived and perceived that this company had wisely chosen the high ground on the east bank of Cherry Creek, they coveted the site, and determined to take possession.

15th Street below Larimer, some time after the Great Fire of 1863. The arched bays of Constitution Hall, which burned down in 1977, are visible on Blake.

After some persuasion, which included vague threats about swinging at the end of a rope, Charles Nichols ceased his vociferous protestations and relinquished any St. Charles' claim to the right bank. His erstwhile comrades, Smith and McGaa, offered him no moral or material support in the confrontation, as they were now situated in relative comfort over on the Auraria side. Another prospector, Sam Curtis, who had been booted out of the original Auraria company for the unpardonable offense of consorting with the St. Charles men, now cast his lot with the new Denver City Town Company. Sam was so glad to be accepted, finally, that he laid out the first streets in the new town, remembering to name one for himself.

In all fairness to General Larimer's Leavenworth party, they ostensibly claimed more lawful credentials than earlier squatters since three of their party had been duly appointed as officers of the newly formed Arapahoe County by territorial governor, James W. Denver. Their interest was in founding the county seat, which arguably gave Larimer's group a quasi-official status. Unfortunately, between the time they left Leavenworth and arrived at Cherry Creek, Governor Denver resigned his post as territorial governor, a fact unknown to them or anyone else in remote Arapahoe County. Nevertheless, Larimer, Ned Wynkoop, E.P.Stout, and the boys proved to be generous and liberally-minded, including Charles Nichols and his partners as stockholders in the new town company. Several town lots were actually deeded to the (now) ex-governor who never quite made it out here until 1882, by which time his lots had been "claim jumped" by others. Denver was a gentleman and never pressed the issue in court, however.

The West had a rough-and-tumble atmosphere. Physical possession meant more than any piece of paper, and a man's rights were enforced with hot lead and a rope. All the early shenanigans, to which Denver owes its existence, were eventually resolved by Congressional action, thus redressing the thorny question, who really owned this land? It was a colorful start to a colorful city, even if a lot of future titles were clouded in the process. Denver never sat on formalities, preferring to operate on the principle that it is easier to beg forgiveness later than to ask permission beforehand.

There must have been something compelling about this particular confluence of creek and river, even before any thoughts of a city existed. I have often pondered why the commercial hub of the West sprang to life at such an unlikely juncture, really no different from a hundred similar watery forks along the river. The site seemed destined for greatness even at a time when it was mainly a campground for indigenous plains Indians, explorers, and mountain men. Early town rivals such as Golden and Boulder were actually more proximate to the gold fields, and even after the railroad arrived in 1870, Golden competed fiercely with Denver, but to little avail.

Denver Public Library, Western History Collection
H-16 Rose & Hopkins
William Newton Byers (1831-1903) raced across the prairie in April, 1859, to found Colorado's first, and oldest, newspaper – the "Rocky Mountain News."

My historical sense is that Denver ultimately prevailed because it was able to attract the necessary human capital. Great cities are places that attract and hold on to talented people. Determined and capable dreamers of empire such as William Larimer, Henry C. Brown, William Byers, and Walter Cheesman, among others, literally "willed" the primacy of Denver. They brought with them the grit and determination to make their venture succeed, whereas typical town promotion schemes in that restless age routinely withered on the vine. Fortune also played a crucial role by smiling on the efforts of these men.

History teaches us that success is just as often the result of luck as pluck. Denver might have stagnated if those early Clear Creek gold strikes had occurred in more remote locations such as the San Juan Mountains in southwestern Colorado. Fate cooperated with Larimer's party, however, and by the time the first train rolled into town, Denver (now combined with Auraria) was the undisputed political and business address for Colorado.

Cherry Creek, flowing northwest, and the South Platte, pointed northeast, form a crude right-angle where the new city was platted. The town fathers laid out streets in the most efficient orientation, at right-angles to the watercourses, thus avoiding triangular lots and blocks: nothing fancy, streets 80' wide, lots 25' wide X 125' deep, divided by 16' alleys. There was only one flaw in the scheme – no white man had a legal title to the land at the time. But the Cheyenne and Arapaho Indians were easy-going landlords and didn't quibble the point. Later Congress cleared the matter up by deeding a 960-acre Congressional land grant to the "de facto" community.

By the time government surveyors, working off of the 6th Principal Meridian in eastern Kansas had laid out orderly rectangular sections based on the four compass points, the street grid was well established, a full 45 degrees off kilter. Practically speaking, the two grids had to reconcile at some point. The points (or lines really) where the twain would meet became Broadway and Colfax Ave. which is why to this day downtown Denver sits catty-wampus to the rest of the city. As a result, a lot of triangular pie slices popped up along the two principal thoroughfares, which explains why the Brown Palace Hotel is shaped like a big cheese wedge. Furthermore, many of the older streets didn't align particularly well with the new ones, a problem that still bedevils traffic planners.

In an attempt to rectify things, at least schematically, the town planners determined that 16th, 17th, 18th, 19th *Streets*, etc. should tie into 16th, 17th, 18th, 19th *Avenues* as they cross Broadway, where everything bends like a dog's hind leg. The nomenclature is subtle, and often confusing, when searching out an address. Numbered *Streets* are used only in the downtown grid west of Broadway (and north of Colfax Ave.), and numbered *Avenues* are used east of Broadway and south of Colfax Ave. In both cases the block numbering begins at Broadway and increases as one moves further away from Broadway (e.g., 600 16th St. is in the downtown grid six blocks northwest of Broadway; 600 E 16th Ave. is conversely six blocks east of Broadway on Capitol Hill).

Denver basks in the shadow of, not one but two, impressive skylines, one man-made, and the other thrown up by forces of nature. It is an interesting coincidence that both skylines, natural and human, are dominated by three peaks which stand head and shoulders above the closest rivals. The natural skyline is the implacable barrier known as the Rocky Mountains, which thrust their granite shoulders so steeply into the Colorado sky that early Denver faced a great commercial disadvantage. There was no feasible way to extend rail lines to the west. Even the early air routes of the 1930s were funneled through Cheyenne, far to the north, in order to avoid the perils associated with flying the mails over the jagged Rockies. As technologies advanced, the mountains were tamed by rail and air.

The alpine barrier that had once seemed such a liability conversely proved to be a tremendous asset. The one thing the arid city needed more than transportation links was water, and those same mountains provided the precious fluid in abundance. They also create the most scenic backdrop of any North American city, a 175-mile panorama of purple mountain majesties and snow-capped peaks.

Colorado has more "fourteeners" (mountains over 14,000' tall) than the other 49 states combined. Most of these are recessed deep within the Rockies, while only four settled along the front ranges. One of the four, Mt. Bierstadt, is hidden in the

penumbra of Mt. Evans so that only three - Longs Peak, Mt. Evans, and Pikes Peak –
are visible from the city. These towering sentinels are widely spaced, about 50 miles
separating each, Longs in the northwest, Evans to the west, and Pikes directly south
of Denver. On clear winter and spring days, their white caps are stunning as they
loom, magnified like a rising harvest moon, over the ebullient city. Longs Peak is the
most prominently situated with respect to downtown, magnificently framed by 16th,
17th, 18th Sts., etc., as through an astronomer's telescope. How fortunate it is that the
early speculators who laid Denver out arrived ahead of the government surveyors,
thus inadvertently conserving this tremendous view.

A mile or so east of the South Platte, the sandy ground underpinning downtown
steepens temporarily to create Capitol Hill, so-named because it is presided over by
the gray granite State Capitol. From here the view fans out to the west, dominated by
the stately mass of Mt. Evans and its ancillary peaks. Sixty-five miles away
Colorado's most famous mountain, Pikes Peak, reigns over Colorado Springs. It
represents the eastern limit of the entire Rocky Mountain chain, extending from
Canada into Mexico, and completes the sweep of nature's saw-toothed skyline which
majestically flanks our city on two sides.

Denver is terminally landlocked, unable to boast a Statue of Liberty in her harbor
or the Golden Gate at her doorstep, but she is guarded by three great sentinels
proclaiming this as a geographic pinnacle, the Switzerland of North America. It is
difficult to conceive a more dramatic setting for a city, lesser perhaps in magnitude
than its great coastal counterparts, but with a distinctly favorable geography upon
which to build and imprint her personality.

A brief sketch of the overall downtown skyline might be helpful. While New York
City evokes the medieval towers of San Gimignano in Tuscany, tall and slender,
Denver, like most American cities, does not possess that quality of lightness. New
York's skyline spreads over a five-mile swath of Manhattan; Denver's is dense and

compact, dropping off suddenly on the edges. This abruptness is a result of several view ordinances south of Colfax, meant to protect the scenic vistas of Mount Evans and the Front Range. Consequently, the only place really tall buildings are allowed is in the core downtown area. These restrictions have created a certain advantage for Denver in giving it a very concentrated skyline, a mass of height, which is surrounded by a ring of moderately-sized five to fifteen-story buildings.

Denver's skyline does not soar so much as it masses, congeals, and closes ranks, especially when viewed from the northwest. From this perspective the whole skyline comes sharply into focus, layered and sculpted, perhaps not a romantic vision but a strong, virile one. From the southwest, buildings spread out along the 17th St. axis, more reminiscent of Manhattan. The view from City Park is undeniably impressive with its mountain backdrop, but my favorite vantage point is from the northwest heights, across the South Platte Valley. Whatever else you may think of its architectural merits, there is no denying the strength of this skyline when viewed from the Highlands neighborhood. No single building is especially remarkable, yet each contributes to the blend. What makes this skyline work is its cohesive compactness. It may lack the delicacy of San Gimignano, but it successfully emulates the huskiness of Chicago without scaling towards brutishness.

Overall, Denver's downtown is a congenial mix of the big city and midwestern Main Street. Victorian-era development was subsequently overlaid by the trappings of an aspiring mercantile city - more cosmopolitan, detectably self-conscious. All that pre-Depression era building, compressed into a 50-year period, attracted much architectural talent, of course.

The dean of early Denver architecture was Frank E. Edbrooke, later joined by his nephew, Harry W. J. Edbrooke, son of the nationally respected Willoughby J. Edbrooke. The Edbrookes were part of a prolific clan of builders originating in Chicago. The gifted brothers William E. and Arthur A. Fisher, who hailed from Canada, were equally prolific and talented builders on the Denver scene, as was the flamboyant Beaux Arts genius Jacques J. Benedict, a Chicago native. Robert Willison and Montana Fallis, an engineering innovator, each worked in Frank Edbrooke's office but later formed their own very productive partnership. Still another team of brothers, Merrill H. and Burnham F. Hoyt, flourished to become, perhaps, Denver's most renowned native-born architects. Burnham was responsible for the Red Rocks Ampitheatre, with its marvelous natural acoustics.

Mention of one more prominent firm, Gove and Walsh, is a must. Aaron Gove grew up in Denver. His future partner, Thomas F. Walsh, began his career with Willoughby J. Edbrooke (brother of Frank) in Chicago. He later spent six years with the famous firm Holabird & Roche before migrating to Denver, where he joined up with Aaron Gove in 1894.

Firms such as these gave Denver a distinct architectural identity and a certain stylistic independence until World War II, after which larger international trends engulfed the profession, reconfiguring the city's face. Surviving remnants of their original works still grace much of the downtown area however, a reminder that Denver may have been isolated geographically, but it was never a backwater. It constantly maintained a viable independence, establishing its own traditions and extending regional influence until the great changes after World War II that dramatically redirected the building professions everywhere.

Chapter 2. Scaling Denver's Buildings 1-10

What makes good architecture? Two things, I believe. First, clarity of vision. The architect, along with the owner, must grasp some vision, over and above strict utility, that is to be expressed conceptually. Gothic cathedrals assume a particular form precisely because they are the result of a single-minded vision. Second, organization of that vision as a logical, unified expression. Without a vision, a building becomes a utilitarian warehouse. Without organization, it devolves into a muddle of disjointed elements. The famous Finnish architect Eero Saarinen put it this way: "Buildings should have 'guts' and direction, and make statements. Neutral buildings do not stimulate man's imagination."

Buildings are the physical stuff of cities and therefore define the city to a great extent. In order to find a method for comparing each building to any other,

Courtesy, David Eitemiller,

Security Bldg. about 1925, by Arthur and William Fisher, 17ᵗʰ & California (demolished). Frank Edbrooke's California Bldg highlights the right foreground.

regardless of style, age, or size – we will consider the universal attributes. Thus we can fairly compare a local landmark with some famous structure, half a continent away if we wish. Such attributes can be extracted through simple observation. Considering only buildings within the urban context, I have identified three primary attributes: *Public Character, Form, and Expression.*

Just as an artist composes a painting on his canvas, setting the subject, foreground, and background in compositional balance, the architect does the same. He must place his subject – a building – on the urban canvas, balancing it against foreground and background, namely the street and surrounding buildings (*Public Character*). Next the artist outlines the figures on canvas, just as the architect outlines the building on the site (Form). Finally the artist adds the color and details that bring the painting into sharp focus, while the architect fills in the frame with windows, walls, doors, and all the trim that creates a detailed finish (Expression). Simply stated, *Public Character* is how well a building integrates with its surroundings, *Form* is its outline, and *Expression* addresses specific details like color, texture, materials, and placement of external elements.

In order to judge these three attributes, we can sub-divide each into its constituent parts, thus giving us six criteria for purposes of rating. A building's *Public Character* is determined by its "street connection" and "public spaces." The *Form* is derived from its "scale" and "mass," and the *Expression* determined by its "integrity" and "imagination." Not all six criteria are equally important, although they are certainly interdependent. I consider that *Public Character* is most important for the people who must use the building. As such, it merits slightly more weight than *Form* and *Expression*. After deriving the six independent scores, averaging them nets a cumulative rating somewhere between 1 and 10.

ARRANGEMENT OF THE FIVE WALKING TOURS

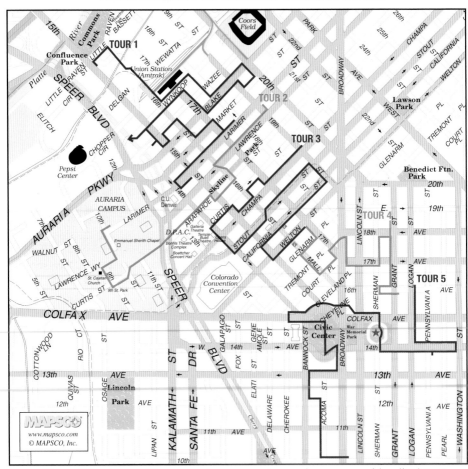

The walking tours utilize a running commentary and are arranged by districts. I have subdivided the downtown area into five smaller districts, which are not arbitrary but reflect the history and makeup of their respective geography. Each district has its own character or perhaps specialized functions unique to it, such as a convention center or live theaters. The historic Lo-Do district, for instance, is very distinct from its surrounding districts because of the age and style of its buildings. Lo-Do adjoins Auraria and Skyline (second tour), which are just the opposite, filled with large, newer buildings but accentuated by a few historic holdover here and there. (Urban renewal "sanitized" these largely historic areas back in the 1960s and 70s, but they have since managed to develop their own unique characters.)

The third district is a healthy blend of old and new, the "heart" of downtown. The fourth district abuts downtown's eastern flank where huge office buildings "feather" out, perhaps a bit abruptly, into the residential Swallow Hill neighborhood. Finally, the fifth district ranges over Capitol Hill, Civic Center, and the emerging "arts district" in the Golden Triangle. I have attempted to string the different walking tours together so that the last building in one chapter is reasonably close to the first building in the next. This way there is some continuity to the flow, especially if you have the time and energy to tackle two or three tours in one excursion.

Using the five subdivisions (Lower Downtown, Skyline, etc.), the top hundred buildings are numbered according to their walking tour order, and identified by name and street address. The original architect(s) is listed with the year the structure was completed. A running commentary will fill in the history, surroundings, interesting architectural features, and give a critical commentary relating to the numeric grades (1 through 10) in each of six categories. The score in each category is then multiplied by its weighted value, either 15 or 20, and added to the others. The cumulative total is divided by 100 to determine a building's final score.

Earlier I stated that good architecture needs two things: clarity of vision (a theme) and organization of the idea (development of theme). The score is a combination of those two requisites, the quality of the theme, or concept, and how well that concept is developed, or applied, in the overall scheme. For instance, if we want to grade how well the XYZ Building "Meets the Street," we might consider it a negative that the loading dock is all that can be seen from the street while the main entry for people is hidden near the alley (a poorly-conceived idea). Furthermore, suppose the sidewalk gets blocked every time a delivery is made (poor organization). We would feel justified in giving that building a low score, perhaps a 2, for how well it "Meets the Street." The table below reflects the meaning of each scale value from 1 to 10.

The values 1 through 10, in all six categories follows these general guidelines:

1. = Failing – terrible concept, thoughtless organization
2. = Poor – uninspired concept, poorly organized
3. = Marginal – poor to mediocre concept and organization
4. = Below Average – marginal idea and organization
5. = Average – credible concept, decent organization
6. = Above Average – acceptable concept, good organization
7. = Good – good concept, very well-organized
8. = Excellent – very good concept, superior organization
9. = Exceptional – artistic concept, exceptionally organized
10. = Masterpiece – sensational concept, masterfully organized

Note: Organization also refers to the quality of workmanship and materials employed in the building.

DENVER'S PREVALENT STYLES

Before beginning our first tour, a brief description of the more common styles seen in downtown Denver might be helpful for the layman. Remember, the actual score given to any building is independent of its architectural style. The important considerations are how well a building interacts with its neighbors, and how truly it reflects its particular style.

Historically, certain design trends periodically sweep across the country, and Denver, being centrally located, was largely affected to some degree by each of them. Here is a short description of some of the more important styles that are represented in the downtown area, excepting the more residential styles such as "Queen Anne," "Bungalow," or even the so called "Denver Squares." Most of our subjects are commercial and institutional buildings in the downtown environment. The following is only the barest thumbnail classification intended for the casual observer. A real in depth breakdown of architectural styles would entail an entire volume or more.

Rocky Mountain big horn sheep carved by Gladys Caldwell Fisher.

Classicism – This is a broad heading that encompasses several styles, from the Greek Revival, which generally spent itself by the Civil War, to Neo-Renaissance and Classical Revival styles that remained popular well into the 20th century. During Denver's early developmental stage, classical styles were frequently translated eclectically, underlining the fact that many of her early architects were not formally trained but pulled ideas out of "pattern books." Columns, friezes, moldings, pediments, and arches were finishing touches generally applied to a blank wall for effect.

The former Post Office, now the Byron White Courthouse, is one of the few exceptions, representing a fully-integrated example of Classical Revivalism. The architect was not local in that case, but worked on the East Coast. Denver's better examples of Classicism tended to be associated with the Beaux Arts movement (see below). Most often, Neo-Renaissance here equates with Italian Renaissance, including its 19th century derivative - the so called Italianate style which, along with the French Second Empire style, captivated the popular imagination before fading prior to 1900.

Gothic Revival – The Gothic Revival gained steam worldwide throughout the 19th century, greatly abetted in the United States by the construction of St. Patrick Cathedral in New York, also influenced by the works of Ralph Adams Cram. (Cram's lone Denver church still stands: St. Andrew's Episcopal at 20th St. and Glenarm Pl.) This movement exerted a substantial influence on Denver's church architecture. The so-called "Victorian Gothic" residential and commercial style never caught on big, however. The finest examples of Gothic Revivalism are undoubtedly its two cathedrals, Immaculate Conception, representing the French tradition, and St. John's, in the classic English style. Both are easily compared, since they sit only blocks apart.

Richardsonian – Often referred to as Richardson Romanesque because of the heavy massing and Romanesque detailing, this style is named after the influential Henry Hobson Richardson who lived and worked in Boston until his untimely death in 1886. His use of rusticated stone, Romanesque features, and heavy, yet handsomely sculpted massing was widely imitated. Trinity Church in Boston is considered his masterpiece, but his Allegheny County Courthouse in Pittsburgh was equally influential. His greatest commercial building was the Marshall Field Warehouse in Chicago, which was demolished after a mere 43 years, a shorter life span than its creator's, who tragically died at the age of 47. Several early Denver architects, notably Franklin Kidder, Varian & Sterner, William Lang, and Frank E. Edbrooke, were undoubtedly influenced by Richardson's work.

Detail of Kittredge Bldg.

Beaux Arts – The *Beaux Arts* movement, which flourished worldwide from the 1880s until the late 1920s, is not really a style of architecture, but a design philosophy that upholds beauty as its primary object. In practice the rigorous *Beaux Arts* training formed a school of architects whose designs are characterized by formal symmetry. The essence of a *Beaux Arts* building is its composition, and all else, including the form, flows from that. Theoretically, the *Beaux Arts* encompassed all styles and periods of architecture, although it generally adhered to Academic Classicism. The architect was free to be as eclectically inventive as he chose, assuming the end result was beautifully composed, ordered, and symmetrical. Therefore, it was permissible to mix and match Doric and Ionic elements, or to place a Gothic spire above a Classical pediment as long as it was done tastefully.

The *Beaux Arts* encompasses the planning process as well as architecture, with respect to a formal visual axis, fixed heights, setbacks, and even landscaping. In a sense, Denver's best example of the *Beaux Arts* would be Civic Center. Individual buildings are essentially elements, a continuation of the pre-ordered layout. Form evolves from compositional order, mathematically determined, not from structure and nature (as the Expressionists would prefer) or function (as the modernists held).

Academically, the *Beaux Arts* wielded its influence through the famous *l'Ecole des Beaux Arts* in Paris, but its popular success in America can be traced directly to the gleaming "White City" of 1893. That seminal Chicago World's Fair exposed countless millions to the philosophy of urban beauty, precisely at a time when wretched industrial cities trapped millions in miserable slums. These same cities were strained to address the problems resulting from rapid industrialization. A major depression also coincided with the fair, further inducing people to long nostalgically for the past. The Arcadian vision caught on, bolstering the *Beaux Arts* ideal, which flourished well into the 1920's as the "City Beautiful" movement.

Denver was especially affected by this wave of enthusiasm for civic beauty and renewal. An opportunistic politician named Robert W. Speer was able to ride that wave into the mayor's office, and he delivered what his constituents wanted – a beautiful city. Corruption and ballot stuffing aside, Speer became the town's most beloved mayor because, over the course of 14 years, in and out of office, he transformed a gritty Victorian town into a beautiful, grandiose city.

The most renowned of Denver's *Beaux Arts* architect was the colorful and flamboyant Jacques J. Benedict, followed closely by Gove & Walsh, and the Fisher brothers, William E. and Arthur A., who created their own remarkable legacy. Each firm experimented with different styles, including Art Deco and early Modernism, with surprising success. Strictly speaking, this was not a violation of the principles of the *Beaux Arts* which allowed for substantial stylistic latitude. Broadly considered, the more eclectic the better, as long as compositional balance, symmetry, and beauty are resultant. The *Beaux Arts* is both an uncompromising and yet flexible form that permits unlimited creativity within certain fixed boundaries.

Expressionism (American) – This is a very broad term, not to be confused with the European Expressionism of Erich Mendelsohn, Antoni Gaudi or Victor Hotra and the Art Nouveau movement. I use it in a purely American context, basically architecture that is informal, organic, and free of classical traditions. Expressionism is neither a school nor a movement, but a loose genre of various vernacular styles that proliferated from about 1880 into the 1920s, roughly spanning the adult life of Louis Sullivan, who certainly personified it.

American Expressionism was essentially non-academic and colloquial, as were many of its gifted practitioners. Consider Louis Sullivan, Charles and Henry Greene, Purcell & Elmslie, Bernard Maybeck, and Frank Lloyd Wright, all of whom tended to design in a distinctly American idiom. Shingle Style, Prairie School, Sullivanesque, and the Craftsman movement, were all were basically informal and home grown; grounded in nature and the ideas of writers like John Ruskin. My intent is not to lump all these indigenous styles into one school but to associate them loosely together because, for one thing, they typically aroused the hostility of the academic establishment.

I imagine that it was not the inherent creativity of these various efforts, but their lack of systematic order that spelled their doom. No self-respecting Beaux Arts or Modernist practitioners were going to give much credence to what they viewed as "seat of the pants" design, no matter how sophisticated it appeared to be. These organic styles lacked a historical pedigree, for one

Merchants National Bank in Grinnell, Iowa. An example of Louis Sullivan's ornamental detail.

thing, and had little in the way of systematic design principles or social philosophy. Like all folk art, they were the intensely personal expression of incredibly gifted and independent-minded men. Each architect seemingly created his own vocabulary.

Denver was blessed by a number of such talented designers, notably Robert Roeschlaub, William Lang, the Baerressen brothers, and John J. Huddart, for whom originality usually trumped stylistic purity. The most "Sullivanesque" member of this loose fraternity was undoubtedly Harry W. J. Edbrooke, Frank's nephew and eventual partner, who had matured in Louis Sullivan's shadow before heading west from Chicago around 1908.

Commercial Style – It would certainly be appropriate to refer to this uniquely American idiom as the "Chicago Commercial Style." Chicago's frontier vitality and the opportunity to build anew from scratch after the Great Fire of 1871 seemed to energize a whole school of engineer / architects who revolutionized the way commercial buildings were designed and constructed. This auspicious group included

William Le Baron Jenney, John Welborn Root, Dankmar Adler, Daniel Burnham, William Holabird, Martin Roche, and the young Louis Sullivan, who was only a teenager at the time of the Chicago Fire. Most of them were trained as engineers, what little formal training they could boast, and their design abilities seem to have been instinctive rather than schooled.

The former Continental Oil Bldg. at 18th & Glenarm Pl. (demolished)

The human catalyst for this remarkable group was the Boston architect Henry Hobson Richardson. Richardson's Marshall Field Warehouse (1887) turned the corner by setting a new aesthetic standard in the city. This powerful statement, part Roman Palazzo; part Renaissance fortress, executed on a modern commercial scale, was soon followed by Adler & Sullivan's Auditorium Building, which it undoubtedly influenced. The massive Auditorium gave Chicago a whole new identity and sense of confidence. Within the decade the modern commercial, steel-framed business block had evolved, with its lean, spartan look, devoid of meaningless historical alliterations. The design proved so efficient that it was repeated endlessly around the world. The only real change over the next century was in the exterior skin, or "wrap." Later architects such as Cass Gilbert and Raymond Hood wrapped the gridded frame in Gothic trappings, or Mies van der Rohe, who used glass and bronze, precisely because the versatile Chicago frame offered such great flexibility.

The architect who popularized the "Chicago Commercial" style in Denver was Frank E. Edbrooke, whose brother, Willoughby J. Edbrooke, maintained a successful Chicago practice. Edbrooke was Denver's dean of early commercial architecture, though not its exclusive proponent. Conditions were somewhat different here, and though the engineering took its lead from developments on the lake, the actual designs in Denver reflected local tastes and building materials.

Art Deco – Just as the American skyscraper style was reaching to the sky and finding its own voice, the market collapsed in 1929. Before skyscraper building faded entirely, however, it combined with the sleek, decorative Art Deco movement to produce some of this country's most enduring landmarks. Art Deco was fond of abstract motifs executed in a streamlined manner. The geometry was flowing and tolerably curvaceous, combining elements of the florid Art Noveau with the abstract angularity of Modernism.

This was the architecture of the "Jazz Era" – buoyant, colorful, and energetic without being overtly academic. Ornament still counted for something, although it tended to be geometrically rather than historically based. New York, Miami, and L.A. are still the primary centers of Art Deco. The Empire State Building and the top of the

Chrysler Building may well represent its culmination but it was nevertheless a far-reaching movement for a time.

Denver's Art Deco catalogue is extremely limited, but thanks to Montana Fallis and Jacques Benedict, the style is at least represented here. It is a uniquely American idiom, which seems to derive energy from Sullivanesque Expressionism, but also exhibits Art Moderne overtones. It evokes vague memories of Prohibition, with its flappers, bobbed hair, and dark-suited hoods peddling bathtub gin.

Modernism – Again we are dealing with an exceptionally broad term that includes many separate developments and styles. Modernism essentially came out of the devastating social / cultural aftermath of World War I. Whether the particular manifestation was Constructivist, Bauhaus, or International Style, these all had one thing in common – a general disassociation from the past. In that sense, Modernism was a utopian experiment from the start: a way to build a new, more perfect civilization on the ruins of the old. Modern technology, rather than traditions, was to be the basis of this new system.

Architecturally speaking, its vernacular is one of extreme geometric simplicity: lines, planes, and angles that replaced the classical orders and motifs. Angularity and minimal expression were equated with a no-nonsense functionality that regarded decoration as bourgeois excess. Even the transitional language of the Art Deco was more or less swept away by the purity of Modernism.

"Dancers" grace the Adams Mark Hotel by I. M. Pei, still one of Denver's finer Modernist efforts.

Modernism was initially a European phenomenon, though it did not really gain a foothold in the United States until the deteriorating political situation in Europe forced many of the Modernist academics, such as Walter Gropius, to emigrate. Although its proponents took the country by storm, its ideals assumed an American flavor. Mies van der Rohe and Skidmore, Owings, & Merrill completely redefined the "gothic tower" skyscraper form, popularizing the "glass box" concept, based on abstract geometry. Historical allusions and ornament were stripped away to reveal pure form and structure.

Modernism actually split into several related but different channels as the horizontal International Style evolved vertically in North American cities. Corbussier and Mies represented two very different approaches to Modernism and each had numerous disciples and imitators. By the 1960s Miesian, Brutalist, and Formalist variations on Modernism had all gained degrees of acceptance.

Because of the Great Depression, Modernism arrived late in Denver, but in the post-war period it took hold with a vengeance, prompted by the early works of the gifted I. M. Pei. Local architects had trouble getting the thing down, however. Their soaring shafts perversely insisted on coming out of the mold looking more like cheap plastic toys than minimalist sculpture. Over the next 30 years, various modern forms proliferated with mixed results locally, the better examples tending to come from outside firms such as S.O.M., Minoru Yamasaki, and Kohn Pederson Fox.

Post Modernism – Sometime in the mid-1960s an intellectual reaction to the repetitive severity of Modernism began to occur resulting in a movement towards eclectic forms and away from the rigid formality of Modernism, which by the late 60s was becoming hopelessly redundant. Robert Venturi and Michael Graves were two of its more articulate advocates. Post-Modernism has since mushroomed on both the planning and architectural levels. While using modern forms, techniques, and materials, it tends to reorganize traditional elements, providing a freer, and sometimes surrealistic, use of ornament. On occasions it elicits a cartoonish quality, but just as often it blends various styles and metaphors energetically, if not always smoothly.

This new eclecticism continues to gain acceptance on the Denver architectural scene. This in turn has encouraged "Retro" and "Historicist" efforts as well. Michael Graves set the standard with the new Denver Public Library and several local firms, such as 4240 Architecture Inc. and Buchanan & Yonushewski, have continued successfully on the path.

In the wake of Post Modernism, Deconstructivism found a hearing, although it seems essentially to be more about sculpture than architecture. The best example is the new Art Museum wing by Daniel Liebeskind, but otherwise it seems to be another European import, with only marginal local influence.

Post-Modern guru Michael Graves extended the Denver Public Library in 1992. It simultaneously shocks and soothes the senses.

TOUR 1: OLD DENVER CITY, i.e. "LO-DO"

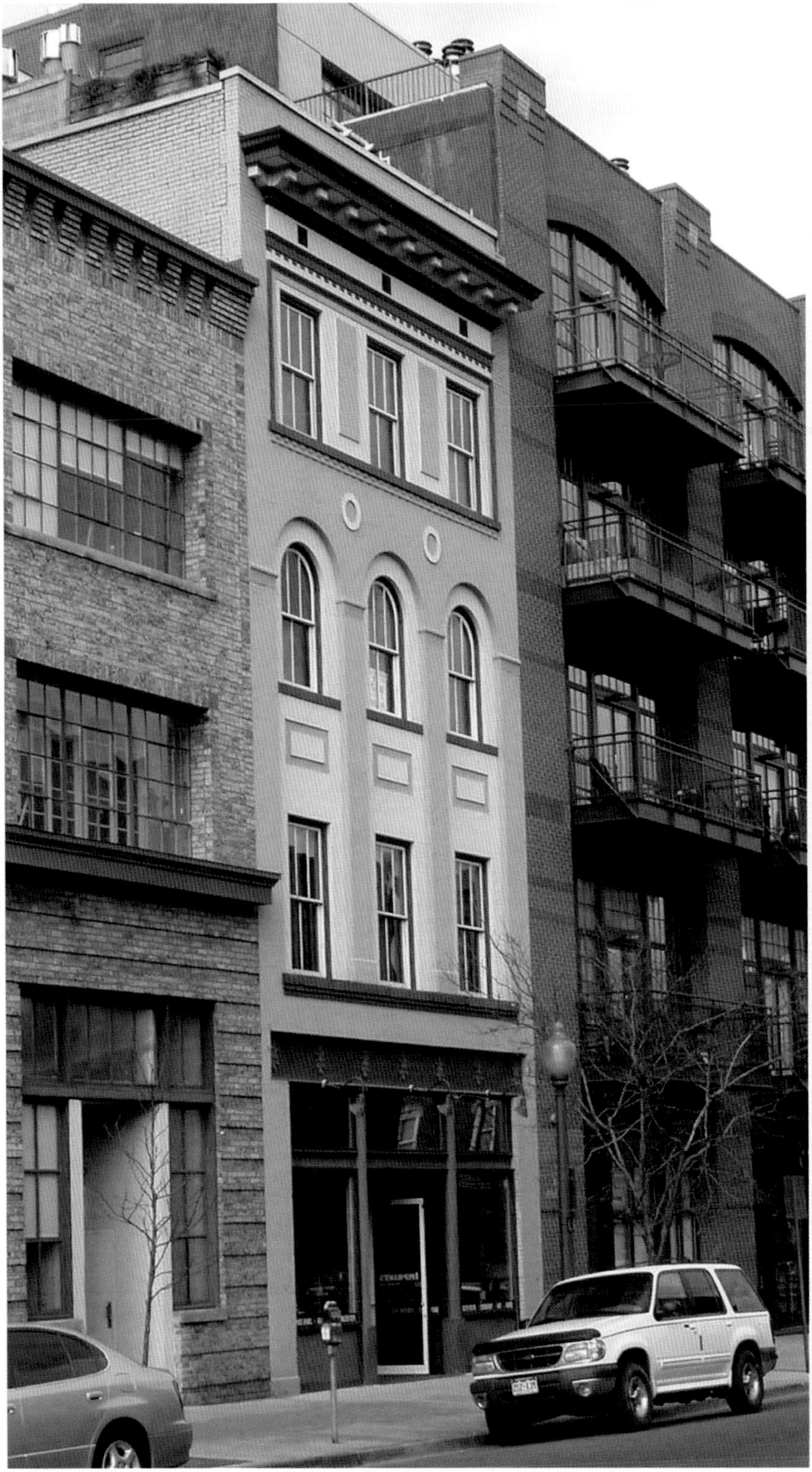

Tour 1. Old Denver City, i.e "Lo-Do"

"Go west young man, go west!" Horace Greeley, 1859

Tour 1.   *Length 2.5 miles.*   Begins at 15th & Little Raven.
Ends at 14th & Larimer.

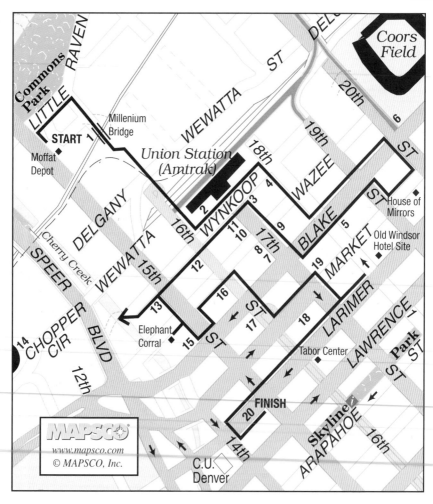

The Confluence, where old and new are juxtaposed, is a natural place to begin. Commons Park and the quill mast of Millenium Bridge herald the 21st century, anchoring a spanking new neighborhood where boxcars once provided the only scenery. This is the locale where Denver's history began to unfold, the confluence not only of streams, but of ideas and cultures as well. Try to visualize the situation during the pleasant Indian summer of 1858 along the meandering banks of Cherry Creek. Cottonwood groves shaded the grassy flood plain, providing shelter from incessant sun and wind. Roving bands of Arapaho, Cheyenne, and Utes camped here regularly, trading with various trappers and mountain men who rendezvoused at the confluence. The restless breeze signified more than a change of seasons however. Bigger changes were in the air. The meeting grounds were teeming with new activity, precipitated by rumors of gold that buzzed around Kansas Territory.

Legend has it that Arapaho Chief Hosa, known as Little Raven, greeted white prospectors with the admonition, "Take the gold! But remember, the land belongs to us, and don't stay too long." The local Arapaho and Cheyenne tribes became restless landlords as the numbers of white men multiplied, almost daily. Within a period less than two months, four town companies were formed. By December, 1858, some 75 to 80 rough-hewn cabins peppered the pastures bordering Cherry Creek. The rightful owners watched warily as the newcomers busily engaged in the surveying, parceling, buying and selling of real estate to which they had no clear title. Gold meant little to the plains Indians, who counted wealth in terms of ponies and the great herds of buffalo, which roamed the plains. In their eyes the land was everything.

Our walking tour begins at the corner of 15th and Little Raven Streets near today's Confluence Park, situated at the point where Cherry Creek is absorbed into the South Platte. In 1858 the river meandered at will over this grassy flood plain, making two great loops, or ox-bows, to the southeast. At the time Cherry Creek branched off some 200 yards south of here. Later on the river straightened out its course, but the old confluence that Little Raven and General Larimer would have known was situated about 100 yards downstream from the railroad bridge, along today's Cherry Creek bike trail. The waterways were so derelict that Mark Twain took one look at the South Platte and quipped, "Why if it were my river, I wouldn't leave it out at night for fear that some dog might come along and lap it all up." This unpromising juncture of two lackadaisical streams was destined to give birth to the great metropolis of the Rockies, however.

Little Raven's Arapaho band, bivouacked at the confluence, formed an unofficial welcoming committee during that balmy autumn. According to early accounts, Little Raven had a keen, inquisitive mind as well as the stoic outlook of a plains tribesman. He was one of the great "Peace Chiefs," along with Cheyenne leaders Left Hand and Black Kettle, all of whom earnestly attempted to pursue a policy of co-existence with the white men. Initially, the greatest mistrust and suspicion was not between settlers and local tribes, but between the embryonic towns of Auraria and Denver City, which squared off competitively against one another. As 1859 rolled around, Auraria, on the left bank of Cherry Creek, held the upper hand, commercially and residentially. Denver City, on the right bank, held the high ground. In the end this proved to be the real trump card. Denver's early historian Jerome C. Smiley wrote, "the one thing that Auraria and Denver had in common was the magnificent setting Nature had given them."

One problem was that the rightful owners had not signed off on the deal, and the 4,749 (by 1860) white residents were technically squatters. Resorting to "after the fact" diplomacy, the United States government attempted to quiet the claim to this magnificent natural setting, including nearby gold fields, by virtue of the controversial Ft. Wise treaty of 1861. The ensuing removal of the Cheyenne and Arapaho peoples to southeastern Colorado discredited the efforts of the "Peace Chiefs" among many of their own people and helped precipitate the tragic "Sand Creek Massacre." Little Raven was camped a safe distance from Sand Creek on that fateful November morning in 1864, but after the slaughter he, too, was pursued by

Colonel Chivington's "Bloody 3rd," fleeing far south of the Arkansas River. Denver's earliest landlord was thus evicted from the promising place, of which historian Smiley waxes ironically that, "over the grandeur and beauty that lay around them... there could be no differences, no dissensions, no strife."

The recently developed **Commons Park** has brought these lowlands full circle, in a sense. Originally, the entire river front from 16th to 19th Sts. was a private park, developed by one of Colorado's more colorful entrepreneurs, John Brisben Walker. Walker's many accomplishments included injecting new life into a struggling publication called Cosmopolitan Magazine, which he later sold for a fortune. The entertainment complex he constructed here was called, simply enough, River Front Park. It boasted several interesting attractions, such as an artificial lake created by damming a section of the South Platte, a horse race-track, and an exhibition hall with an unwieldy name — **Castle of Culture and Commerce**. Simply called **"Walker's Castle,"** it was a stone structure standing approximately where the new pedestrian footbridge crosses the river at 16th St. Curiosities from artwork to industrial exhibits and gemstones were displayed within. The castle fell into decline and eventually burned down in 1951.

River Front Park faded into an industrialized no man's land over the years but Walker's larger legacy was more enduring. He not only donated the land for Regis University; he also helped pioneer the Denver Mountain Park system along with Mayor Robert Speer. Red Rocks Park, Walker Ranch Park on Mt. Falcon, and Inspiration Point Park, all owned by Walker, eventually became Denver public parks. Today's Commons Park resurrects John Brisben Walker's vision for the Platte Valley, now relieved of the grimy switching yards and bare concrete warehouses.

To our left, the little red brick **Moffat Road Train Depot** sits forlornly astride the 15th St. underpass. This is the sole surviving evidence of another heroic yet tragic saga: one man's dream to push a railroad west from Denver through the seemingly impregnable Rocky Mountains. The dreamer was David Moffat and his railroad was the Denver, Northwestern & Pacific, which never actually got much past Craig, Colorado. (Typical of the beleaguered railroad's fortunes, a wealthy English investor who had just committed to completing it from Craig to Salt Lake City returned to England on the *Lusitania* when it was fatally torpedoed in May, 1915.) The "Moffat Road," as it was popularly known, was shut out of Union Station early in the 20th century because the powerful Union Pacific didn't like the idea of competition, thus forcing Moffat to build his own depot. By 1904 this quaint, brick, commercial-style structure became the end of the line for freight and passengers.

Courtesy, Colorado Historical Society   F-8289

Banker, David Halliday Moffat (1839-1911), was involved in three railroads - the Denver Pacific, the Rio Grande, and the Denver, Northwestern & Pacific, his final venture.

Ultimately, the exorbitant costs to maintain the line over lofty Rollins Pass, where winter snow slides marooned or swept away entire trains, forced the Moffat Road into bankruptcy, leaving the dream of a tunnel under the Continental Divide unfulfilled. Moffat died tragically, possibly by suicide, in March of 1911, after a fruitless quest to convince Wall Street that his dream was fundamentally sound. Ten years later, through a strange set of circumstances, a devastating flood in Pueblo finally broke the political logjam that had stalled the tunnel project in the legislature. Funding was approved, and by 1929 the Moffat Tunnel was a reality. But it was not until the 1934 Dotsero cutoff was completed that Denver achieved its dream of direct transcontinental rail service. In 1947 the Moffat Road was merged with the rival Denver and Rio Grande Western Railroad. Union Station was no longer "off limits" to David Moffat's railroad. The tunnel provided Denver with an added benefit, diverting precious western slope water into Denver's reservoirs for the first time ever.

Strolling north along Little Raven Street we approach 16th St. where the first of our hundred top buildings peers out over its green, park setting.

1. Riverfront Tower – 1590 Little Raven St. – 4240 Architecture Inc. – 2002

Score 6.3

Meets the Street – 6	Scale – 7	Integrity – 7
Public Spaces – 5	Mass – 7	Imagination – 6

Try to imagine a swath in the very heart of the city, largely un-built upon for nearly 150 years, and supporting weeds and tightly packed train yards, nothing permanent. In that barren environment East West Partners and 4240 Architecture teamed up to create a signature piece for the brand new Riverfront Park neighborhood. Riverfront Tower rises 13 stories to its illuminated clock tower. Cut sandstone, brick, and various setbacks give it a traditional, grounded flavor — still within the Post-Modern idiom.

Two smaller buildings join it, outlining the pleasant little courtyard that accesses the new Millenium Footbridge. Courses of red and buff brick echo the 1904 era "Moffat Road" Station, thus tying past and present together.

Ascend the stairs, perhaps suggestive of the Spanish Steps in Rome, to the deck of **Millenium Footbridge**. The raised platform provides stimulating views of Lo-Do, Auraria, and Union Station. The bridge itself, supported by cables attached to the white, pencil-like shaft, looks vaguely maritime. Don't be fooled — it's a one-legged suspension bridge floating nearly a mile above sea level — an amazing balancing act. One sincerely hopes that the engineers got all their calculations correct. At night the illuminated, quill-like shaft creates a dramatic visual icon. The footbridge traverses the main consolidated trunk line, serving the Union Pacific and Burlington Northern / Santa Fe railroads, as they haul thousands of tons of freight and coal through the heart of Denver each day.

From the spacious bridge deck, view the train platforms and west face of the *Beaux Arts* **Union Station** which straddles 17th St. The station demarcates Lower Downtown, or Lo-Do, the old warehouse district where Denver began. Spurred by the opening of **Coors Field** in 1995, most of the warehouses have been renovated into lofts and commercial space, while newer buildings (under strict architectural review) have filled in many open lots. Lo-Do, a neatly defined rectangle six blocks long and four wide, was formerly sliced by a series of antiquated viaducts, which came down in the 80s. The Wynkoop vista magically opened up as a result. The street is now one of the finest expanses of late 19th and early 20th c. commercial architecture in America.

2. Union Station - 17th St. & Wynkoop - wings: W.E. Taylor – **1881** -
      concourse: Gove & Walsh – **1914**   **Score: 6.6**

Meets the Street – 6	Scale – 8	Integrity – 6
Public Spaces – 5	Mass – 8	Imagination – 7

Passenger rail service was in its heyday when the "City Beautiful" movement stormed the country after the 1893 World's Columbian Exposition. The *Beaux Arts* style, which spearheaded that movement, influenced many of the period's train stations, Denver's Union Station being a fine example. Though modest in scale, it asserts a commanding presence at the foot of 17ᵗʰ St., over which it presides like a dowager queen. The present structure has elements from the original 1881 Victorian station (seen in the two wings) and the 1914 grand concourse, in the *Beaux Arts* tradition, centering the whole mass. After a fire in March of 1894, the old station was rebuilt with more subdued roof-lines and a Romanesque tower that only lasted 20 years.

Expanding passenger traffic necessitated the reworking of the entire station environment, including track layout, platforms, and the adjacent 16ᵗʰ St. viaduct. Gove and Walsh made no effort to reconcile the new concourse with the pre-existing wings, executed in rose colored rhyolite — quaintly rustic in contrast with the pedigreed, *Beaux Arts* hall to which the wings attach.

This odd juxtaposition of Classicism with Victorian elements illustrates Denver's coming of age in the early 20ᵗʰ century. Having passed through its wilder, formative years, the self-conscious young city was anxious to present itself to the world as cultured and sophisticated. The city had just been through a major skyscraper boom and was developing a monumental Civic Center. Two Gothic cathedrals, a new, full-block Post Office / Federal Courthouse, and a state-of-the-art civic auditorium were in various stages of completion. This was the era of Boss Robert W. Speer's "city beautiful" experiment, and the expansion of Union Station was a central element in the plan.

In fact the whole country had assumed a new consciousness by the eve of World War I. The United States had arrived as a world power. All over the country great train stations were going up — in Washington, Kansas City, and New York: physical testimonies to our industrial might and unquenchable confidence. While nowhere near the scale or grandeur of the contemporaneous Grand Central Station in New York, Union Station has managed to maintain its dignity somewhat better. Grand Central is now engulfed by brassy high rises, which seem to sprout literally from its roof, thus diminishing its symbolic power.

Denver's Union Station still holds its own on the street, where it really sparkles (the interior is rather disappointing — a spartan, three-story atrium). Gove and Walsh reserved all the glory to the exterior, as an advertisement for the railroad industry. The intricate relief, carved into the pale green terra cotta that resembles stone, allows it to float above the surrounding, down-to-earth, commercial architecture. An enormous steel awning, suggesting a train shed, is supported by massive tie rods angling from the replicated stone. A parapet wall is surmounted by the de rigeur public clocks, front and back, which are over-topped by blocky, orange signs, arched like rainbows over the roof-line, that proclaim "UNION STATION." Further inducements to "Travel by Train" ornament the dentil ledge in the same carnival orange, plugging an industry which essentially went defunct 40 years ago. The signs, dating from 1951, when train travel was experiencing its post war decline, were undoubtedly a public relations attempt to revive a flagging industry.

In a sense the signs, brightly illuminated at night, deface the classic facade, but over time their presence has become integral to the station's image. Better to strip Times Square of its blazing marquees than to trifle with such a venerable accretion. Union Station is, after all, the embodiment of architectural assimilation, holding a special place in the city's pantheon of proud buildings, like an eccentric uncle who always shows up at Thanksgiving, but without whom the party would never quite be complete.

From Union Station bear left along Wynkoop, enjoying the view that New York architectural critic Paul Goldberger hailed as the finest surviving warehouse row in the country. This unbroken array of late 19th and early 20th century structures is one of Denver's architectural treasures. In a sense it anchors, in conjunction with Union Station, the entire Lo-Do district, thanks to its flowing continuity. Few American streets have achieved this level of architectural harmony. Stand at the front entryway of Union Station and gaze down the entire length of 17th St., the "Wall Street of the West." The first building on the left-hand corner is our next entry.

3. Sheridan / City Railway Bldg. – 1720 Wynkoop – Baerresen Brothers – 1882, 1892   Score: 5.3

Meets the Street – 5	Scale – 6	Integrity – 6
Public Spaces – 5	Mass – 6	Imagination – 4

Originally this building was a stable and barn for the City Railway Company, which ran a horse-car service around early Denver. As horse-cars were gradually replaced by cable cars, then electric streetcars, the building was given a new facelift by the Baerresens in 1892. It became the main plant and warehouse of Hendrie & Bolthoff, a firm that supplied mining lift equipment, electrical motors, and devices of every kind. A century later the building was again retro-fitted, this time as a retail and loft development. The fenestration (window styles and placements) along the Wynkoop and 17th St. facades is seemingly unrelated, a consequence of the 1892 renovation that created a "false front" along 17th St.

4. Wynkoop Brewery / Brown Mercantile – 1634 18th St. –
Gove & Walsh – **1899**   **Score: 5.5**

Meets the Street – 5	Scale – 6	Integrity – 6
Public Spaces – 5	Mass – 6	Imagination – 5

One of the many great warehouse buildings lining Wynkoop, this one was constructed for Brown Mercantile, a large grocery wholesale operation. Gove & Walsh received several commissions for warehouse structures in this area, following the success of their **Morey Mercantile Warehouse (#12)** in 1896. Wynkoop Brewery has relatively clean, simple lines with round-head windows on the fifth floor, giving the structure a very dignified presence. Decorative corbelling under the cornice terminates the facade with a flourish; however, the sandstone molding on the fifth floor detracts from the clean vertical lines. This is conservative, commercial architecture, executed in warm earth tones — basic but effective. About 1988 Denver's brew pub phenomenon was introduced here, which proved so successful that it has since been widely emulated — not to mention catapulting its innovative founder, John Hickenlooper, into the mayoral office in 2003.

Architecturally this area still has a late 19th century feel although in reality much of what we see dates from the early 20th century (very few first generation structures survived even to 1920). A good example is the building on the right, currently known as the **18th St. Atrium** (1621 18th St.) by Fisher & Fisher, 1919, a straightforward commercial warehouse, one of the last built along Wynkoop Row. Originally it was called the **Bourk, Donaldson, & Taylor Bldg.** This is one of Fisher & Fisher's classic "purple cast" buildings, similar to the Weicker Warehouse at 14th and Wynkoop (now **Steelbridge lofts**).

The recessed mortar joints, a device they frequently used, lends more texture to flat walls. The fourth-story roundel windows delineate a shorter "attic" floor, adding visual interest to a finely proportioned building. The flared parapet is quite experimental, effectively capping the stout walls without resorting to historicism (emulated detailing). The initials of the original owners can be seen in the medallions ornamenting the facade on 18th St.

Across Wynkoop stands the muscular **Beatrice Lofts / Cold Storage Warehouse**, constructed in 1902 by the firm of Gove & Walsh, and further expanded about 1912. Originally it was called the Littleton Creamery. The thick masonry walls literally had to thaw out for several weeks before renovation could proceed back in 1984. The facade is highlighted by intricately woven brick patterns that visually lighten the building's heavy mass.

Turn right onto 18th St. Proceed two blocks southeast to Blake, then turn left towards 20th St. Notice the three- story building on the opposite corner.

5. Blake Street Bldg. / General Electric Bldg. – 1441 18th St – architect
unknown – **1906**   **Score: 6.9**
Meets the Street – 7   Scale – 8   Integrity – 8
Public Spaces – 5   Mass – 7   Imagination – 7

Listed on the National Register of historic places, this three-story, Sullivanesque jewel features a beautiful articulated facade using a blend of brick to achieve its warm, speckled tones. The design is simple yet graceful, exhibiting a harmonious composition of elements. The tiled spandrels between second and third-story windows feature inverted, motivic triangles, which effectively counterpoint the open and closed circles under the rounded arches. A clean projecting cornice provides definition and neatly frames the underlying abstract geometry. The design is simple but fluid and expressive, a great study of form and composition. This is a good example of American Expressionism in a commercial application.

Lo-Do evolved from a down-and-out warehouse area into a trendy night life district within a surprisingly short period after the construction of the new ballpark. This stretch of Blake has since become the main approach to the stadium, accounting for the numerous entertainment establishments. Two blocks brings us to 20th St., dominated by **Coors Field's** retro ballpark profile.

6. Coors Field – 2005 Blake – Hellmuth, Obata, Kassabaum (HOK) –
1995   **Score: 6.9**

| Meets the Street – 7 | Scale – 7 | Integrity – 7 |
| Public Spaces – 7 | Mass – 7 | Imagination – 6 |

Coors Field is the second structure on this site to act as a catalyst for growth and development. Denver's first train depot was built here 125 years before the stadium opened in 1995.

Coors Field followed immediately upon the success of Baltimore's Camden Yard, also by Hellmuth, Obata, Kassabaum, Sports Facilities Group in Kansas City. The traditional baseball park theme subsequently became a nationwide trend. Lots of red brick and green, structural lattice work blend it nicely into the old, surrounding warehouses. The stadium was a major catalyst in neighborhood renewal over the past dozen years. It doesn't feel as large as it really is, thanks to the sunken field and generous setbacks along Blake and 20th St. A former storage warehouse was actually incorporated into the stadium's right field extremity. Although the site covers the equivalent of five square blocks, it feels intimate and completely integrated into its neighborhood. In fact, it has come to define the surrounding neighborhood, while becoming one of Denver's best-known structures.

The railroad actually played an important early role at this site. Denver's first train station back in 1870 was a simple brick structure located approximately where the right field fence joins the foul pole. That early station served the Denver Pacific and Kansas Pacific lines, which consolidated with the Union Pacific — under the control of the notorious robber-baron, Jay Gould. The old depot functioned for about a decade until the new Union Station opened in 1881. No doubt the settling of Denver's red light district only two blocks away on Market had something to do with proximity to that original depot. Turn right and walk up 20th St. to Market.

The light stucco building at **2009 Market** (north side of 20th St.) is one of only two Market St. brothels that can still be positively identified from the red light days. 2009 was built by Mattie Silks, Denver's queen of prostitution, who retired in 1915. Earlier, about 1880, she had sold it to rival *madam*, Jennie Rogers, who was equally shrewd and prosperous in the flesh trade. From the 1870s well into the 20th century, this entire street between 19th and 22nd Sts. was lined with high class "parlor houses" and ghastly "cribs" — filthy hovels where the cheaper prostitutes plied their abysmal trade. Alcoholism, opium, and suicides were a way of life in the cribs. The successful operators like Jennie and Mattie sheltered their girls from that more degraded existence, so long as they remained attractive and profitable.

Silent faces in stone tell no tales, but their presence raises intriguing questions about the origins of the House of Mirrors.

The most famous pleasure palace on Market was the House of Mirrors, which went through several re-incarnations as a Buddhist temple, a warehouse, and now a nightclub. The **House of Mirrors** sits mid-block at 1946 (originally 1942) Market and is easily distinguished by its gabled, white facade. The belief is that Jennie Rogers financed it by blackmailing a wealthy Denver businessman who coughed up $17,000 to build the opulent parlor house, bedecked in mirrors. It became famous throughout the West for its comforts and its glamour. Jennie brazenly had the figures of herself , her dupe financier, as well as his two wives carved on the front of the house where they remain to this day, leering like grotesque gargoyles over the street.

Jennie built the House of Mirrors in 1888 and worked it until her death in 1910. After that it fell to the queen of the street, Mattie Silks, but times were already changing. Reform was in the air and steps were being taken to outlaw prostitution. Slowly the city began to apply pressure. Mattie shuttered the House of Mirrors in 1915. Within three years all the Market St. bordellos were gone. This stretch became just another part of Denver's wholesale produce district, filled with warehouses. In the 1990s this one-block stretch resurrected as a nightclub mecca. Through the worst times one of Denver's oldest jazz clubs, El Chapultepec, lingered on the corner of 20th St. & Market as it does today, still tough and seedy, but filled with "bluesy" strains.

Turn right on 19th St. for a block, then left, backtracking along Blake. The **Windsor Farm Dairy Bldg.** at 1855 Blake is a notable Fisher & Fisher structure from 1918. On our left is the former Crocker Cracker Factory, an Italianate business block typical of the 1880s. A century later it was incorporated into a newer office building.

A block away the **Blake Street Bath & Racquet Club**, 1732-70 Blake, was designed by J. W. Roberts and is notable for the 1881-vintage soft orange brick common to the period. The design is subdued and simply conceived for Victorian sensibilities. Back in the 70s this building became one of the early conversions to loft homes, at a time when Lo-Do was still a warehouse / gin mill district. It succeeded and helped to prove the viability of residential rehabs in Lo-Do, however.

7. Barth Hotel – 1514 17th St. – Frederick Eberly – **1882**   **Score: 5.8**

| Meets the Street – 6 | Scale – 6 | Integrity – 6 |
| Public Spaces – 5 | Mass – 5 | Imagination – 7 |

The Barth is the only remaining building downtown associated with William and Moritz Barth, German brothers who made a fortune selling boots to the early miners, then shrewdly invested their profits in Denver real estate. A few years after Moritz built this warehouse, the Barth brothers built an impressive four-story commercial building, way uptown at 16th St. & Stout, to take advantage of the business migration towards Brown's Bluff, now Capitol Hill. In the late 1880s this structure was converted into a hotel.

In the 1930s Moritz Barth's son, Allen Barth, repurchased the property and re-named it the Barth Hotel. It was recently restored to its original glory and again exudes the Victorian flavor of the old railroad city. It is worth noting that each floor manifests a different window pattern: round-head windows on the second floor, half-arched on the third, square lintels on the top story. The fourth-floor windows are extremely narrow, while random moldings decorate an eclectic facade that is as unpredictable as it is lively.

8. Millenium Bldg. – 1550 17th St. – Parkhill, Ivins Architects –
2000   **Score: 7.6**

Meets the Street – 8	Scale – 6	Integrity – 8
Public Spaces – 8	Mass – 7	Imagination – 8

This is one of the more compelling facades downtown. How to lure a big 17th St. law firm from its sleek, high-rise environs into a funky, low-rise gaslight square district? Provide brand new digs in a distinctive building, which echoes commercial buildings of old. It feels "retro" and timeless, producing a lively dialogue with Frank Edbrooke's stocky **Oxford Hotel (#10)** just across the street. The elaborate, brick texture adds distinction, and its light charcoal hue ties it admirably to the **Sugar Bldg. (#16)** down the block. The two main facades are broken at midpoint by pairs of six-story masts, tilted slightly outward as if awaiting sails to catch the wind. The suggestion is very maritime, a feeling which is reinforced by the stylized fish market awnings protruding a story above the sidewalk. They recall the old Seattle Fish Market that thrived on nearby Market for several generations. The interior lobby is as well appointed as the richly articulated facade. The Millenium Bldg. is one of Lo-Do's most successful in-fill projects, and very satisfying architecture.

9. **Mayer House** – 1702 Wazee - Olson Sundberg Architects –
1998   **Score: 8.4**

Meets the Street – 8	Scale – 9	Integrity - 9
Public Spaces – 7	Mass – 9	Imagination – 9

Mayer House hints at how Frank Lloyd Wright might have interpreted the urban town houses of Boston and Chicago had he been more disposed to cities. (Wright once cracked to his Denver audience that cities were only good for two things: making money and meeting women.) This witty town-home is most expressive, though sparsely ornamented. The beige aggregate and red sandstone, articulated by deeply inset openings, give it a regional flavor and lend it a sense of timeless permanence. It is certainly one of Denver's more articulate architectural statements.

Built by Fred Mayer as a private residence, the house has museum quality written all over it, which may well be the owner's intent (just as the Henry Clay Frick mansion in New York became the Frick Collection). It is the sort of building that plays colors off nicely at different hours of the day or in changing weather conditions.

Immediately next door, the **Titanium** at 1720 Wazee, by Joe Simmons (Olson Sundberg Architects – 2002) tries bravely to capitalize on its urbane neighbor, but it's simply made of poorer stuff. The main face on Blake creates some interest, incorporating an old facade, but the overall design is de rigeur Post-Modern. The five-story titanium columns (hence the name) lift the eye momentarily but cannot sustain visual interest for long. It filled a dreadful hole in the streetscape, but ends up more a cliche than an original statement.

10. Oxford Hotel – 1600 17th St. – Frank E. Edbrooke – 1891

		Score: 6.5
Meets the Street – 6	Scale – 6	Integrity – 7
Public Spaces – 7	Mass – 7	Imagination – 6

Now listed on the National Register, the Oxford was one of Denver's leading hotels for better than 60 years, until the decline of train travel reversed its fortunes. The hotel made a dramatic recovery with the rediscovery of Lo-Do, and today it is again one of downtown's premier hostelries. It is even reputed to have its own resident ghost who occasionally wafts about the third floor.

Frank Edbrooke created a very pure, straightforward design here. The paired windows are deeply inset within the dark, chocolate masonry which gives it a somber, weighty appearance. In order to offset this sobriety, Edbrooke inserted a tier of Roman arched windows on the fourth floor (out of five). The parapet

Colorfully bedecked, the Oxford has re-claimed its position among Denver's premier hotels.

fancifully suggests a crenelated fortress. The building's strong walls and rigid, ordered geometry show a definite early Chicago School influence. The decorative terra cotta relief, highlighting the masonry above the windows, feels Sullivanesque, though not as smoothly integrated into the structure as per Sullivan's works. The Oxford pre-dates Edbrooke's **Brown Palace (#68)** at the opposite end of 17th St. by a couple of years. This design takes a more sober approach than the Brown, whose real glory is the interior court.

Denver's grandest Art Deco relic may not be a building but a popular tavern, the **Cruise Room** by Charles Jaka, located just off the Oxford's main lobby. The sleek, moderne 1935 decor celebrated the end of Prohibition with an international theme. Ways to raise a glass in 11 different cultures are enshrined in relief on the walls, from the English "Cheerio" to Japanese "Banzai", Norwegian "Skal," and the colloquial American toast, "Bottom's Up."

10 a. Oxford Hotel Annex – 1624 17th St. - Montana Fallis –
1912		**Score: 6.5**
Meets the Street – 7	Scale – 6	Integrity – 6
Public Spaces – 5	Mass – 7	Imagination – 8

No attempt was made to emulate Edbrooke's dark, husky model across the alley when Montana Fallis was commissioned to expand the Oxford. Instead, he turned to a classical motif, executed in glazed tiles, and tucked six floors into the space of five on a narrow lot behind the **Struby-Estabrook Bldg. (#11)**. A four-level "bridge of sighs" spans the alleyway, picturesquely tying the annex to the older parent structure. A wide, gently rounded, projecting bay gives the front side a light, floating sensation. This feature, rising four floors to the parapet, and the satin white cast, give the Annex its real distinction.

The porcelain Oxford Annex nestles between the original Oxford (left center) and Struby-Estabrook Bldg. (foreground).

11. Struby-Estabrook Bldg. – 1660 17th St. – attributed to
Frank E. Edbrooke – **1885**		**Score: 6.0**
Meets the Street – 6	Scale – 6	Integrity – 7
Public Spaces – 6	Mass – 6	Imagination – 5

A charming structure, epitomizing the commercial vitality of the railroad era, direct and straightforward, it exudes a sense of warmth with its rich sandstone and brick tones. The most compelling feature is the use of variegated stone in the first-floor arches. The individual bays along 17th St. are recessed, suggesting an arcade. The unequal arch spans are jovial, visually, and strike a chord with the classic Roman arches that illuminate Union Station's great hall. Like the Sheridan / City Railway Bldg. across the street, Struby-Estabrook models two distinct fenestration patterns (window openings) on its primary facades.

Turning left on Wynkoop, we stroll down to 16th St. where the **Barteldes, Hartig Building** by Gove & Walsh (1906) stands at number 1600 Wynkoop. The small windows and heavy masonry massing indicate that this was in fact another warehouse for wholesale fruits, seed, and grains. The heavy load-bearing walls were capable of supporting an immense 600 lbs. per square foot load. The most interesting design features are the extensive use of decorative corbels that facilitate a slightly projecting cornice, executed in brick and stone. An arched main entry sits illogically on the second floor, directly opposite a similar elaborate cutout in the **Morey Mercantile Bldg.** — mute testimony to the raised viaduct that once ran along 16th St., and into which these marooned apertures once connected.

12. Tattered Cover / Morey Mercantile – 1536 Wynkoop – Gove & Walsh
– **1896**   **Score: 5.4**

Meets the Street – 5	Scale – 6	Integrity – 5
Public Spaces – 6	Mass – 5	Imagination – 5

Wynkoop Row is named for an early Denver sheriff and Civil War officer, Major Edward Wynkoop. The Tattered Cover / Morey Mercantile Bldg. is the buff colored structure at center.

Although it vaguely suggests Italian Renaissance form, this former grocery warehouse is a no-nonsense, turn-of-the-century commercial building, typical of period warehouses. It feels a bit fortress-like, solid and heavily massed. The massing, within the context of Wynkoop Row, is certainly appropriate. Heavy, rough-dimensioned lumber, which makes up the interior framing members, lends a rustic flavor to the Tattered Cover's retail store. It's an honest treatment, revealing its gritty, former warehouse character. While it is not Gove & Walsh's most sophisticated design, it still deserves respect.

Morey's historical significance stems from this being the first large building to be undertaken after the silver crash and Panic of '93 — which many thought would be the end of Denver's greatness. In a sense it was a harbinger of the new mercantile era, which re-defined the city's economic role as it gradually moved away from mining and smelting, relying more on transportation and distribution. It also represented a turning away from the exuberant, pre-crash architecture to a far more conservative style of buildings.

The proprietor, Chester S. Morey, was an enigmatic figure. Born in 1847, he fought for the Union in the Civil War at Petersburg and in the Virginia campaign. He was on the field at Appomattox when Gen. Robert E. Lee surrendered to Gen. Ulysses S. Grant. His father was killed in the Virginia campaign, and with the little money from savings and inheritance, he went into the grocery business in Chicago. Morey migrated to Colorado in 1872 because of poor health.

By 1875 he had recovered sufficiently to become the Denver agent for the Chicago firm and eventually a partner. In 1884 he formed the C. S. Morey Mercantile Company which remained a major grocery wholesaler in the mountain states until 1956 when it was bought out by Continental Foods. Morey himself was a civic activist, especially in public education. As a member of the Denver School Board, he was the driving force behind the creation of the Manual Training High School.

A block down Wynkoop we see the **Steelbridge Lofts**, formerly the **Weicker Warehouse**, at 1700 15ᵗʰ St., by Fisher & Fisher (1918). A relatively newer building within the old district, it nevertheless manages to converse amiably with the Victorian neighbors. The "purple cast" brick and flared parapet resembles the **Bourk, Donaldson, & Taylor Bldg.**, three blocks up Wynkoop at 18th St. Colorado Saddlery still manufactures riding saddles on the opposite corner, as it has since 1945. Its customers have included ordinary cowboys as well as illustrious riders such as John Wayne, Ken Curtis, and Lorne Greene.

13. Edbrooke Lofts – 1450 Wynkoop – Frank E. Edbrooke – 1906, 1910   Score: 5.4

Meets the Street – 5	Scale – 6	Integrity – 6
Public Spaces – 4	Mass – 6	Imagination – 6

Smooth red brick and understated lines make this former grocery warehouse a significant addition to the "Wynkoop Row." The building was actually built in two stages, four years apart. The upper two floors are slightly different, visibly later additions. The roundels here soften the angularity of the facade. Edbrooke paired all the windows to strengthen the piers and give the building more lift, then capped it with a strong projecting cornice. The old water tower is still perched high above the southwest corner, recalling the industrial character which is so much a part of Lo-Do's history.

A short distance up Wynkoop past the old railroad bridge, we can see the Pepsi Center, which is the city's principal indoor sporting events venue. Rather than attempting to cross busy Speer Blvd., a description from here will suffice. Pepsi Center can also be viewed from the **Tivoli Student Center (#21)** on the Auraria campus at the beginning of the next tour.

14. Pepsi Center – 1000 Chopper Pl. – H.O.K. Sports Facilities Group – **1999**

Score: 4.9

Meets the Street – 5	Scale – 5	Integrity – 4
Public Spaces – 6	Mass – 4	Imagination – 5

Denver's posh, Post-Modern events center is situated practically on the site of **"Indian Row,"** Auraria's first permanent settlement dating to the late summer of 1858. A number of cabins were already clustered in the present day parking lots between the Pepsi Center and Cherry Creek before things got going on the higher, Denver City side of the creek. The wet spring of 1864 proved the wisdom of the Denver City men, when Cherry Creek jumped her banks and flooded Auraria. William Byers' **Rocky Mountain News**, unwilling to favor either side, positioned its offices right in the creek bed. Their printing press was eventually located a mile or so down the South Platte, buried in the river's bed.

Modern day flood controls have pretty well contained both streams, permitting the arena as well as an extensive amusement park to occupy the flood plain. Pepsi Center is surrounded by parking lots, so it hardly feels urban in the strict sense. The site was originally a train yard, accounting for its general openness. The building has definite "front" and "back" profiles, the front side being far better. From the back side it resembles a pre-war aerodrome. The main face features stylized rosette columns bisecting a plane of green glass. These mock columns are in-filled with more glass and surmounted with a minimalist cornice, also in metallic green. The combination of colors, materials, and geometry is an agreeable Post-Modern compromise. That much said, the various elements don't congeal into a cohesive statement of purpose, coming across as paste-on decorations.

The interior public concourse is spacious and substantial. Thanks to all that glass, the concourses receive natural light and offer tremendous vistas of the downtown skyline. The building is a monument to the new American sports culture, far removed from the roughhewn days of wooden benches that seemed more apropos to rough and tumble contests like ice hockey. Alas, grit is a thing of the past, and slick is in. Sporting events today feel more like Las Vegas floor shows than rugged athletic events, due in large part to pampering palaces like the Pepsi Center.

Proceeding left up 15th St. we come to one of frontier Denver's more important intersections, 15th & Wazee. Half a block up Wazee, at #1444, stood the famous **Elephant Corral**. Back in the days before the railroad, 15th St. was the route used by most of the overland trails entering the city, especially the Smoky Hill Trail and the pikes to Boulder and Golden. A transit hub for horses and wagon trains quite naturally developed just off 15th St., close to the traffic - a sort of courtyard arrangement known as the Elephant Corral. Plenty of livestock watered here for sure, but no elephant visits were recorded.

The name derived from a popular expression at the time, "going to see the elephant," which meant heading out West to prospect in the gold fields of California, Nevada, or Colorado. For a time the Elephant Corral was also a notorious gambling den, and a game of cards was generally chased by a shot of whiskey, also plentifully supplied. After the fire of 1863, urban refinements came and the games of chance moved to more substantial establishments such as the Palace. The reconstructed corral continued to function as a carriage and livery stable, well after the railroads had drained away most of the overland freight. The old name stuck, along with the familiar courtyard arrangement, even after a more permanent rebuilding occurred in 1902.

15. Palace Lofts – 1499 Blake – RNL Architects – **1998** – **Score: 6.9**

Meets the Street – 6   Scale – 7   Integrity – 7
Public Spaces – 6   Mass – 8   Imagination – 8

Architecture scored a victory when this 10-story ziggurat loft project began rising on the site of a former printing supply house, formed of ugly pre-cast concrete panels, fronted by an uglier parking lot on 15th St. Palace Lofts conjures up images of New York City's West Side, perhaps Chelsea along the Hudson River. The two-tone brick, set off against greenish window mullions, gives it a very urbane sense. Despite rising several stories higher than its surroundings, it doesn't feel overbearing. Setbacks are so expertly handled that, close up, the top four stories fade from consciousness. From a distance the pleasingly sculpted profile advertises Lo-Do better than any billboard. The retro styling doesn't grate against nearby historic buildings, even the two-and three-story neighbors. In that regard this is one of Lo-Do's more skillful in-fill projects.

Palace Lofts takes its name from one of early Denver's most celebrated gambling/ entertainment halls. The area was filled with gambling dens like the Criterion, the Occidental, and the Progressive Club, but **The Palace** was built as a high class establishment by the big wheel of gambling, Ed Chase, in 1864, not long after a fire had cleaned out this whole area. The Palace attracted such prominent customers as Senator Ed Wolcott, H. A. W. Tabor, and even the amiable Eugene Field on occasion. The bar was reflected in a 60' mirror, and a separate theater featured 750 seats and curtained boxes. The show girls were often showered with tokens of affection, jewels and furs among them. But every now and then a jealous paramour was libel to go berserk, as Palace girl Effie Moore learned the hard way. One night she was shot dead by a disgruntled admirer, while she performed on stage. Generally though, the Palace was an upscale operation and bullet-ridden bodies were not allowed on the premises.

Denver Public Library, Western History Collection   X-24703
The famous Palace Theatre was Denver's early high class entertainment venue, including a popular gambling hall that lured high rollers like H.A.W. Tabor.

Chase eventually sold the theater to former lawman Bat Masterson. As the carriage trade moved uptown, Chase followed and opened newer establishments, like the Arcade at 16th & Larimer, where Masterson, Deadeye Dick, and the confidence man Soapy Smith congregated. The Palace casino closed up in 1889, the same time that Chase bought the Arcade. The building survived another 40 years before coming down, while the theater section lasted through the 1950s.

The opposite corner of 15th & Blake, now a parking lot, is the site of **Constitution Hall**, so-called because the state's constitution was drafted there in 1876. It had originated in 1865 as the home to Denver's 1st National Bank, headed by Jerome B. Chaffee. The landmark endured for the next century until a disastrous arson fire, set by a former employee, claimed it in the spring of 1977.

Author's Collection
On April 24, 1977, an arson fire consumed Constitution Hall, where Colorado's constitution was drafted in late 1875. Efforts to save it failed, and the smoldering ruins were demolished shortly thereafter.

Backtrack one block to15ᵗʰ St. & Wazee, inhabited by some of the city's oldest surviving structures. In 1863, Denver consisted mostly of frame buildings, hastily constructed as the new city burgeoned outward. On April 19, 1863, a fire broke out at the rear of the **Cherokee House Hotel**, where the Palace Lofts now sits. The conflagration spread quickly, and before the Great Fire of '63 was contained, a four-square block area was in smoldering ruins. The city passed new regulations, mandating brick construction on future buildings. That decision later extended to residential areas as well, giving Denver a unique appearance for decades to come. The city rebuilt quickly, in brick of course, starting with the two- and three-story buildings seen along this stretch of 15ᵗʰ St., and around the corner on the east side of Wazee. Not many Civil War era structures survive here, apart from this small patch that somehow managed to slip unnoticed through frenetic waves of construction after the railroad arrived in 1870. As wagon trains slipped into obsolescence, the area around the old **Elephant Corral** drifted quietly, unmolested by progress, through the generations.

16. Sugar Bldg. – 1530 16ᵗʰ St. – Gove & Walsh – 1906-12   Score: 6.8

Meets the Street – 6	Scale – 7	Integrity – 7
Public Spaces – 7	Mass – 6	Imagination – 8

Denver's only remaining open-cage elevator is reason enough to poke your head inside the Sugar Building. Besides that, this is one of the more interesting Denver examples of "Sullivanesque" architecture. The building's name refers to one of Colorado's more successful agricultural ventures, the sugar beet, which was pioneered by Charles Boettcher, among others. Boettcher created the Great Western Sugar Company in 1905 to consolidate beet processing, just one of his numerous industrial enterprises. Agricultural products eventually replaced mineral wealth as the mainstay of Colorado's economy, and a large part of that new wealth came from the sugar beet. In fact, Charles and his wife, Fannie, had smuggled the beet seeds in their luggage, after a visit to their native Germany.

The Sugar Building went up four stories in 1906, but as expansion was required, Gove & Walsh added the top two stories in 1912, and the adjoining red brick warehouse, which topped off in 1916. The beautiful geometric designs in the brick as well as the orderly massing of piers and finely-detailed cornice pay tribute to the influence of Louis Sullivan. The base and lower stories are simple, yet beautiful; geometric patterns highlight the three upper floors, creating increased visual excitement as the eye lifts. An imaginative frieze fills the void between the top story and cornice.

The building is really two, a back section finished in red brick that distinguished the packaging and warehouse functions from the offices occupying the front building. This warehouse section is simply ornamented, but it speaks a strong vertical language, using narrow windows and projected pilasters. The gaunt, almost minimalist Chicago School influence is quite apparent here.

Proceed up 16th St. Mall one block to the corner of Blake. The large, buff brick structure, **16 Market Square**, is situated where Barney L. Ford, a 38-year-old former slave who arrived in Denver in May, 1860, constructed the **Inter Ocean Hotel**. Ford, a natural businessman, started out by cutting hair and later opening two restaurants, one just down the street at 1614 Blake. By 1873 he was able to build the hotel on this site, and another in Cheyenne in 1875. Early Denverites were color blind regarding the popular entrepreneur, whose wife was even listed in the Denver Social Register. The industrious and hard working Barney died of a heart attack in the winter of 1902, age 80, suffered, not surprisingly, while at work shoveling snow.

Barney L. Ford, an enterprising, escaped slave, built a respectable business empire in Denver, and gained social acceptance.

Courtesy, Colorado Historical Society F 6323

17. 16 Market Square – 1400 16th St. – Hartman & Cox with
David Owen Tryba – **2000**   **Score: 7.0**

Meets the Street – 7	Scale – 7	Integrity – 7
Public Spaces – 7	Mass – 8	Imagination – 6

A plaque posted in the lobby reads, "God is in the details," attributed to Mies van der Rohe. Details are abundant at 16 Market Square which fills the former eyesore that edged RTD's Market Street Station for years. The eight-story "retro" design recalls the days of McKim Meade & White, circa 1910. It respectfully tips its hat toward the area's older, historic structures. A rounded corner bay on Market recalls the stately Central Bank Bldg. that once graced 15th St. & Arapahoe. Buff colored brick echoes the restored Sugar Building, a block hence, actually making a transition to red brick along the flanks just as the Sugar does. 16 Market Square contributes admirably to the texture, color, and scale of a busy public square straddling the Market Street Station. Strategically situated where downtown high-rises fade into the warm intimacy of Lo-Do, it visually buffers the historic district from the huge monoliths nearby. Whatever 16 Market Square may lack in a contemporary feel, it compensates for in crafting and sensitivity to its environment.

The southeast corner of 16 Market Square marks the location of **Clark, Gruber & Company**, which opened for business on July 20, 1860. This enterprising partnership was the only financial venture in U.S. history to combine both banking and minting operations together. After all, there was a lot of gold dust pouring down from the mountains, and it made perfect sense to coin it into useable cash. After nervous government lawyers determined that there was nothing illegal about Clark, Gruber's activity, the partners agreed to sell the minting operations to the United States government – which then took over the building. The banking arm of the firm moved a block away to 16th St. & Blake, where the new state constitution would be framed, some ten years later, thus the name Constitution Hall.

The bank became the First National Bank after receiving the state's first bank charter and went on to become the dominant financial institution in the Rocky Mountains, under the management of David H. Moffat, Walter Cheesman, Jerome Chaffee, and George Kassler – among other early pioneers. **The Denver Mint (#92)** eventually relocated to Civic Center on West Colfax Avenue, where it continues to stamp out billions of coins to this very day.

An important step in the redemption of Lo-Do was the restoration of the 1600 block of Market, which had once been slated for wholesale destruction as part of a typical 1960s freeway scheme. Mercifully, that proposal died a premature death for lack of funding. Slowly, one building, then another, found new life as demand for funky space grew through the 1970s and 80s. By 1982 a couple of inappropriate high-rises had infiltrated Lo-Do over on 17th St. The Regional Transportation District (RTD) committed itself to Lo-Do when it constructed the underground **Market Street Station** as a part of the 16th St. Mall project. Above ground, two older buildings on the block were renovated as headquarters for the transit district.

18. Market Center – 1600 block Market – various architects – 1878-1893   Score: 6.4

Meets the Street – 7   Scale – 7   Integrity – 7
Public Spaces – 5   Mass – 7   Imagination – 6

After Larimer Square, Market Square is the most comprehensive collection of Victorian-era buildings to be rehabilitated, en masse. All of the structures in this row were raised during the 15-year period before the 1893 crash, giving us a representative glimpse into how the old "railroad city" must have felt. Market was the historic produce center, and these were typical of the commercial structures that housed various wholesale trading companies.

My favorite is the former **Columbia Hotel** (1878) situated on the corner of 17th St. The architect is unknown today, true of all six buildings, yet this is the most ornate of the group. The style is Victorian Commercial, exemplified by the imaginative cornice and exotic brickwork. Notice the alternating window treatments and decorative black string-courses running horizontally between windows.

Next door are two unnamed buildings (1884-85) slightly newer than the Columbia. The larger one lost its pressed tin cornice somewhere along the time-line, which gives it a slightly more severe look. The three-story **McCrary Bldg.** (1884) at 1634 Market is somewhat deceptive as to its origins. It was given a new face, probably including the roundhead windows, about 1905, when Mr. McCrary's wholesale grocery business moved out. The second-story windows are probably truer to the original look. Next to it stands the **Liebhardt-Lindner Bldg.** (1881) which features doubled windows and a raised, center bay parapet. It is well-composed and sober by Victorian standards, but allows the maximum amount of light to enter.

The Lieberhardt-Lindner Bldg. (left) and Hitchings Block testify to pre-"Silver Crash" exuberance. This was part of Denver's wholesale grocery district through the 1960s.

Perhaps the most eclectic member of the row is the **Hitchings Block** at 1620 Market (1892). This unusual structure was built as an investment by the Rev. Horace B. Hitchings — Episcopalian canon of the Cathedral of St. John's in the Wilderness.

Rev. Hitchings is best remembered for eulogizing Captain Silas Soule, who was murdered in cold blood on the streets of Denver in the spring of 1865. Soule made enemies by testifying against Colonel John Chivington regarding the terrible massacre at Sand Creek. His murderer, an ally of Chivington named Squiers, simply left town and was not pursued. Captain Soule had been married only a few weeks before he was killed. This was only days after the assassination of Abraham Lincoln, and Soule is considered the last Civil War casualty in Colorado. His name is inscribed on the Civil War memorial, west of the state capitol.

Rev. Hitchings erected his building some 27 years after those melancholic events, crowning the fantastic parapet with a gothic finial, in keeping with the bizarre collection of motifs set under it. One suspects that the good canon was a dabbler in architecture. The building opened shortly before Denver took its severest economic plunge, in 1893, and the city would never again witness this kind of fanciful, 19th century design. It truly marked the end of an era for the ambitious young city.

19. Alamo Plaza – 1401 17th St. – Clothier, Weber & Assoc. –

1982		Score: 4.9
Meets the Street – 5	Scale – 3	Integrity – 4
Public Spaces – 6	Mass – 5	Imagination – 6

The significance of Alamo Plaza may be that it galvanized the city's conservation movement and effected a special B-7 ordinance. B-7 down-zoned the Lo-Do district, thus cooling speculative development pressures at a critical moment in its re-birth. The building strives for interest, but the tan aggregate and protruding bays don't quite achieve it. Its 15 stories feel awfully tall in the low slung neighborhood, and the aggregate doesn't mesh well with all that surrounding red brick. Chamfered corners soften the angularity but ultimately the building seems out of place here, which explains why it created such a negative reaction when it first went up. The bulk of its half block site is devoted to a ho-hum parking garage, further aggravating neighborhood relations.

Walk one block over to Larimer where the "Three Ugly Sisters," a trio of residential high-rises, line the west flank of Larimer. No, this isn't public housing. Incredibly, all three towers qualify as "luxury" units. The worst of the lot is undoubtedly **The Windsor** (1777 Larimer), which pilfered a fine name from a fine old hotel with a colorful past. The original **Windsor Hotel** was situated across 18th St. from its cheesy,

Denver Public Library, Western History Collection   WHJ-1574 William Henry Jackson
Englishman James Duff built the Windsor Hotel, then leased it to William Bush and H.A.W. Tabor. It opened in June, 1880. Tabor also gave it notoriety by keeping his mistress, Elizabeth McCourt (Baby) Doe, ensconced here while in Denver. Despite its colorful history, it gradually faded and was demolished in 1959.

stucco namesake. A fenced, grassy knoll, fronting the VOA apartments, is where silver king H.A.W. Tabor and Baby Doe carried on their torrid love affair under the nose of Tabor's first wife, Augusta. Tabor eventually married Baby Doe, and even died in the Windsor years later, Baby Doe faithfully at his side. A young bartender named Harry Tammen also started out here, but went on to greater things. Tammen, with his partner Fred Bonfils, turned a struggling newspaper called the *Denver Post* into a regional journalistic force. Still later, the Windsor turns up in Jack Kerouac's 50s beatnick odyssey, "On the Road," truly a hotel with a rich tapestry of legend and lore.

Its modern, bland, vanilla namesake would endure about a decade in Las Vegas before getting blown up for something newer and bigger. The shabby cosmetics and pseudo-glitz make this Windsor insufferable. Considering the bargain its builders got on the taxpayer-subsidized land, it should be called the Windfall.

The Barclay by Barancik, Conte & Associates, 1625 Larimer,   is likewise misleading geographically. The original Barclay Block sat in the next block occupying the west side of 18th St., face to face with the Windsor Hotel - to which it was connected by an underground tunnel. The legend is that this tunnel allowed the state legislators, who convened at the Barclay before the State Capitol was built, to traipse unseen to the Windsor's fabled bar. In truth it served another purpose. The Barclay had an extensive Roman bath / gymnasium in the basement, which was frequented by guests from the Windsor Hotel. An even longer tunnel reputedly connected these important early buildings to Union Station, four blocks away. By the time legislative functions found a permanent home in the new capitol building, around 1896, this stretch of Larimer was in decline. The sensational, uptown Brown Palace supplanted the Windsor as the city's hotel of preference. 18th and Larimer faded into obscurity as a respectable business address, abetted by the raucous gambling and red light activities nearby.

The modern Barclay, nearly two blocks and a century removed from its namesake, possesses all the charms of a grain elevator. Nevertheless, it is the most humane of the sisters, featuring such welcome amenities as street level retail space, mixed uses, and strategic setbacks from the property line. Its stark whiteness could be easily remedied by a splash of color, allowing the blank monolith to blend more happily into the earth tones surrounding it.

Denver Public Library, Western History Collection   Z-2955
Herndon Davis

The Arcade as rendered by Denver Post artist, Herndon Davis, who painted the famous "Face on the Bar-room Floor" in Central City's Teller House. By this time, around the 1940s, Larimer was rife with indigents, rescue missions, and plenty of gin mills.

The new Barclay itself overlays much early history. The first **McClintock Bldg.** resided here, home to the First National Bank before 1880. This block also housed some of early Denver's more infamous gambling halls, as well as the photographic studios of William H. Jackson, whose lens so vividly captured much of the early West. The most nefarious of the gambling dens was the **Arcade**, at 1609 Larimer, built by the kingpin of the city's gambling fraternity – "Big Ed" Chase. The Arcade routinely hosted such old West luminaries as Soapy Smith, Deadeye Dick, and Bat Masterson. A sensational killing occurred here when one of the Arcade's faro dealers shot his best friend in an ugly gunfight, not over cards, but a woman. He was acquitted on the basis of self-defense. The Arcade was respectable, however, compared to its next-door rival, appropriately nicknamed the "Slaughterhouse," which had two famous murders to its credit. This is where the West was really wild.

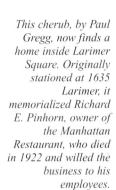

This cherub, by Paul Gregg, now finds a home inside Larimer Square. Originally stationed at 1635 Larimer, it memorialized Richard E. Pinhorn, owner of the Manhattan Restaurant, who died in 1922 and willed the business to his employees.

The opposite side of Larimer figured greatly in Denver's early development as well. Walter S. Cheesman's handsome, five-story business block sat at the corner of 17th & Larimer. Cheesman is the pioneer you can thank whenever you take a shower, since he was quite instrumental in developing Denver's water supply, allowing the arid city to blossom and grow.

At the other end of the block, where the Cheesecake Factory anchors **Tabor Center's** retail mall, the **Tabor Block** raised its majestic crown. Completed in 1880, the Tabor Block marked the transformation of Denver from a raw cow-town to a real city. Standing five stories tall and trimmed in cut limestone, it instantly became the premier business block in the city. Just as important, Tabor brought the gifted architect Frank E. Edbrooke to Denver to supervise its construction in 1879. Over the next 30 years, Edbrooke became the city's leading commercial designer and left a lasting imprint on Denver. This building and the **Tabor Grand Opera House**, which followed it by a year, were both designed by Frank and his brother Willoughby J. Edbrooke, of Chicago.

The Tabor Block was an ambitious design, featuring Corinthian pilasters capped by classical pediments, more evocative of Second Empire Paris than dry, dusty Denver.

In its waning days, the Tabor Block assumed a haunted appearance, though still structurally sound. Legend has it that H.A.W. Tabor, a former stonecutter, helped dress some of the elaborate cut stone.

It must have dazzled a budding metropolis composed of simple two- and three-story business blocks. In tandem with Tabor's Grand Opera House, the two buildings changed Denver's whole perception of itself, evidenced by the ensuing building boom that turned Denver from a cowgirl into a Victorian matron. That was more Edbrooke's doing than Tabor's in the final analysis, but without Tabor's introducing the eager city to this gifted architect, who knows?

David Moffat took over the presidency of the First National Bank in 1880, moving it into Tabor's new business block (Tabor was the largest shareholder at the time). For some 30 years, Moffat guided it through panics and depressions, putting up $2,000,000 of his own money to pull it through '93, and built it into regional dominance. One of the bank's more colorful incidents occurred here on May 28, 1888 when Moffat was robbed of $21,000 by a steely-nerved perpetrator who threatened to blow the place to smithereens with a flask of nitro-glycerin. Moffat never discerned whether the robber was bluffing and, although the holdup man was never apprehended, it was later believed through underworld tipsters that he was one Robert Leroy Parker, alias Butch Cassidy.

The Cheesman and Tabor Blocks were ripped down in 1972 by the urban renewal authority in one of the more savage acts of urban vandalism perpetrated on Denver. There was no question of their historical and architectural importance to the Queen City and, in fact, this site was one of the very last to be redeveloped in Skyline. Unlike L.A., we didn't even get a little plaque to commemorate the site's significance.

Larimer Place by Lombardi & Associates, 1551 Larimer, represents total architectural narcissism. Its gravest sin is a faceless, impenetrable wall, compounded by an ugly loading dock, opening directly onto the 16th St. Mall, a shocking example of civic indifference. The building squeezes every possible amenity from the surroundings, but offers zero public benefits in return, not even an attractive entry.

Denver's first genuine skyscraper, the Railroad Building, once raised its head on this block. The iron skeleton was certainly innovative, but its stone facade was plain and lusterless. An investment by the Evans family, it proved to be a financial disappointment. Governor Evans miscalculated in his conviction that the center of Denver would always remain near its origins, at 15th St. and Larimer. As the business moved steadily uptown, the Railroad Bldg. was left far behind until its only neighbors were gin mills and furniture warehouses. The Evans family finally let the place go for a mortgage during the Great Depression.

20. Larimer Square – 1400 block Larimer – 19th cen.   Score: 6.7

| Meets the Street – 7 | Scale – 7 | Integrity – 7 |
| Public Spaces – 7 | Mass – 6 | Imagination – 6 |

Had it not been for Dana Crawford, who tenaciously fought City Hall back around 1965 in order to reclaim the 1400 block of Larimer from the jaws of bulldozers, the impetus for preservation in Lo-Do might never have gained sustaining momentum. Happily, her efforts to create Larimer Square succeeded brilliantly, gaining widespread public acceptance, which further encouraged historic renovations in the area. Larimer Square is a story in its own right, situated on an immensely important block in Denver's early history. Architecturally, it preserves the flavor of the Victorian "railroad city" better than any other downtown block.

Before examining the square's architecture, we ought to set the stage by scrolling back to the late autumn of 1858. General William Larimer, Charles Lawrence, E.P. Stout, and Dick Whitsitt with their band from eastern Kansas had just arrived to survey the promising townsite. From the brow of a rise, not quite a hill, overlooking the cottonwoods hugging the South Platte, they surveyed several Indian encampments and a handful of recently built cabins across Cherry Creek. The high ground was all theirs. Some 250 yards to the west a half– finished cabin stood, hewn from rough cottonwood logs, and belonging to Charles Nichols. Both Nichols and Larimer were town promoters, a breed of opportunists intent on making a lot of money subdividing real estate. Nichols' presence created a problem, though not an insurmountable one, for General Larimer who had the advantage of numbers. The St. Charles Town Company had staked this claim, improved it (the unfinished cabin), and retired to eastern Kansas, leaving Charlie Nichols to hold the fort until spring.

The new group had a different idea, which necessitated jumping the St. Charles claim. They immediately organized a Denver City Town Company and started surveying blocks and lots for immediate sale. Nichols protested of course, but after threats and a show of force by the Denver group, he reluctantly agreed to sell out the St. Charles interest to Larimer's party, heading east with the bad news. Larimer, Lawrence, et al got to work building a town which really consisted of a few cabins for shelter against the impending winter. The spot they chose was right here, 15th & Larimer.

The two Will Larimers (father and son) initially occupied Nichols' unfinished cabin until their own 16' X 20' cottonwood palace was ready. It featured Denver's first, real glass-paned window, and a high end dirt floor and dirt roof! Denver's real estate boom was off and running. 15th St. (originally named F St.) was at the center of gravity. Larimer constructed his new digs on the site of the present day Granite Building, near the alley. It was not actually the first completed dwelling, however. That honor went to a double cabin erected by Messrs. Moyne and Rice, immediately across 15th St.

from the Larimer home, where Writer Square now sits. That cabin straddled the property line allowing Moyne and Rice to share a party wall and save on construction costs. Denver's first residence was actually a duplex, a building style that would be frequently repeated here.

The concept was so good that two other intrepid builders, Charles Lawrence and Folsom Dorsett, built themselves a double cabin on the north corner of the intersection, facing its prototype across Larimer St. The busy intersection was finished off by Hickory Rogers, who erected his cabin on the west corner, opposite Larimer's domicile. The president of the Denver Town Company, E.P. Stout, settled in a block yonder, on the triangular site at 14th St. & Larimer where Denver's old city hall is still commemorated by a bronze bell. Denver thus officially began right where today's Larimer Square is situated.

Denver Public Library, Western History Collection   X-19273

Early Larimer, about 1864, looking north toward 16th St. Teams of oxen park nonchalantly before W.D. Daniels' dry goods store and the U.S. Post Office. Two rough log cabins are visible at left, similar to the early Lawrence, Dorsett, and Larimer cabins.

The rough-hewn cabins were but a makeshift beginning. Within a couple years the block was filled with commercial structures, mostly wood, but a few of brick. The oldest survivor is probably not on Larimer, but a block down the hill, behind Larimer Square. A little one-story brick structure on the corner of 15th St. & Market rests on the foundations of the Holladay (later Wells Fargo) stage lines. During 1862 the Overland Mail & Express Company had slid into bankruptcy and was taken over by its largest creditor, Ben Holladay. His total investment in the company was around $700,000, a princely sum in 1862. Apparently Holladay was a managerial wonder and he turned the faltering express company around – reorganizing and setting it up on a clockwork schedule. In the process he built the office that is still partially extant, and made Denver a hub of operations.

Within four years the Holladay Overland Mail & Express Company was a booming concern. Holladay then sold his investment to Wells Fargo for $1,800,000, realizing a $1,100,000 return. An appreciative city council renamed the street, formerly called McGaa, after Holladay. It retained the name for several decades until its reputation became so sordid, due to the congregation of brothels, that Ben Holladay's family petitioned the city to rename it again. This time they called it Market, although further down it reverts to Walnut, giving it the most confusing etymology of any street in Denver. Wells Fargo constructed the present building in 1874, though it later lost the two upper floors.

By that time Hickory Rogers' cabin (at 15th & Larimer) had been replaced by a two-story brick drug store owned by William Graham. Graham's City Drug Store served another purpose, however, during the years when law and order were having a tough go of it. A vigilance committee met here, "unofficially" helping out pioneer sheriff Ed Wynkoop dissuade some of the horse thieving and indiscriminate killings that were plaguing this youthful metropolis. That extra-legal body managed to hang several miscreants from the bridge over Cherry Creek, thus getting the word out to drifters and con men that Denver wasn't a good place to shop for horses. About 1970 the old drugstore building began to fail physically. It became necessary to replace it with the current facsimile structure, although it is not a true replica.

Next to this are three of the more ornate examples of early commercial Victorian style, dating from the early to mid 1870s. The Crawford Building at #1439 and the **Gallup & Stanbury** at #1451 both feature flamboyant bracketed cornices, culminating in daring apexes. Continuing down the west side of Larimer we pass the ornate

Congdon Building at #1421. Take away the elaborate pressed-tin cornice and you can see the conservative style typical of Denver's early commercial buildings – a simple brick face with arched windows on the second story. The city evidenced very little architectural daring until the arrivals of Horace Tabor and Frank E. Edbrooke in 1879. They finally introduced Denver to something more than the western cow-town vernacular.

Next door at #1415 is **Lincoln Hall** – a dignified, restrained Second Empire design. Lincoln Hall sits about where the first theater in the Pikes Peak gold country was established in 1859, Apollo Hall. Besides drinking, the Apollo provided two other types of entertainment – one on the stage floor and the other as the town's first city hall.

The corner of 14th St. & Larimer features the conservative, brick **Miller Block**, which faced Denver's old **City Hall**, situated across 14th St. from 1883-1936. It was here, in the spring of 1894, that a quarrel between Governor David Waite and two political appointees escalated into the "City Hall War." For a couple of days these streets were filled with state militia and artillery arrayed against several hundred policeman and political supporters, hunkered inside the rustic walls of city hall. A pitched battle was averted only by the intervention of the state's Supreme Court, spoiling

Lincoln Hall (far right) and the Miller Block, home to Gahan's Saloon, which went underground, literally, during Prohibition. It continued to slake the thirst of Denver's city government officials, including policemen!

many wagers that the cannons would open fire on city hall. This showdown was all the more senselesse considering that Colorado was in the throes of its worst financial crisis ever. The politicians were offering comic relief when they should have been concerned about economic relief.

That incident actually spurred the movement for home rule which Denver finally achieved in 1904 when it also became its own county. The bell, which later hung in the old city hall, was cast in 1906 and marks the site well. Meanwhile the Miller Block housed Gahan's Saloon, a favorite watering hole for politicians, reporters, and policemen. During Prohibition (1919-1933) Gahan's went dry, but the rumor was that the basement became one of the town's favorite speak-easys, right across from City Hall!

The east side of Larimer Square is slightly newer vintage, but it still has several buildings of interest. The two-story **Kettle Building** at #1426 dates from 1873 and is a unique structure. Its thrifty builder, George Kettle, simply constructed a front and rear wall, using the two neighboring structures for side-wall support. Pass through the Kettle Arcade and enter the charming inner courtyard of the Bear and Bull. Notice the Cherub Fountain that once graced the sidewalk in front of the Manhattan Restaurant at 1633 Larimer. The courtyard is named after the bear and the bull that can be seen in the wall to the left of the fountain. These carved figures are all that remain of the Mining Exchange Building that once graced 15th & Arapahoe.

Next door at #1430 is the 1880 **Sussex Building**, a conservative, no-nonsense commercial structure sitting on the site of Denver's first post office — as well as William Graham's original drugstore (1859). Graham later moved across the street as business grew. Next to this is another conservative-looking business block, built in two separate phases, 1890 and 1908, as the **Buerger Brothers Building**. The Buerger

The Granite Bldg. announces the beginning of Larimer Square with colorful fanfare.

Brothers barber supply would later move over to Champa St. after commissioning the city's favorite Art Deco landmark by Montana Fallis (#36). Finally we retrace our steps to 15th St., anchored by Larimer's sauciest Victorian.

The **Granite Bldg.** (1882) was constructed by George W. & William Clayton on the site of General William Larimer's cabin. This may be Larimer Square's most exuberant Victorian building. The four-story pile is a liberal mixture of dressed stone (three varieties) and pink rhyolite, which give it a colorful, airy quality in spite of its heavy massing. Chamfering allows for a corner entryway as well as providing a prominent nameplate for the Clayton brothers. This building wonderfully dramatizes the optimism and eclectic tastes of the 1880s, at the height of the "Gilded Age." The forerunner of the Denver Dry Goods began here as the McNamara Dry Goods, before relocating to 16th & California in 1889.

Courtyard of the Bear and Bull in Larimer Square.

Mention should be made of one of early Denver's more celebrated buildings, the 1885 **Chamber of Commerce Bldg.**, an early work of Frank E. Edbrooke. Located across the alley behind Larimer Square, at 14th St. & Lawrence, this Richardsonian Romanesque 3½-story structure boasted clean, articulate lines and graceful Roman arches, repeated at half scale on the top floor. General Roger Woodbury, one of early Denver's most ardent boosters, was the president of the Chamber. The city's first library, called the Mercantile Library (a forerunner of the Denver Public Library), was instituted on building's top floor. Unfortunately this structure, so important both historically and architecturally, was lost to a parking lot.

Larimer Square ends this Chapter and tour #1. In order to proceed to tour #2, walk west on Larimer, crossing Speer Blvd. and Cherry Creek. The distinctive **Tivoli Student Center**, (#21) can be seen three blocks away.

TOUR 2: AURARIA & SKYLINE

Tour 2. Auraria & Skyline

"There are too many brutal buildings today." Minoru Yamasaki

Tour 2. *legnth 1.5 miles.* Begins at 10th St. & Larimer (Tivoli).
Ends at 19th St. & Larimer.

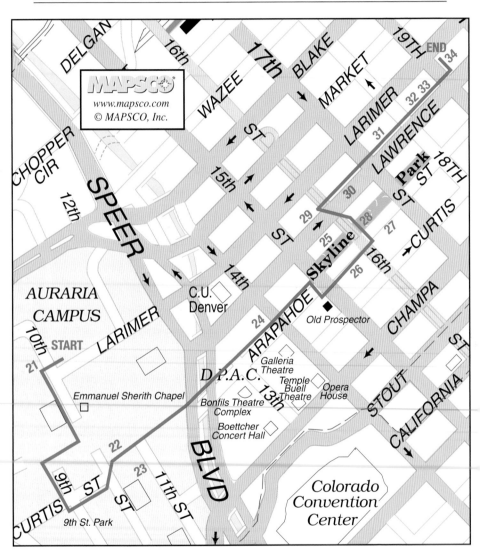

The Skyline Urban Renewal district resides where the Victorian railroad city once hummed with commerce. This historic node was virtually obliterated around 1970, much the same way Bunker Hill in Los Angeles was antiseptically reformatted into a car-oriented business zone. Denver's civic leaders had to resort to an original bit of political chicanery in order to acquire the necessary federal funds to wipe this 25-block slate clean. Conservative voters had denied a bond issue needed to provide local matching funds for federal aid but they had earlier (unwittingly?) approved bonds for a new convention hall. Savvy local politicians pushed a bill through Congress permitting convention centers to qualify for matching funds. Presto! The $14,000,000 already committed to build Currigan Hall was then credited to Denver as urban renewal seed money.

Federally-funded bulldozers moved in shortly thereafter, and a significant portion of Denver's early history was carted out to the landfill. Over the ensuing 16 years most of Skyline was successfully rebuilt, but with noticeably less character. Larimer, Denver's original "Main St.," was hard hit by the wrecker's ball. The replacement structures are a bland lot compared to their splashy Victorian predecessors. The sidewalks are grudging at best, shaved back to 10' from the standard 15' downtown sidewalk. The old Larimer had lots of color and street life back in its skid row days, a hard-bitten mixture of gin mills, flop houses, and furniture outlets.

Skyline today brims with predictable corporate containers, but in the midst of chaos, the slender, graceful outline of the Daniels & Fisher Tower soars like a mast or church spire, gently reassuring our bludgeoned senses. A handful of older structures, like the old Cable Railway Bldg. managed to survive the saturation bombing, wryly termed "urban removal." I am reminded of Henry James

Photo by J. J. Karius,
Arapahoe Street, before the urban renewal onslaught, sometime in the early 1960s. Skyline Park replaced this stretch of store-fronts.

lamenting over the razing of the old landmarks on lower 5th Ave. and discovering, with almost fanatical joy, that a couple of old churches had survived the carnage intact.

"Half the charm of the prospect... is in their still being there, and being as they are; this charm, this serenity of escape and survival positively works as a blind on the side of the question of their architectural importance... they illustrate again, supremely your grasped truth of the comparative character, in such conditions of beauty and interest. The special standard they may or may not square with signifies, you feel, not a jot:" ("The American Scene," 1905).

James' florid Victorian prose notwithstanding, the intensity of his conviction is clear. It is just such landmarks that anchor us to a once-familiar place. Their architectural merit is secondary to the happy fact that they somehow survived to remind us what kind of neighborhood once thrived where we now stand.

I was amused when strolling recently through the Bunker Hill section of downtown Los Angeles where colorful little plaques reminisce about the hill before it succumbed to "urban cleansing." Plaques, however nostalgic, are hardly a fitting substitute for the real thing. Skyline was Denver's "urban cleansing" experiment, not unlike the old truism about suicide, "a permanent solution to a temporary problem." It disconnected Denverites from a great deal of their historical past. Denver was fortunate, and Skyline eventually bounced back as a fully integrated neighborhood of residents and businesses. The creation of Skyline Park and the 16th St. Mall, dual axes intersecting at the restored D & F Tower, provided some civic restitution. And the convention center that made it all possible? In a twist of Byzantine irony, Currigan Hall was itself bulldozed amid howls of protest (it too had attained landmark status). After an abbreviated life span of 35 years, it was replaced by a terminally nondescript parking garage / exhibit hall. The gods have their ways of exacting revenge.

Our walking tour actually begins in a neighboring urban renewal zone, the Auraria Higher Education Center. Auraria is the oldest part of Denver's settlement. It was here that Denver was born in the summer of 1858 on Cherry Creek's west bank. By the early 1970s, the triangle-shaped neighborhood bounded by Colfax Ave., Cherry Creek, and the S. Platte River had evolved into a grab bag of industries, warehouses, and few hundred residents, mostly Hispanic. Proximity to downtown made it an ideal site for an urban college campus, shared by three institutions – the University of Colorado at Denver, Metropolitan State College, and the Community College of Denver.

Once again it was the people vs. the bulldozers, but a few historic buildings were salvaged including three churches, an historic brewery, and a full block of early Victorian-era residences. At first, the juxtaposition of modest 1870s houses engulfed by modern, block-sized classroom buildings was a little disconcerting. Today, the campus has filled in with verdant landscaping and mature trees; old and new co-exist peaceably, providing a sense of contrast and context for one another. The tour begins at the student hub of the sprawling campus, a former brewery that now houses student union functions and the campus bookstore.

21. Tivoli Student Center – 1342 10th St. – Harold Baerresen –
F.C. Eberly – H.O.K. – **1882, 1890, 1984**   **Score: 5.3**
Meets the Street – 4   Scale – 6   Integrity – 5
Public Spaces – 5   Mass – 6   Imagination – 6

It seems fitting for an old neighborhood of German immigrants to be overshadowed by a brewery. Tivoli is the largest of a handful of structures that survived the transformation of the old Auraria into a spanking new college campus. This block-square complex is actually a combination of new and old buildings. The more important elements, historically and architecturally, are those facing 10th St. on the east side of the block. A central two-story section dates back to 1882 and was the West Denver **Turne Halle**, a German social center. The designer, Harold Baerresen, was a Danish immigrant and ship's carpenter by trade, who became a self-professed architect after arriving in Denver in 1879. With his brothers who came later, he developed a very successful building practice (see **Sheridan / City Railway Bldg. #3**).

A brewery existed here long before Turne Halle, as early as 1859. By 1860 entrepreneur John Good had purchased it, naming it Tivoli after the famous gardens in Copenhagen. The venture prospered and by 1890 the brewery constructed the towering structure adjoining Turne Halle. A merger in 1901 created the Tivoli-Union Brewing Company which continued operating until 1969. The brewhouse itself is an eclectic Second Empire pile with castle-like crenelations and Italianate-style central tower. The architect was Frederick C. Eberly. Other sections were added at different times.

After years of neglect, an ill-fated effort to revitalize Tivoli as a specialty retail center did manage to pull all the elements together around an interior central court in the 1980s. The venture failed financially however, and in 1991 the student body infused new life into Tivoli by converting it into a student center. With 40,000 students using the campus, the place virtually hums with activity. The facade has recently undergone a renovation that finally stripped away generations of paint to reveal the natural brick color, so that now we get a sense of the buildings in their original splendor.

A block to the south, at the corner of 10th St. & Lawrence, we come upon **Emmanuel - Sherith Israel Chapel**, the oldest surviving church building in Denver. It was constructed in 1876 as Emmanuel Episcopal Church and later sold to Congregation Sherith Israel in 1902, explaining why it has both Christian and Jewish symbols on its face. Despite its modest proportions, the rusticated stone walls stand out boldly against the modern campus buildings. Although it's nominally Victorian Gothic, the heavy walls and pencil thin window openings give it a slightly Romanesque feel. Today it serves as an art gallery for the campus while continuing to be a strong visual anchor. Incidentally, the Tabors – Horace and Baby Doe – lived quietly in a tiny duplex (now gone) just a couple of doors down 10th St. from the church, in the mid 1890s, after they lost everything in the 1893 Silver Crash.

Glancing down Lawrence towards the mountains you can hardly miss the Spanish Colonial Revival **St. Cajetan Church** by Robert Willison, 1926. St. Cajetan is the youngest of three Catholic parishes that once populated the Auraria triangle. One of Denver's more interesting stories centers around an Irish immigrant who virtually founded and built a parish for the poor Hispanics who were migrating in from southern Colorado and New Mexico. John K. Mullen was a self-made millionaire who had made his fortune in flour milling. His Hungarian Flour Mills were in fact one of Auraria's largest industries. Mullen and his family lived on 9th St. where the former St. Cajetan rectory still stands. By 1923 the family had moved to a beautiful mansion at 9th & Pennsylvania (now demolished), but Mullen still owned the old West Denver homestead.

St. Cajetan's Mission Revival style lends an air of antiquity to the modern college campus. Despite appearances, the former parish church is a mere 80 years old.

Hispanic Catholics were attending Mass in the basement of the Irish church, St. Leo's (demolished in the 1960s) at 10th St. & Colfax. Ever sympathetic to the less fortunate, Mullen donated his former home as a site for a new Hispanic Church. By the time the building was completed in 1926, he had invested an additional $65,000 into the project, most of the building's cost. The church became the center of Hispanic social and cultural life in Denver, and when threatened with destruction by the impending higher education center in the 1970s, parishioners rallied to save the historic building by getting it designated as a landmark. The resourceful congregation later relocated to a new location in southwest Denver and thus kept the parish alive. The old church was subsequently made into a performing arts hall for the colleges, in which capacity it has functioned ever since.

The architect, Robert Willison, was an immigrant from Scotland who became the city architect and building inspector under Mayor Robert Speer, later serving as a state legislator. He designed a Revival-style church that reflected, on a grand scale, many of the churches in the San Luis Valley, the oldest settled part of Colorado. Willison is equally famous for the imposing Neo-Gothic Church of St. Dominic, a short ride across the Speer Viaduct in North Denver. His most important achievement is undoubtedly the **Municipal Auditorium (#44)**, constructed in 1908. Where else but America could a Scot and an Irishman collaborate to create an ethnic church serving native Hispanics, who were generally the object of extreme prejudice? Sometimes the melting pot culture fostered unusual alliances, in this case resulting in a happy ending.

Turning left at St. Cajetan Church we pass an un-assuming brick duplex that was moved to this site to escape demolition. Originally located in the old Jewish neighborhood on West Colfax, it once housed a North High School student who later

The 9th Street Historic Park provides a fascinating glimpse of early Denver residential neighborhoods.

became prime minister of Israel, Golda Meier. At Curtis St. we approach the **9th Street Historic Park**, a full-block collection of restored Victorian, Second Empire, and Italianate homes, some as early as 1873. This block is a primer on Denver's early residential architecture, representative of the tastes and social aspirations during the early railroad period. Each building has a plaque identifying the original owners and styles, but special note should be made of three: the **Stephen Knight House** at 1015

9th St., the **John Witte House** at #1027, and the **Jeremiah Gardner House** at #1033. Turn east along Curtis and pass under the classroom building bridging the street. To our left, at the very heart of the Auraria campus, the Auraria library can be seen.

22. Auraria Library – 10th St. & Curis to Lawrence – C.F. Murphy
and Helmut Jahn – **1977**   **Score: 5.5**
Meets the Street – 5   Scale – 6   Integrity – 6
Public Spaces – 5   Mass – 6   Imagination – 5

This is the only modern building on the campus that really creates any "buzz," with its white aluminum skin that distinguishes it from the nondescript classroom buildings. The horizontal flow of the building is enhanced by the white louvers that screen the sunlight and add a bit of texture to the smooth curtain wall. Two interior courtyards allow light to penetrate the interior recesses of the library. The generous landscaping helps to soften the streamlined surface.

The library was always intended as a kind of visual and academic focal point on campus, and within its rather severe context it literally glistens. The design hardly seems daring today, but in 1977 it made Helmut Jahn a star. It provides welcome counterpoint to the heavy brick "education factory" that surrounds it and advertises its function well, especially at night when the stacks are clearly visible from a considerable distance. Its lightness also defers graciously to the solid, Romanesque form of **St. Elizabeth Church** immediately across the way.

23. St. Elizabeth Church – 1060 St. Francis Wy. (11th St.) – Fr. Adrian, O.F.M.
– **1898**   **Score: 6.7**
Meets the Street – 7   Scale – 7   Integrity – 7
Public Spaces – 6   Mass – 6   Imagination – 7

This is actually the second church building on this site. St. Elizabeth of Hungary is Denver's second oldest Catholic parish. It was established in 1878 by Father Frederic Bender, who founded no fewer than seven parishes over his long, productive career. Within 20 years St. Elizabeth's had outgrown the small brick building that stood here. The gifted friar, Father Adrian, OFM, arranged the plans for this beautiful Romanesque Revival church whose 162' bell tower still dominates Auraria. This stout, grounded structure, built of rusticated Castle Rock rhyolite is visible all along Arapahoe, making it a landmark in the true sense. An unfortunate interior remodeling from the 1970s removed the original intricate stained glass and many of the beautiful frescoes, reredos, and pulpit. The exterior is original, however, and St. Elizabeth's is the only active parish out of three that once served Auraria.

The church's history is quite unique, stemming from a sensational assassination reminiscent of Thomas Becket's murder at Canterbury. In the early morning gloom of Sunday, Feb. 23, 1908, the youthful German pastor, Father Leo Heinrichs, was shot to death at the communion railing by a fanatical anarchist, Giuseppe Alia. Alia had vowed to execute a priest merely on principle, and after spitting out the host during the early 6:00 a.m. Mass, he fired a revolver pointblank at Father Heinrichs' heart. The mortally wounded priest staggered to the altar before dying. Two off duty police officers who happened to be attending Mass apprehended the fleeing assassin.

The entire city was horrified at the brutality of the deed, and tens of thousands – Catholic and Protestant alike – turned out for the priest's funeral. Feelings were so strong that Alia's trial had to be moved to Colorado Springs to assure fairness, and possibly prevent a lynching. Alia was later executed in Canon City. Father Leo's vestments, bullet holes intact, are still in custody of the parish.

Proceed towards downtown on Curtis, which becomes Arapahoe once we cross the Cherry Creek bridge, and returns us to downtown proper. To the right we see the **Denver Performing Arts Complex (#44)**. Straight ahead, on the left side of Arapahoe, we climb a slight incline past the former **Tramway Bldg. (#24)**.

24. Hotel Teatro / Tramway Bldg. – 1100 14th St. – Fisher & Fisher –
    1911   **Score: 6.5**

Meets the Street – 6	Scale – 7	Integrity – 7
Public Spaces – 6	Mass – 6	Imagination – 7

This location was closely connected to the pioneer Evans family for nearly a century. Dr. John Evans, a physician from Cincinnati, Ohio, was a successful promoter of early Chicago railroads and real estate in the 1850s. As a renowned physician, he was deeply involved in the founding of Northwestern University in Chicago, which he initially headed. In 1862, President Abraham Lincoln appointed Dr. Evans to be the second territorial governor of Colorado.

Governor John Evans was a successful medical doctor, railroader, and educator who left Chicago in 1862 to oversee Colorado Territory. He stayed on, promoting education, industry, and railroads until the day he died, in July, 1897.

Denver Public Library, Western History Collection Z-2873

The first governor, William Gilpin, had gotten embroiled with Congress over the unauthorized issuance of script to pay for the Glorietta Pass campaign in New Mexico, which actually saved Colorado from invasion by a Confederate army. Nonetheless, Gilpin was sacked and replaced by Evans, who was not only an ambitious man, but also quite wealthy. For the young city of Denver, it turned out to be a fortuitous match. Evans, ever the practical dreamer, threw all his energies into his adopted city.

The **Evans House** sat right here, where Colorado's first family entertained visiting dignitaries such as President Ulysses S. Grant in the parlor. The Evanses, being good Methodists, it is not surprising that the city's first Methodist Church sat just across 14th St. at Lawrence. The **Colorado Seminary** (also Methodist) was located directly across Arapahoe. After a tenuous start and a forced closing lasting several years, this embryonic institution was resurrected as the University of Denver. The main campus began relocating to distant University Park in 1891, but the original building continued to shelter D.U.'s School of Arts and Music well into the 20th century.

Around 1887, when classroom space was getting tight, the four-story **Haish Bldg.** was constructed on the opposite corner (currently the Executive Tower) to house Medicine, Law, and Dentistry. Dr. John Evans remained president of the board of Denver University until his death in 1897. It should be noted that the great, snowcapped peak hovering to the west of Denver is named in honor of Evans, as is Evanston, Illinois, home to Northwestern University. Dr. Evans was obviously an energetic man of many abilities, but his greatest lifetime project was the city of Denver itself.

Another Evans interest, the Denver Tramway Company, was owned and managed by John Evans' son, William Gray Evans, known locally as "Tramway Bill." By 1910, the senior Evans was dead. William had settled his family at 13th Ave. & Bannock St., in a house purchased from Rocky Mountain News founder, William N. Byers (now the Byers-Evans Museum #98). Although 14th St. was no longer prime residential property, Tramway Bill figured that the old family homestead would be an ideal location for the center of his streetcar operations. It was strategically situated one block from the "Loop" at 15th St. & Lawrence, where the inter-urban lines from Boulder and Golden intersected with the Denver streetcar system. Even better, the sloping topography allowed the stabling of streetcars on two levels, a marvelous efficiency. By 1911, the brothers Fisher had completed a block-long complex of offices and car barns.

Fisher and Fisher were never ones to do things in a slipshod manner, demonstrated by the well-balanced and appointed details we see. The building exhibits a solid and confident character. The deep red brick piers enclose white-tiled window bays, creating a two-tone effect. The vernacular is vintage 20th century Commercial, interpreted in a classy Fisher and Fisher idiom. The grouping of windows, three per bay, has a vague "Chicago" resonance. In fact, this is more reminiscent of their University Building (16th St. & Champa) which went up at the same time. Both buildings have strong corner piers, for instance, which mask the structural grid rather than amplifying it, and both artfully blend terra cotta with brick. There is a fully functional auditorium on the second floor, just west of the tower. A marble staircase adorns the main entry foyer as one enters the building. The extensive car barns stretching to 13th St. were long ago converted into classroom and office space, but one can imagine what a beehive of activity they were during the heyday of streetcars.

Denver's last streetcar was retired in 1950, after which the building spent four decades as the University of Colorado extension. It was then rehabbed, this time into a boutique hotel. A ninth-story penthouse floor was integrated so expertly into the original structure that you would never guess it was not original. In a sense, Hotel Teatro anchors the 14th & Arapahoe vicinity, not because of its size, but by its street presence and strong character. The immediate surroundings are hardly cohesive, and today Tramway Bill's monument stands like a tuxedo in a crowd of blue jeans, dressing up a singularly drab environment.

A block away **Brooks Tower** looms ominously, significant as the first downtown high-rise apartment building (1967). This was the pet project of Central Bank president Ellwood Brooks who imagined it revitalizing a sagging neighborhood. Unfortunately, this required the leveling of the 1891 **Mining Exchange Building**, by Kirchner and Kirchner, one of Denver's more elaborate Victorian commercial blocks. The great rounded corners and Romanesque entry arch (reminiscent of Sullivan's Midwest Stock Exchange in Chicago) softened the otherwise heavy, Richardsonian massing.

The Mining Exchange featured a central tower topped by the "Old Prospector," a grizzled 12' miner leaning smugly on a pick handle as he ponders the chunk of gold resting in the

Denver Public Library H-567 Rose & Hopkins
Denver's finest Richardsonian Romanesque building, the Mining Exchange, was traded off for a soulless apartment building in the mid-1960s.

palm of his outstretched hand. The "Old Prospector" was sculpted by Alphonse Pelzer out of a quarter-ton slab of copper. At present he waits stoically at the main entrance to Brooks Tower, whose 43 stories of dark chocolate brick and ho-hum balconies create zero visual excitement. Attempts to energize the two-story podium produced an unconvincing throwback to Sunset Boulevard poised incongruously on 15th St. Brooks Tower connects happily to the street but is otherwise as soulless as a ledger sheet.

Denver Public Library   MCC-2705 Louis McClure
Jacques J. Benedict's graceful Central Bank Bldg. anchored 15th & Arapahoe for 80 years. Its needless demise in the summer of 1990 was a civic tragedy.

The northwest side of Arapahoe once hummed with the Loop Market and Jacques J. Benedict's graceful **Central Bank and Trust**, circa 1910. A designated landmark, it became a pawn in a tangled web of corporate self-interest when an out-of-state owner defaulted and the lenders (including Central Bank) panicked. They decided to demolish it, despite vigorous protests by the mayor and city officials who even offered to buy it, all to no avail. To make matters worse, the urban renewal authority was threatening at the same time to raze the historic **Denver Dry Building** on 16th St. a tactic which only heightened the political tension.

The ensuing demolition of Central Bank in July of 1990 outraged the citizenry and spurred the city to enact strict legislation that protected all landmark buildings in the Central Business District. It requires a one-year waiting period and an approved building permit in hand before a demolition permit could be issued. That ordinance now protects many of downtown's older structures, and encourages adapting them to new economic uses.

25. Park Central – 1515 Arapahoe - W.C. Muchow & Assoc. –
       1973   **Score 5.3**
Meets the Street – 4   Scale – 7   Integrity – 4
Public Spaces – 5   Mass – 7   Imagination – 5
    Some mention should first be made of this block's history. It was home to "Newspaper Alley," so-called because several of Denver's many newspapers lined it

back in the 1880s, notably the *Denver Times* and the *Denver Tribune*. The *Tribune*, though short lived, had a glorious history owing in part to its managing editor for a two-year period, Eugene Field. Field arrived in town around 1880 from Kansas City but before he left for Chicago and literary fame, he had gained a reputation as the city's crown prince of mischief and practical jokers. He once reviewed a local Shakespeare production of King Lear, castigating the leading actor with barbs such as, "he played the king like he expected his opponent to play the ace."

Another time Field induced his editor to impersonate visiting celebrity Oscar Wilde. Unknown to the populace, Wilde's train had been delayed. Field brazenly paraded the impostor around town, passing him off as the more famous personage to the adulating crowds. When Wilde finally did arrive, tired and out of sorts, the crowd had all retired, leaving no greeting committee at the station. Oscar was not amused by the prank, but Denverites never forgot it. Field now has a library named after him; Wilde came up empty-handed.

Park Central sits where Gene Field once scribbled, his feet resting comfortably in lounge slippers conveniently tacked to the wall. The structure is really three interlocking cubicles, rendered credibly enough in a modern vernacular by a respected local architect. The lines are clean, the scale is tolerable, and the geometry is reasonably eye catching, but on the whole it belongs in an office campus. It shrugs off Lawrence like a service alley, and the dull, black aluminum skin feels flimsy.

Park Central was inadvertently a part of the complex financial machinations that ultimately led to the senseless demise of Jacques Benedict's *Beaux Arts* **Central Bank Bldg.** In the end, one of Denver's finest landmarks was traded off against its inferior offspring. The loss of the original Central Bank actually cheapened the visual drama of Park Central itself, whose blocky geometry formerly played off tolerably well against the classic bank structure. Nowadays, Park Central feels like a one-legged sailor hobbling sadly around the park.

One of Denver's more important business blocks, the **People's Bank Building**, was located at the northwest corner of Park Central on 16th St. & Lawrence. Frank E. Edbrooke designed this nine-story tower, constructed in 1890. It was one of Edbrooke's more mature and successful office buildings, featuring a light stone base and seven stories of finely articulated brickwork that gave it strong vertical emphasis. Later called the **Interstate Trust Building**, it met its fate by implosion in 1970.

Skyline Park, 1700 block of Arapahoe. The old Arapahoe High School, 1872, was situated mid-block, just behind the seated couple. Later it became part of the six-story Club Bldg, after a new high school was erected at 19ᵗʰ & California.

Skyline Park was originally designed by Lawrence Halprin and opened in 1968 as a key element in the Skyline urban renewal project. This linear park fronting Arapahoe from 15th to 18th Sts. focuses on the stately **Daniels & Fisher Tower**. Halprin designed a playful series of manmade canyons and fountains whose irregular geometry was modeled impressionistically on nearby mountains. An uninspired reconstruction retained only vestiges of Halprin's original scheme. The largest and most engaging of the water sculptures, at 15ᵗʰ St., was ruthlessly annihilated and replaced by a barren patch of lawn. The block between 15ᵗʰ and 16ᵗʰ Sts. is now as sterile as a Turkish eunuch. On sunny days it looks hotter than the Sinai Peninsula as it basks in splendid desolation.

The middle segment, fronting the **Westin Tabor Center**, creates more sense of intimacy and retains one of Halprin's smaller fountains. The hotel is also a plus, providing a lively urban backdrop. The third segment, from 17ᵗʰ to 18ᵗʰ Sts., fares little better than its barren 15ᵗʰ St. counterpart, except that the stair-stepped water sculpture at the far end gives it some sense of climax and definition. There is no real dialogue between the park and the three aluminum buildings that stare blankly at this public space as if it were an intrusive neighbor.

On the plus side, some practical improvements emerged in Skyline Park, such as the addition of real sidewalks along Arapahoe's right bank. Hallelujah! Another plus was the replacement of concrete surfaces around the fountains with soft road-fill, which not only discourages kamikaze skateboarders but has the added benefit of providing a more rustic context.

Denver's first public high school, **Arapahoe School** (G.E. Randall, 1872), sat mid-block between 17ᵗʰ and 18ᵗʰ Sts. For a time it was the city's tallest building, with three stories, plus ornamental cupola, as well as a source of great civic pride. The former **Federal Reserve Branch Bank** was located at the 17ᵗʰ St. end of the same block, along Arapahoe, before it succumbed to the Skyline bulldozers around 1968. The Neo-Renaissance facade, clad in Colorado Yule marble, gave it an imposing presence on the street, despite its modest scale. Its successor (#26) is hardly a worthy replacement.

26. Federal Reserve Bank – 1020 16ᵗʰ St. – Donald Prezler and
W.C. Muchow & Assoc. – **1968**   **Score: 4.2**

Meets the Street – 3   Scale – 6   Integrity – 4
Public Spaces – 3   Mass – 5   Imagination - 5

Ouch! Not one, but two of early Denver's grand edifices, the **Tabor Grand Opera House** and **Old Post Office Building**, bit the dust for this intrusive, Lego-Land parody that effectively interrupts the retail continuity of 16ᵗʰ St. If ever a building looked dated, this one does, right out of 1968 when it plopped itself onto the scene, a cheap rendition of Boston's more famous City Hall (1963) by Kallmann, McKinnell, & Knowles. The "Fed" aspires to wittiness, but only acts busy in a purposeless manner. Deep recesses, voids, and projections give it a sculptured quality, but draping it in common aggregate only diminishes what little authority it tries to muster. The Feds bought a pig in a poke back in '68 and threw away a charming Neo-Renaissance palace only a block away, callously abandoning it to its fate with a wrecking crew. This was a deal where the citizens lost heavily, all the way around.

Denver Public Library, Western History Collection   MCC-236 Louis McClure
For 85 years, 16ᵗʰ & Curtis was ruled by the Tabor Grand Opera House. Its demolition was an example of shocking bureaucratic indifference. The crowning achievement of Denver's Victorian "Railroad Era," it brought culture to the rough, aspiring metropolis.

The **Tabor Grand Opera House** was an integral part of Denver's history for too many years to adequately chronicle here. Along with the Tabor block, built simultaneously around 1880, these two seminal structures gave the raw, frontier city its first taste of real urban life. Equally important, these projects were the catalyst that brought Frank E. Edbrooke to Denver from Chicago. His brother Willoughby J. Edbrooke undoubtedly had a hand in the exuberant Second Empire designs, but it was Frank who came out to supervise construction. He stayed, and subsequently endowed Denver's commercial architecture with his unique and indelible stamp. Denver turned an important corner with the arrival of Frank E. Edbrooke, yet if it hadn't been for Horace Tabor's grandiose ideas, who knows how differently things might have turned out? One thing is certain, however, the **Tabor Bldg.** and Tabor's Opera House put Denver squarely on the social / cultural map for the first time. The opera house also influenced other important buildings like the fabled Windsor Hotel, with its Second Empire corner tower and mansard roof-line.

Denver Public Library, Western History Collection   X-21980, 22027

Ill-fated lovers. Horace Tabor met the beautiful, young divorcee, Elizabeth McCourt Doe, in Leadville during the Spring of 1880. An infamous love affair ensued, followed by a blissful marriage - after Tabor maneuvered a divorce from his first wife, Augusta, in 1883. Baby Doe remained ever constant to the much older Tabor. Some 36 years after his death she was found frozen in her Leadville cabin, near his defunct Matchless Mine..

Aside from its connection with the Tabors, the opera house established Curtis as the "Great White Way," Denver's fabled theater district and center of night life for decades. Likewise, it was instrumental in pulling business in the direction of upper 16th St. Above all, it became the focal point of the city's cultural life, unchallenged until the exuberant, "Sultanesque" Broadway Theater was constructed in 1889, way uptown on Brown's Bluff, three years before Henry C. Brown completed his hotel. Tabor made all those future developments possible by establishing a market for "high brow" entertainment, thus proving that the frontier city of 35,000 souls would support something more than dance halls and gambling salons.

The building's hodgepodge Victorian frumpery, surmounted by a flashy corner tower, reflected the flamboyance of H.A.W. Tabor and his (then) mistress, Elizabeth "Baby" Doe. Tongues certainly wagged on opening night when Tabor's wife, Augusta, was conspicuously absent. A veiled figure, decidedly not Augusta, sat mysteriously in the

*The old Post Office & Federal Bldg. as it was when Horace Tabor became
Postmaster. Tabor's star was waning just as promotional genius Harry H. Tammen's
was rising. Tammen's successful curio establishment can be seen next door. The
biggest fish Tammen ever lured was Fred Bonfils. Together they reaped millions,
running the influential Denver Post.*

back of the private box, adding fuel to the fire. Box "A" was inscribed with the Tabor
name, and regularly occupied by H.A.W. and Baby Doe, after they were formally
married, until the fateful year 1893 when Tabor's fortunes slid away along with his
beloved opera house.

The **Old Post Office / Custom House** played a role in Tabor's rags / riches /
rags saga as well. The Post Office occupied the Arapaho end of this site, just
across the alley from Tabor's Grand Opera House. That building, commenced in
1884, took eight years to complete because of political and bureaucratic
ineptitude. Even then, it was considered inadequate and disorganized when it
finally did open. Old photos show a squat, clumsy Neo-Renaissance attempt,
surmounted by an equally ill-proportioned cupola, but in time, it mellowed and
took its place as a landmark. It was here that Horace Tabor worked the last 15
months of his life, after being rescued from abject poverty by his old friend,
Winfield Scott Stratton. Stratton was a former carpenter who had made millions
in the Cripple Creek gold fields. He advanced Tabor $15,000 and helped influence
Senator Ed Wolcott, who had known Tabor since his Leadville days, to get Tabor
appointed as Denver's postmaster.

Horace and Baby Doe Tabor returned full circle, moving back into the Windsor, where they lived comfortably and respectably, until April, 1899. Tabor died from an attack of acute appendicitis (he might have lived, but Baby Doe was afraid to let the doctors operate). Tabor's luck had finally run out for good, but the legacy he left Denver endured for decades. The words inscribed on the Arcadian curtain of the Tabor Grand Opera House proved amazingly prophetic, "So fleet the works of men, back to the earth again. Ancient and holy things fade like a dream."

27. Independence Plaza – 1001 16th St. - Seracuse, Lawler, & Partners – 1973   Score: 5.1

Meets the Street – 6	Scale – 6	Integrity – 4
Public Spaces - 6	Mass – 5	Imagination – 3

One of the earliest privately financed Skyline developments, Independence (originally Prudential) Plaza was the first to mix retail with office space. The tower is unspectacular, capped by a heavy, protruding mechanical penthouse. The smaller plaza buildings are somewhat more refined but sport the typical 70's rough aggregate finish. A renovation in the 90s extended the retail facade out from the original setback, creating a more interesting but still marginal retail face along 16th St. To its credit however, Independence Plaza pulls back from 16th St., opening a visual promenade for the historic **Daniels & Fisher Tower (#28)**. The massing is respectful: low, three-story buildings along 16th St. with the 25-story tower pushed far away from the fragile looking D&F. White aggregate keeps the overall feeling bright, but Independence still resembles a chunky farm girl regardless of how hard they try to make her over into a slender princess.

28. Daniels & Fisher Tower – 1101 16th St. – Frederick Sterner & George Williamson – 1911   Score: 8.3

Meets the Street – 8	Scale – 9	Integrity – 9
Public Spaces – 7	Mass – 9	Imagination – 8

The Daniels & Fisher Tower is one of the better variations on a Venetian campanile, thematically popular just after the turn of the 20th century. Other well-known imitators include the University of California at Berkeley and the Metropolitan Life Tower on Madison Square, New York. The year 1910 was an exciting time in the young city of Denver. Optimism filled the air as Denver's skyline crept steadily upward. Merchant prince William Cooke Daniels, busily expanding his 16th St. retail emporium into a Renaissance Palazzo, set a soaring campanile above it all.

The tower is a ¾ scale model of the celebrated bell tower of San Marco in Venice. Modifications

William Cooke Daniels, merchant prince and son of W. B. Daniels, envisioned a towering, Venetian mast, which has been synonymous with Denver for nearly a century.

included the use of a yellowish, buff brick and the addition of fenestration for offices (very un-Italian), but Frederick Sterner pulled it off with plenty of élan' and good taste. D & F's larger New York cousin, the Metropolitan Life Tower, is more than double its scale, yet the D & F soars effortlessly and unperturbed thanks to its simpler, more flowing window arrangement. Also, the placement of the timepiece proportionally higher up gives it a more ordered prominence than Met Life's clock. Both structures are certainly landmarks of the first order, positioned dramatically within their respective urban frameworks: Met Life reigning prominently over Madison Square, and the D & F Tower situated strategically at the nexus of 16th St. and Arapahoe.

It's hard now to imagine that back in the 1970's it sat derelict and in real danger of the wrecking ball for the better part of a decade. Notice that the lower six floors in the north and west faces are differentiated by reddish brown brick. This marks the profile of the original D & F department

The stately D & F Tower framed (left) by the Westin Tabor Center and Aluminum Chase Tower.

store, which attached here to the tower itself. Rather than mask the old wounds from the razed portion, the developer chose to outline it, thus giving us a historical glimpse, much like shadow buildings from the past.

If brick and mortar can claim a soul, then downtown Denver's soul undoubtedly resides in the D & F Tower, perhaps the city's premier icon. Once towering over the skyline, it claimed to be the nation's third tallest when it opened in 1911 (Met Life was the first). Today it looks like your grandmother huddled among the L.A. Lakers. If certain buildings give cities their unique character, then there is no doubt that, even lost among the giants, the D & F Tower remains one of Denver's most important and distinctive landmarks.

29. Writer Square – 1500 Larimer – Barker, Rinker, Secat & Partners –
1981   **Score: 7.2**

Meets the Street – 7	Scale – 8	Integrity – 6
Public Spaces – 7	Mass – 8	Imagination – 7

The use of a rust-colored brick lends a warm ambiance to Writer Square. A retail pedestrian lane connecting 16th St. Mall to Larimer Square dovetails nicely with the Tabor Center's urban storefronts. The brick arches hearken back to Larimer in its heyday as Denver's first Main St. An engaging plaza at 16th and Lawrence draws pedestrians into the shopping promenade. Fashionable town-homes above the stores are reminiscent of a European town. This appealing project is a healthy mix of residential, retail, and office functions; sensitively scaled to historic Larimer Square and representing Skyline's best effort to create a real neighborhood.

Like many of the Skyline blocks, a significant amount of history is associated with this one. Banking tycoon David Moffat once sold stationary at his Lawrence St. establishment. Another early civic promoter, Roger Woodbury, owned the parcel of land mid-block along Lawrence which was the birthplace of the famed *Denver Tribune*, later absorbed into the *Denver Times* which was also located at 1547-51 Lawrence.

The earlier building on that site however is where Woodbury brainstormed with George Francis Train back in 1867 when it appeared that the Union Pacific Railroad would bypass Denver. With Woodbury's encouragement, Train prepared his famous *"The Lord helps those who help themselves"* speech that convinced the aspiring young city to build its own railroad, the Denver Pacific. The city leaders responded positively and Denver subsequently became the rail hub, and premier city of the Rocky Mountain region.

30. Tabor Center – 16ᵗʰ St. & Lawrence – Urban Design Group / Kohn
   Pederson Fox – **1984**   **Score: 7.4**
Meets the Street – 7   Scale – 6   Integrity – 8
Public Spaces – 8   Mass – 8   Imagination – 7

Glancing from the slightly raked plaza, this Post-Modern office tower (Kohn Pederson Fox), replete with alliterative flashbacks to the days of Art Deco, stands out handsomely in the disjunct architectural environs. The durable look of Tabor Center, which includes the brick and glass Westin Hotel across Lawrence, interposes an element of order into the corporate urban clutter. From Tabor's intimate, granite plaza, the upper stories of the D&F Tower are neatly framed by Tabor's buildings, lending a sense of timelessness.

Tabor Center fills two city blocks at the geographic node of Skyline. In a sense it rescued an urban renewal experiment that was rushing headlong into that unhappy condition which urban advocate Jane Jacobs coined "the blight of dullness." Tabor breaks decisively with Skyline's predictable, over-planned and under-designed "model city" image. The choice of colors and finishes is refreshing: olive green glass and metal effectively contrast, with buff-colored brick and concrete. Red polished granite sills and lintels frame office windows, creating an articulate and cheerful facade. The hotel and office building both sit well back from 16ᵗʰ St., which features a three-story retail pavilion, originally done in a greenhouse motif. The newer version gestures theatrically towards 16ᵗʰ St. It allows more store frontage directly on the mall and improves the interior connections to office tenants and 17ᵗʰ St. The retail component defers respectfully to the D & F icon while still generating a sense of excitement on the street.

What makes Tabor Center a great complex? A host of details such as quality materials, conveying a sense of durability, spacious public lobbies, and suitable connections to the surrounding streets. This is the only place in Denver that remotely feels like 5ᵗʰ Avenue or Rockefeller Center. I feel a little pampered every time I walk through its doors, which is how any great building ought to make one feel.

The Westin Hotel, handled by Urban Design Group, is equally important, providing 24-hour activity to the Tabor Center. It anchors the 17ᵗʰ St. end of the project and gives Skyline Park its best definition. The Westin occupies the same ground as one of Denver's more important early hotels, the **Markham**, which began its existence as the **Grand Central Hotel** in 1872. The Grand Central became one of the early city's more elegant hostelries, entertaining such guests as President Ulysses S. Grant and General James W. Denver, who visited his namesake city only once, in 1882. Years earlier

Denver had traded his governor's hat for a general's stars as the Civil War erupted. He played an interesting role after the war's conclusion.

James Denver was one of the defense counsel for Captain Henry Wirz, C.S.A., commandant of the infamous Andersonville, Georgia prison. In the summer of 1865, Wirz was tried by a military tribunal, headed by General Lew Wallace, for war crimes. It seems that the whole trial was a diversionary tactic designed to draw attention from the terrible conditions in Union P.O.W. camps such as Elmira, N.Y. Wirz was apparently convicted in the panel's mind well before the trial began; requests for a normal trial before a civilian jury were denied. The bias was so obvious that General Denver quit the disgraceful proceedings in protest before the actual trial even began. The conclusion was predictable, Wirz was condemned and hanged, but the ordeal left a bad taste in the public's mouth. No further recriminations were attempted against other Southern leaders such as Robert E. Lee or Jefferson Davis, whom radical Republicans were hoping to convict of treason. Denver, however, came out of the sordid affair with his honor and reputation intact.

The Westin Hotel sits where the Grand Central Hotel once hosted President Grant and General James Denver, who lent his name to the Queen city of the plains.

From all accounts the former general and governor enjoyed visiting the precocious city named after him. Shortly after Denver's visit, the Grand Central was purchased by V. D. Markham and Thomas Patterson, and greatly enlarged, surviving as the Markham Hotel until the Skyline bulldozer leveled it nearly 100 years after its historic origins. Patterson, who owned the *Rocky Mountain News* for years, installed the *News'* business office on the ground floor of the Markham.

Across the street the banded glass and aluminum **Chase Tower** at 1125 17th St. by Skidmore, Owings & Merrill, seems to mimic the **1670 Broadway Bldg.** (#73) dominating the far end of 17th St. The gently rounded corners salvage a listless design by softening the otherwise harsh corners. Two low-slung companion structures absorb most of the site, pre-empting any meaningful human activity (several restaurants have failed, despite fronting Skyline Park). Although it outperforms most of the clunky neighbors, in truth this tower could be situated anywhere without a real sense of displacement.

The site is historically significant. One of Denver's earliest pioneers, George W. Clayton, lived here until 1886 when the property became so valuable that Clayton tore down his house and constructed the three-story **Clayton Bldg.**, a handsome commercial structure that survived well into the 1970s. Clayton and his brother, William (Denver's sixth mayor in 1868-69), were both active on the early vigilance committee, formed to combat the rash of frontier lawlessness in the wake of the Civil War. George resigned from the committee after an incident in which he felt the committee's decision was a little too hasty in light of the thin evidence.

He was also a director of the Denver Union Water Company, the First National Bank, and a founder of the Denver Club. The four-story **Granite Bldg.** in **Larimer Square (#20)**, also constructed by the Clayton brothers, is still intact. William served as Denver's sixth mayor, in 1868-69. George Clayton's memory and endowment continues at the Clayton College for Youth in Northeast Denver.

31. 17ᵗʰ St. Plaza (Excel Energy) – 1225 17ᵗʰ St. - Skidmore, Owings &
        Merrill – **1982**   **Score 4.9**

Meets the Street – 4	Scale – 4	Integrity – 7
Public Spaces – 7	Mass – 4	Imagination – 3

A kinetic sculpture enlivens this spacious plaza, marking the site of the Gumry Hotel disaster, Denver's worst. Twenty-two people died when an untended boiler erupted.

17ᵗʰ St. Plaza feels like a transplant from the Windy City: broad, big-shouldered, its uncomfortable bulk set well back on an expansive plaza, reminiscent of Chicago's monolithic city hall. An insensitive, suburban, two-story garage tacked onto the rear tarnishes its sense of urbanism. The dark, polished granite and bronze tinted windows give it a rich, somber texture. The smooth, monotonous facade is broken only by recesses at the top and base. The plaza is thoughtfully contained, taking advantage of the sloping topography for a shady, sequestered green. An active pedestrian causeway fills the southeast. This intelligent plaza, enlivened by a kinetic sculpture, offsets the building's heavy girth and institutional formality.

Denver's worst hotel disaster occurred here on the Lawrence side of this plaza. The **Gumry Hotel** was leveled on August 18, 1895, by a huge boiler explosion and fire which killed 22 people, including the owner, Peter Gumry. Gumry was a Swedish immigrant who also happened to be the superintendent of construction on the new state capitol building which was then rising on Sherman St. Investigations revealed that a 22-year-old building engineer, Helmuth Loescher, was not only undependable but had little working knowledge of boilers. At the time of the explosion he was across the street getting a beer.

The real scandal, however, was that the city boiler inspector had certified the boiler the previous May without verifying that crucial repairs had in fact been made. Gumry, as a construction superintendent, should have realized the danger, the city inspector had been undeniably lax, and Loescher was derelict in the duties for which he was patently unqualified. The scandal resulted in a tightening up of inspection procedures as well as establishing qualifications for building engineers.

32. City Cable Railway Bldg. – 1201 18th St. – 1889   Score: 6.3

Meets the Street – 6	Scale – 6	Integrity – 8
Public Spaces – 6	Mass – 5	Imagination – 7

Thoughtfully renovated by James Sudler in 1974, this red-brick, Romanesque Revival power station became his architectural firm's office, and included a popular restaurant downstairs. The building's historic associations are at least as important as the architecture, with its intricate brick patterns and extensive corbelling.

An extensive cable car system called the Denver City Cable Railway Company began operating three lines, powered from this building, on Nov. 1, 1889. The Welton line ran from 16th St. to 38th Ave. and Gaylord St., powered by a 38,000' cable which was then the longest continuous cable in the world. The company also built the original 16th St. and Larimer viaducts, connecting the north and west sides of Denver with the city.

Before San Francisco's cable cars "rode halfway to the stars," Denver was the cable car capital of the world. The system operated out of this former powerhouse on Lawrence.

The firm eventually operated 29 miles of cable road plus 10 miles of electric and two miles of horse-car trams. The panic of '93 forced its consolidation with Bill Evans' rival Denver City Tramway Company which independently operated other cable lines from its powerhouse at Colfax and Broadway. By 1900 the entire system had been converted to electrical trolley lines, and the old cable no longer hummed a few inches beneath the streets, but for a time Denver, not San Francisco, was the cable car capital of the world.

33. AT & T Bldg. – 1875 Lawrence – Skidmore, Owings & Merrill –
1983   **Score: 5.8**
Meets the Street – 5   Scale – 7   Integrity – 7
Public Spaces – 5   Mass – 6   Imagination – 5

*Old and new co-exist amicably, making the AT&T Bldg. one of Skyline's
more successful in-fill structures.*

This is corporate architecture with a suggestion of humanity. The red brick exterior
ties in well with the 1889 City Cable Railway Bldg. at the opposite end of the block.
Banks of windows inset from spandrels and columns give it a nice sense of texture,
even from a distance. The building is not oversized but still manages to assert itself
thoughtfully, restrained yet dignified. It may lack postcard drama but the crimson cast
and edge-of-downtown location give it great contrast against the skyline backdrop. In
my opinion this is S.O.M.'s best effort out of three attempts in Skyline.

34. Sakura Square – 1255 19th St. – Bertram Burton & Assoc. –
1972   **Score: 6.1**
Meets the Street – 7   Scale – 7   Integrity – 5
Public Spaces – 6   Mass – 7   Imagination – 4

The Japanese genius for instilling a flat, featureless building with a touch of
urbanity is aptly illustrated by this little slice of Tokyo. The success lies in careful
attention to details on the two main levels which are retail oriented and skillfully
integrated into the Japanese style plaza, skillfully landscaped to soothe the eye. The
spatial relationships among buildings, streets, and plaza are very well thought out,
mitigating the potentially oppressive qualities of a non-descript 20-story concrete hull
on the visitor. A very effective use of open space, arcades, walkovers, and shrubbery
creates a whole that is better than the sum of its parts.

Governor Ralph Carr (1939-43), who spoiled his political career by inviting interred Japanese-Americans to remain in Colorado after World War II, is memorialized in the plaza. Many ethnic "Nisei" took the courageous governor's advice, and did stay to become successful farmers, businessmen and community leaders. After sipping tea in the refreshing Japanese garden, walk up 19th St. towards the sky-scraping core of central downtown. A three-block walk jaunt up 19th St. brings us to the starting point of the third tour, the Alfred A. Arraj Federal Courthouse.

Twilight in Skyline makes the D & F Tower shimmer like some storm-tossed lighthouse.

Tour 3. Retail / Financial Core

"Now that the architect has had his fun, let's throw the design into the wastebasket and begin all over again." Lewis Mumford

Tour 3.	*length 2 miles.*	Begins at 19th St. & Champa.

Ends at 16th St. & Glenarm Pl.

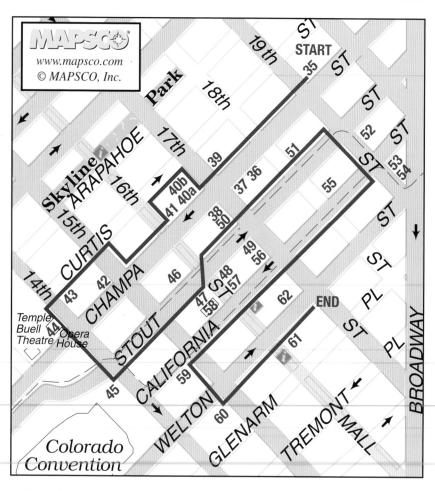

Alongside Wynkoop Row's masonry palisade, Champa qualifies as downtown's other "architecture row." Virtually every period and style from Victorian to Post Modern is represented. Wynkoop delivers more consistency, but Champa titillates with its smorgasbord of variety. Champa (an indecipherable Indian word, presumably one of William McGaa's wives), situated just inside the line demarcating the sanitized Skyline district, escaped the ravages of urban renewal bulldozers, in part, because the powerful Colorado National Bank protected it.

The Boettcher interests also owned properties just across the street at the time. Consequently, the historic structures within the protective penumbra of all that institutionalized money had a better than average chance of surviving.

While a great many of Denver's quality architects are represented on Champa, mention of one noteworthy firm is a must. Fisher & Fisher enjoyed extraordinary prestige from 1892, when William Ellsworth Fisher established the practice, until his son, Alan B. Fisher, died in 1978. William's younger brother, Arthur Addison Fisher, joined the firm in 1907 and carried it on after William's death in 1937, partnering with his nephew Alan. Champa contains numerous examples of this versatile firm's work, such as the University Bldg. with its highly expressive vernacular. The Edbrookes, Frank E. and nephew Harry. W.J., contributed a pair of significant designs to Champa – including the Gas and Electric Bldg. – whose illuminated facade enjoyed substantial fame throughout the United States.

The next two streets going east, Stout and California, also boast a melange of architectural variety. But later, large–scale projects landed here

Like exiles from ancient Babylon, exotic beasts protrude from the Colorado Business bank at 17th & Champa.

more frequently, impairing that human sense of scale which Champa generally managed to retain. These streets form a "counter axis" to the main 16th/17th St. downtown axis. California presents a more corporate face than Champa; Stout fits somewhere between the two, geographically and architecturally. 16th to 17th Sts. on Stout constitutes downtown Denver's ground zero – the heart of the heart, with its bustling energy. Clanging streetcars jostle with shoppers and well-heeled businessmen. If Denver had a Times Square or State Street, it would fit here. So let's take the pulse of the city.

35. Alfred A. Arraj Federal Courthouse – 901 19th St. –
Anderson, Mason, Dale / H.O.K. – **2002**   **Score: 8.1**

Meets the Street – 7	Scale – 9	Integrity – 8
Public Spaces – 8	Mass – 9	Imagination – 8

It's refreshing to see symbolism in Federal architecture again. The Alfred A. Arraj Courthouse blends into downtown's corporate culture, while clearly stating its public function. The architects consciously express the Western landscape, suggesting sage, mountains, and plains through the mediums of color, texture, and indigenous materials. Contrasted with these arid elements, the supreme importance of water is metaphorically confirmed in the glassy, aqua curtain wall. Silvery basket-weave mullions, brick precipices, and a strong limestone base are meticulously crafted. The region's newness is suggested by the absence of older historic references, while the building's strong lines give it a character associated with rugged pioneer settlers.

The courthouse basks in Denver's sun drenched climate like a native, managing to dress up the bleak, bus station environs. A contemporary sundial, more perfunctory than useful, reinforces the building's

Alfred A. Arraj Federal Courthouse and the sleek 1999 Broadway skyscraper dress up 19th St. with a sense of the urbane.

public persona. This intelligently conceived structure manifests the Western American heritage: a climactic, social, and geographic profile of its region. Its ethos is clearly modern and functional, but hardly sterile. Louis Sullivan might well have created such a building, had he lived another 80 years.

Proceed southwest, beyond the marble Courthouse, to 1732 Champa.

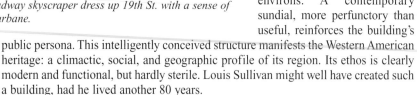

36. Buerger Bros. Bldg. – 1732 Champa – Montana Fallis –
1929   **Score: 6.8**

| Meets the Street – 7 | Scale – 7 | Integrity – 7 |
| Public Spaces – 6 | Mass – 6 | Imagination – 8 |

The scale is very modest, and its mid-block location obscures the Buerger Building's real significance, but don't let size or location fool you. This former barber supply house may be Denver's most representative example of Art Deco. Ornate pilasters outline each bay, flaring out like surreal fronds at the apex. Decorative medallions and spandrels are colorfully executed in abstract geometric patterns. The building's facade is a virtual museum of terra cotta craft. This was a significant contribution to Denver's architectural scene by one of its more celebrated designers – engineering wizard, Montana Fallis.

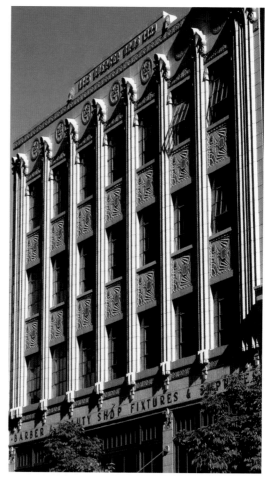

Next door (1726 Champa) stands the **Chamber Lofts (Chamber of Commerce Bldg.)** by Marean & Norton – **1910**. The Chamber moved uptown from 14th St. & Lawrence in 1910, reflecting a business trend that had been accelerating since the mid 1880s. Its new headquarters reflected the changing taste among Denver's second generation power elite. The pioneers were rapidly passing on. John Evans died in 1897, Walter Cheesman in 1908, David Moffat and Charles Kountze

Art Deco is rare but not entirely foreign to Denver streets. The Buerger Bldg.'s modest scale hardly diminishes the elaborate, colorful ornamentation.

would not survive 1911. Tabor, Palmer, Larimer, Byers were all figures from the past. Their heirs and successors, determined to leave their own mark on the maturing city, were of a more conservative bent. The Chamber Bldg. demonstrates a fundamental shift away from wildcatting to sober asset management.

Its Classical Revival facade is less than daring; the elements are not even well integrated. Light bulbs, highlighting the upper bays, give it a slightly vaudevillian air. Despite the veneer of confidence, the building appears layered, perhaps a reflection of the social stratification that Denver itself was experiencing. Mrs. Crawford P. Hill ruled Denver's "Sacred 36" society nobs resolutely from her Capitol Hill mansion (still intact at 10th Ave. and Sherman). Beneath the glittering social strata, however, mine output was dwindling and labor was in a state of agitated unrest. Four years later it exploded violently, in the tiny coal camp of Ludlow, Colorado.

The Chamber Bldg. seems to reflect the irony of its age – tranquillity and prosperity on the face of things, uncertainty and social unrest festering under the surface. Only a few short months after 18 men, women, and children died in the shocking massacre at Ludlow, the First World War ignited in a faraway Balkan province called Bosnia. It ushered in a drastically altered modern world that Denver, despite its smug sense of isolation, would have to contend with. Forever changed were the realities, social attitudes, and morals that would determine its future development.

37. Colo. Business Bank (Ideal Bldg.) –821 17th St. – Montana Fallis – 1907, Fisher & Fisher – 1927   Score: 8.1

Meets the Street – 8	Scale –7	Integrity – 8
Public Spaces – 9	Mass – 8	Imagination – 8

Not surprisingly, the first reinforced concrete high rise west of the Mississippi was constructed by Charles Boettcher as a "poster building" for his Colorado Portland Cement Company (later known as Ideal Cement Company). His equity partner in the venture was Fred Bonfils, probably the most despised figure in the business community. Bonfils, who ran the *Denver Post*, was not above extorting advertising revenues from businessmen by threatening to expose the more unsavory sides of their personal lives. For this particular project, Boettcher and Bonfils teamed up with engineering genius Montana Fallis. In order to demonstrate the new building technology, they resorted to a typical Bonfils "publicity stunt." During construction, the floor was loaded to 65,000 lbs., then an intense, 1,800–degree fire was stoked in the basement. This was allowed to burn for 75 minutes in order to demonstrate to the building department (and prospective tenants) just how fireproof a building could be. Not a crack was found in the floor that refused to deflect more than .03 of an inch under all that weight and heat.

Twenty years later the sturdy building was sold to the Denver National Bank. The bank promptly hired architects Fisher & Fisher to re-configure the structure, expanding it into a bank. The former "Chicago Style" facade with its heavy bracketed cornice was stripped away. An eight–story extension rose along Champa, and a svelte new look was created, using lots of stucco and travertine quarried in Colorado. Two enormous cast bronze doors, weighing a ton apiece, highlighted the central bay. A spacious banking floor with a huge basement vault (now the Broker Restaurant) was carved out. A ninth-story penthouse floor was squeezed in at the top, delineated by petite Roman–arched windows, grouped in threes. The main face on 17th St. is also subdivided into three parts, the center part featuring three arched bays. Horizontal and vertical elements are reconciled admirably, allowing it to soar gracefully. Richly carved travertine wraps the first two floors, which are dramatized by barreled porticos announcing the main entry.

If you view the building after banking hours, soak in the splendid bronze doors, which recall Lorenzo Ghiberti's famous baptistry doors in Florence. Twenty-eight relief panels demonstrate various native American dance forms. The banking floor within is luxuriantly decorated and should be viewed if possible. Numerous artists were employed to decorate the ceiling and columns (made of iron, painted to look like natural stone). Artist Arnold Ronnebeck was commissioned to create the bas relief, depicting the history of money, high above the banking floor. In the end, Fisher & Fisher deftly transformed an ordinary office building into a unified work of art.

Fisher & Fisher also designed the Classical Revival **US Bank #40** and early Modern **Hotel Monaco #39** on the two corners, opposite Champa. William and Arthur Fisher, more innovators than imitators, demonstrated a mastery of the creative process normally associated with more famous names. Their contribution to Denver's early stylistic independence is enormous.

38. Boston Lofts – 828 17th St. – Andrews, Jacques, & Rantoul – 1890   Score: 6.8

Meets the Street – 6	Scale –7	Integrity – 7
Public Spaces – 6	Mass – 7	Imagination – 8

The Boston is considered one of the city's finest examples of the 19th century Commercial style. Its historical significance stems from the fact that it helped spur development of 17th St. as an uptown business address. Originally an office block, it was recently converted into loft apartments, after serving for decades as the financial nerve center of the Boettcher empire. The architects, like the builders, hailed from Boston — hence the name. Essentially Richardsonian Romanesque, it was executed in soft Manitou Sandstone, requiring the eventual removal of many decorative elements that weathered poorly. It may have been a blessing. The building now exerts a more powerful vertical thrust than when horizontal string courses wrapped it like a corset. The pairing of floors within arched bays and doubling the window apertures on the top two floors make it float like a great Roman aqueduct. Windows are deeply recessed, exposing the massive thickness of the bearing walls and heightening the sense of drama. Much of the ornate tracery and ornamental columns, successfully preserved around the main entry and lower floors, is well worth examining.

This is an unusual case of less becoming more. Old photos show a rather fussy facade, featuring rusticated stone blocks mounted up to a third floor molding. An Italian Renaissance style balcony was propped incongruously over the main entry. The original lines were broken and fussy. Today, absent any extraneous ornamentation, the

Boston Lofts details project a decidedly Roman feel.

lines are strong and clean, revealing a harmonious balance. Excessive frills actually worked against the Boston Building, since it didn't really need all that gingerbread to make a strong artistic statement, thus affirming the inherent soundness of Andrews, Jacques, & Rantoul's original concept.

Prior to the Boston Bldg., this site contained **Wolfe Hall**, a seminary (i.e., a finishing school) for young women founded by the Rev. George M. Randall, first Episcopal bishop of Colorado. In 1867 he obtained funds for the school from John D. Wolfe and daughter, Catherine, of New York City. The 2 $^1/_2$–story Victorian Gothic building once housed the largest denominational school in the state. When the property was sold to developers in 1889, Wolfe Hall moved to Capitol Hill – near the present **St. John's Cathedral (#85)**.

Next door is the 1916 **Kistler Bldg.**, at 1640 Champa, by Harry W.J. Edbrooke. Built as a printing house by William H. Kistler, with a stationary store on the ground floor, this is a more theatrical version of Edbrooke's **Rio Grande Lofts (#46)** on Stout. Heavy printing equipment required super–strengthened floors above, so the place is built like a fortress. The current entry is ill–defined and unappealing, and mirror glass gives the facade a blank, brittle face, detracting from its natural charm. The original warehouse-style casements were more honest. But despite the incompatibility of modern "improvements," the naturally sanguine Kistler still manages to shine.

39. Hotel Monaco (Railway Exchange Bldg.) – 909 17th St. –
Fisher & Fisher – **1937** **Score: 6.1**

Meets the Street – 6	Scale – 7	Integrity – 5
Public Spaces – 5	Mass – 7	Imagination – 7

Denver's first truly International Style building was designed as a billboard for the passenger train business. Originally the **Railway Exchange**, it aspired to identify rail travel with all that was modern, sleek, fast, and comfortable. The (then) new Modernism, just recently arrived from the German Bauhaus, fit the bill perfectly, and so Fisher and Fisher honed their drafting pencils once again, plunging into a new dialect. They didn't do badly for a first try. In fact, they captured the streamlined spirit so well that 70 years later the building still looks young and fresh. The production of a predominantly horizontal design was compounded by the need to tie into a pre-existing, glazed tile wing on Champa. The two sections don't exactly mesh perfectly, but the color and roof–line are close enough to suggest harmony.

Hotel Monaco, left, and the Colorado Business Bank across Champa highlight the versatility of Fisher & Fisher.

Denverites, grinding through the Great Depression, must have been dazzled by the optimistic futurism this building represented. Today it has been successfully re-incarnated as an up-scale, boutique hotel. The building's unpretentious sophistication reflects Modernist principles without indulging in the gaunt severity or abstract functionalism of many Bauhaus designs. It retains an optimistic outlook and human sensibilities, softened certainly by the rounded, *Moderne* curves. The old **Denver Post Bldg.** at 15th St. & California attempted to emulate the same Modern idiom 10 years later, but I think less successfully. It didn't survive for comparison purposes, but of the two buildings representing the genre, I believe the better one is still with us.

40a. U.S. Bank (Colorado National Bldg.) – 900 17ᵗʰ St. – Fisher &
Fisher–**1915**, Hoyt & Hoyt–**1926**, Rogers & Nagel–**1964**   **Score 6.7**

Meets the Street – 6	Scale – 6	Integrity – 5
Public Spaces – 8	Mass – 7	Imagination – 8

Formal Classicism had nearly run its course in the United States when the first edition of the Colorado National Bank reared stately Ionic columns three stories over 17ᵗʰ St. Fisher & Fisher's original bank covered only about half the area occupied by the expanded building, but it established the image that the bank has projected ever since. Within ten years, the need for expansion was apparent, so Colorado National retained another talented pair of brothers, Burnham and Palmer Hoyt, to double the working space. Hoyt & Hoyt tied the original structure seamlessly into the new, endowing the three–story banking hall with unequaled splendor. The form is reminiscent of an ancient Roman basilica. Large panels set above the galleries and the south end of the main nave are decorated with dreamlike scenes titled *Indian Memories* by the renowned muralist, Allen True. A false rotunda in the ornate ceiling marks the center of the original 1915 banking hall.

In 1964, more space was needed, so Denver architects Rogers and Nagel (forerunners of RNL) expanded the place again, this time using the rooftop as the point of departure. Instead of piling on another layer of Ionic columns, they abstracted the column theme, using rectangular columns, slightly beveled to insure lightness. These newer columns resolve directly into gently rounded arches capped by a clean, resolute cornice. In essence a modern structure was grafted onto a marble temple, reconciled by the marble itself and dark bronze mullions framing the windows. The new tier is respectful of the base, maintaining the same proportions, alignments, and materials; ingeniously adapted with superb craftsmanship.

The bank itself is Denver's second oldest, dating back to 1862. It was founded by the Kountze brothers, Luther and Charles, who four years later obtained the territory's second national charter, renaming it Colorado National Bank. Charles ran it until his death in 1911, ironically the same year that his chief competitor at the First National Bank, David Moffat, died. The Kountze family maintained an affiliation with the bank for well over a century. When the bank moved into its Greek temple at 17th & Champa in 1915, it adopted the slogan, "the bank that looks like a bank." Eventually it was absorbed into the nationwide banking chain that controls it today.

Walk one block west on 17th St. to the tower immediately behind the "bank that looks like a bank."

40b. U.S. Bank (Colorado National) Tower – 950 17th St. – Minoru Yamasaki – 1973   Score: 7.5

Meets the Street – 7	Scale – 7	Integrity – 7
Public Spaces – 8	Mass – 8	Imagination – 8

In my opinion, this is the World Trade Center designer's most refined skyscraper. Here, Yamasaki opened up wide bays filled with windows, belying his personal acrophobia. This building exhibits a clean, straightforward vertical order – base, shaft, and crown. In Dallas or New York the developers would have scaled it to 40 or 50 stories, destroying its singular proportions. At 26 stories, packed neatly into the relatively modest Denver skyline, it has a chance to be noticed and admired. Bronzed windows contrast dramatically with granite clad columns. Unfortunately, the original white marble cladding was replaced some years ago. The tower lost some of its luster as a result (as well as visual compatibility with the older bank).

Yamasaki related that he enjoyed older buildings because they could be so "elegant, delightful, and serene." He thus made a new structure that converses amiably with its older neighbors. His stated design philosophy here was simply, "I just want to add some delight to life." The building also pays tribute to Mies, but it goes beyond his rigid boundaries to find its own expression. The strong piers, spaced unevenly so as to avoid redundancy, reveal an economy of structure and energize the facade. The cantilevered corners create tension and a sense of restrained drama. It is an articulate building, deserving of admiration.

Proceed southwest along Curtis for one block to the 16th St. Mall. This stretch of Curtis was once the heart of the live theater district, boasting such entertainment palaces as the **Empress, Paris, Iris**, and **New Isis Theaters** – all huddled together along Denver's "Great White Way." The anchor venue was the **Colorado**, formerly **Tabor's Grand Opera House (see #26)**, dating back to 1881, at the corner of 16th St. & Curtis. Curtis was Denver's equivalent of Times Square, but the Depression and new uptown movie palaces such as the **Paramount (#66)** eventually killed the vaudeville circuit. At one time Curtis boasted eight marquees between 15th and 18th Sts. Today it is once again the center of live theater, though two blocks removed, in the **Denver Performing Arts Complex** which straddles what was once Curtis, south of 14th St. Now turn left and proceed one block to Champa.

Denver theaters lined Curtis in the 1920s. The marquee at left is Horace Tabor's Opera House, re-christened the "Colorado." Baby Doe Tabor was still alive at this time, occasionally frequenting 16th St. No doubt the scene stirred many poignant memories in her heart.

41. University Bldg. – 910 16th St. – Fisher & Fisher –
1911   **Score: 8.0**

| Meets the Street – 8 | Scale –8 | Integrity – 8 |
| Public Spaces – 7 | Mass – 8 | Imagination – 9 |

The University Bldg., built as the Foster Bldg., exemplifies the high aesthetic standards of the Fisher brothers and is undoubtedly their liveliest work. This is possibly the most exciting and original skyscraper to appear in Denver prior to World War I. The rich colors and textures combined with ingenious terra cotta motifs create a decorative marvel. Charcoal–brick piers contrast vividly with the creamy terra cotta ascending unbroken from the 3rd through 12th floors. The tripartite grouping of the slender windows gives the structure an added sense of lift. Rounded window apertures, at the top, play imaginatively with the boldly flared cornice, capped by pyramidal parapets. Decorative geometric motifs abound and fanciful frieze work – executed in blue, green, and gold – fills in the voids above and between the shapely windows.

While the idiom is 20th century Commercial, it has certain *Art Nouveau* overtones, although its tight geometry is not so fluid. The originality evident here demonstrates the relative, regional independence of Denver architects at the time. This 1910 design tackles the considerable aesthetic problems associated with skyscrapers candidly, yet with sophistication.

The scheme is a bit fussy to be considered monumental (contrasted with Sullivan's Wainwright and Guaranty buildings), but in its tight urban container, limited to short range vistas, it boasts pleasing definition. William and Arthur Fisher experimented with a broad range of palates, evident in the diverse array of their Denver buildings. The University Bldg. harmonizes multiple elements, mixing textures, forms, and colors as masterfully as any Chicago or East Coast designers of the day. Possibly Fisher & Fisher's *opus magnum*, it may well represent the culmination of Expressionism in Denver.

Just two doors further down Champa, the Victorian **Odd Fellows Hall** (1543–45 Champa), featuring highly-dressed limestone, surprises the casual passerby. This 1889 building, designed by Emmett Anthony, also boasts a unique history. It was long reputed as the home of the Old Dutch Mill, a popular cabaret – later a cafeteria during Prohibition – that finally succumbed to the Great Depression in 1935.

During its heyday it was an important jazz club. Legend has it that the popular song

"Melancholy Baby" was sketched out on a napkin by one of the Old Dutch Mill waiters. It later debuted right here, by singer George Morrison, who frequented the place. A thoughtful restoration / expansion was executed in 1982 by Denver architect David Owen Tryba, who added a non–intrusive penthouse without disturbing the original Victorian facade.

42. Gas & Electric (Insurance Exchange) Bldg. – 910 15th St. – Frank and Harry W.J. Edbrooke – **1910**   **Score: 6.3**

Meets the Street – 6	Scale – 6	Integrity – 6
Public Spaces – 6	Mass – 7	Imagination – 7

7619 GAS AND ELECTRIC BUILDING AT NIGHT, DENVER, COLO.
BEST LIGHTED BUILDING IN THE WORLD

Attributed to the Edbrooke firm, this became a giant billboard for the Denver Gas and Electric Company. It seems to favor Harry W.J. Edbrooke's other Expressionist works, and it quickly became one of the more recognized buildings in Denver, gaining substantial fame as the "Best Lighted Building in the World." The terra cotta facade is wired for over 13,000 light bulbs, ranging from 5 to 200 watts, which give it a glowing personality at night. Its dedication on Nov. 10, 1910 drew over 75,000 spectators (better than a third of the city's residents) to witness Mayor Speer throw a switch that bathed the new tower in effervescence. The lights continued to illuminate Denver nights until Sept. 25, 1943, when wartime security concerns blackened them.

After Japan's surrender in 1945, the firmament at 15th & Champa lit up again. Denver Gas & Electric, merged with the Public Service Company of Colorado in 1924, moved up 15th Street to its new building on Welton in 1963 (see #60). The lights were darkened for the next 30 plus years as the visual drama of "the best lighted building in the world" faded from collective memory. Finally, in the 90s, the wiring was re–worked and old bulbs replaced so that once again, 15th St. glows every night at dusk.

The building is early 20th century Commercial style and features a flamboyant projecting cornice arching gracefully over the sidewalk. The rounded windows on the top floor almost seem to intersect the curving arc of the cornice, a sensation enhanced by the circular *oeil-de-boeufs* or "bull's eyes" – lighted apertures centered above each window and dramatically back-lit. Even by day the thousands of geometric voids housing countless light bulbs ornament the facade in a freckled fantasy. The Gas and Electric Bldg. is part theater, part architecture, but every town ought to be lucky enough to have a late night show like this one.

Turn right and walk one block to Curtis. The second building to the right, at 1512 Curtis, is the **Bauer Bldg.**, circa 1890, a restored Victorian Commercial structure, famous for the innovative confectioner and restaurant owner, Otto Paul Bauer. Bauer, another talented German immigrant, brought the dusty cow–town its first taste of real cuisine. Much later he invented the ice cream soda, right here, on a hot summer day before the advent of air conditioning. His best–remembered product was undoubtedly the candy that carried the Bauer name for decades.

43. Mountain States Telephone (Qwest) – 931 14ᵗʰ St. –
William N. Bowman – **1929**   **Score: 6.9**

Meets the Street – 6	Scale – 6	Integrity – 7
Public Spaces – 8	Mass – 7	Imagination – 7

Denver's last pre–Depression skyscraper dominated the city's skyline in terms of sheer bulk for a quarter century. The 1950s building boom finally challenged it. Commentators from the time called it "American Perpendicular," although "Telephone Gothic" is more succinct. Bowman, a gifted local architect, also designed the Cosmopolitan Hotel, Denver Theater, and the Colburn Hotel on Grant St. The **Telephone Building**, with a volume of 5.2 million cubic feet, was decidedly the most ambitious building venture ever attempted in Denver, up until its time. Curiously, this was the only Denver "setback" building, designed to take advantage of a zoning loophole that allowed extra height, over and above the normal twelve story height limit. For every foot of setback the upper portion could rise three additional feet. At 16

"Telephone Gothic" expresses the corporate American culture of the 1920s, before depression, war, and a hoard of intellectual exiles from Europe steered architecture in an entirely new direction.

floors, it looked down on every other downtown structure, excepting the State Capitol dome and the pencil-thin D & F Tower. Its mass was further emphasized by the off-center location on 14ᵗʰ St. The extensive use of yellow terra cotta, 18,000 tons in all, gives it a striking presence, even in today's milieu of modern spires.

Of notable interest are the wonderful depression era murals, decorating the entry

Denver Public Library, Western History Collection X-26399

Dry goods baron William B. Daniels built this ornate mansion on Curtis, only to lose it in a divorce settlement. An octagonal cupola crowned the edifice. Notice the unpaved street and typical children, congregating along the fence rail.

porticos, by prolific artist Allen True. True, a Colorado Springs native, depicts various modes of communication from the frontier era to the present (circa 1929), executed in his characteristic style. Romanticized images of progress and industry lend heroic proportions to the brawny laborers, who ply a seemingly quasi–religious vocation of work. The **Telephone Building**, flanked by lesser expansions, maintains its strong character nonetheless. Finely sculpted Gothic corner towers raise it a notch above most telephone exchanges of the era, creating an elegant expression of verticality.

Apparently the site on which it sits started out as an Indian encampment. As far back as 1860, early eyewitnesses found Arapaho campfires on the site. Later, department store proprietor William B. Daniels built an elaborate Italianate style mansion at 1422 Curtis. After he surrendered the property in a divorce settlement, it eventually devolved into an upscale gambling den called the Inter-Ocean Club. The Inter-Ocean was a part of "Big Ed" Chase's gambling empire, which also included the **Navarre (#72)**. It later turned into a boarding house. The corner was occupied by David Moffat's mansion, featuring an ornate Mansard corner tower commanding 14th St. After the Moffats moved to new digs at 17th & Lincoln St., it also became a boarding house. Later hemmed in by cheap storefronts, it began to take on a spooky, "haunted" appearance before its razing sometime in the 1920s.

Denver Performing Arts Complex – 14th St. & Curtis – Kevin Roche / John Dinkeloo, and Hardy Holzman Pfeiffer – **1976 to 1997**

The most successful thing about the Denver Performing Arts Complex is the arts center concept, which has won rave reviews. DPAC is the largest performing arts center in the country after Lincoln Center in New York, with over 10,800 seats scattered throughout its various halls. These include a major concert hall, opera house, Broadway theater venue, several playhouses, and a grand ballroom – all wrapped around a utilitarian parking structure. The buildings are joined together by the Galleria, an open–ended, barrel–vault that protects patrons from rain and snow, but not necessarily capricious winds.

DPAC started out fairly bleak, but persistence and continued infusions of cash in the 90s produced much improved results. Boettcher Concert Hall, a minimalist shoe box that emphasizes interior spaces, received a badly-needed lobby extension, including additional bathrooms. The improvements ate up a lot of the dead plaza and connected it psychologically to the neighboring venues. The vanilla, *Moderne Civic* Arena, built in 1951, was then gutted and given a new face, resurrecting as the **Temple Hoyne Buell Theater**, a 2,800–seat playhouse for Broadway–style productions. It was named after Denver's dapper, millionaire playboy-architect, who sported a singular handlebar mustache, Temple "Sandy" Buell.

Temple Buell (1895–1990) hailed from a socially prominent Chicago family, but the effects of tuberculosis, compounded by his being gassed during the First World War, sent him to Colorado in 1921. He recovered marvelously, married his wealthy fiancee, and stayed on, living nearly 95 years. "Sandy" founded a very successful firm that designed numerous schools, the **Paramount Theater (#66)**, and several government buildings. In 1925, he purchased a weed–filled plot that citizens used as an impromptu dump. By 1950, the area around the dump was rapidly developing, so Buell turned developer and built Cherry Creek Shopping Center on it. This American prototype opened in 1952, the first of its kind. Cherry Creek became a gold mine, spawning a whole new genre of shopping centers wrapped around open–air pedestrian malls, later enclosed.

Long-time residents may recall the intriguing, silver Buell Building at 14th St. & Stout, where Sandy maintained his practice. The main entry was guarded by a towering knight in full, medieval armor, brandishing a large broadsword in its glassy alcove. Temple Buell was an irrepressibly colorful individual, as well as being a noted philanthropist.

Buell Theater sports a glassy facade, pushed out into the Galleria, narrowing the space and giving it a lively European street flavor, a good example of "less is more." The **Helen Bonfils Theater**, countering Boettcher Concert Hall, tries to create a little stir with its dealer-shade awning, fanning out from the bare concrete elevations. Overall the DPAC, absent any unifying theme, is an architectural grab bag, but as a cultural hub for the performing arts and a night life generator, it is unparalleled.

Quigg Newton Denver Municipal Auditorium is the final act in the 30-year odyssey of DPAC construction. The Municipal Auditorium is now in its third incarnation, as the Ellie Caulkins Opera House, after a $92 million reconstruction, literally from the inside out. Only the historic shell was retained, while an entirely new structure was raised within.

44. Quigg Newton Denver Municipal Auditorium – 14th St. & Curtis –
Robert F. Willison – **1908** – reconstruction – Semple Brown Design –
2005   **Score: 5.9**

Meets the Street – 5   Scale – 6   Integrity – 6
Public Spaces – 7   Mass – 6   Imagination – 5

The original Civic Auditorium was a convertible, multi-purpose structure accommodating everything from organ concerts and opera to sporting events and conventions. Mayor Robert Speer lay in state here, mourned by thousands, after his unexpected death in 1918. This building had been his proudest achievement, out of all the many projects he inspired.

Back in 1908 the still-unfinished Auditorium had to be hurried up to host the Democratic National Convention, which nominated William Jennings Bryan, the Free Silver populist, a third time for president. For the third time, Jennings failed to get elected, a record of frustration equaled only by Henry Clay – and perhaps the Denver Broncos. The building's exterior was brilliantly lighted at night by thousands of light bulbs, and for forty some odd years it was Denver's civic showpiece.

That first age of glory ended around 1955, when an abysmal, "functional" reconstruction turned the building into a mediocre theater / concert hall. This particular incarnation featured the acoustics and charm of a high school lunchroom, but for the next 50 years Denverites put up with it. Fed up voters finally approved a bond issue to help re-configure the hall as a first–rate opera house. The building was once again gutted to its outer walls and perhaps, as they say, the third time is a charm.

The new theater takes the form of a traditional Italian opera house, lyre–shaped to enhances vocal acoustics, and insures that no spectator is more than 113' from the main stage. Horseshoe galleries are outlined in cherry wood, executed in a simple, modern idiom. The public spaces are ample and bright, although stark as a modern art gallery. Beneath the spacious lobby, a basement meeting hall exposes the original stone foundation walls to great effect, and features an upscale restaurant.

The exterior, listed on the National Register of Historic Places, has been largely restored to its former glory, including outline lights which sparkle at night. The structure's Renaissance Revival tendencies are expressed in an early 20th century vernacular. Imposing brick pilasters sprout musical Corinthian capitals, while carnival–like pleasure domes originally marked the corners, reminiscent of old Atlantic City (removed in 1955, the cupolas are to be replaced when funding materializes). The bracketed cornices, made from pressed metal, are notable effects.

The building has really come full circle as Denver's principal opera house. The history of local opera can be traced back to 1915, when a young Italian priest named Fr. Joseph Bosetti staged *Cavalleria Rusticana* here. Bosetti hailed from Milan and migrated to Denver around 1911. His musical talents were quickly recognized by Bishop Nicholas Matz, who made him the founding director of the Cathedral Choir. When Fr. Bosetti arrived, grand opera had faded from the scene down at the **Tabor Grand Opera House**. He mounted his first production on an $800 budget, using amateur singers, stagehands, and musicians. The results were anything but amateur. Out of these early efforts, the Denver Grand Opera Company emerged in 1931.

Bosetti's annual productions, here at the Auditorium, became the toast of the town, until a stroke forced him to quit opera productions in 1952. It seems fitting that the Auditorium once again takes its place at center stage, today as home to Opera Colorado, a brainchild of the late Nathaniel Merrill – who launched it in the early 1980s in a less than ideal environment, Boettcher Concert Hall. Today, Denver plays a larger role in the opera world, thanks to Mayor Speer and Father Bosetti, who first laid the foundations.

Courtesy, Archdiocese of Denver

Monsignor Joseph Bosetti (1886-1954) grew up in the shadow of Giuseppe Verdi's "Casa Reposa" in Milan, Italy. Migrating to Denver in 1911, he enjoyed a meteoric career as a choral director, opera producer, and vicar general of the Catholic diocese. On several occasions he was even decorated by the Italian government for his cultural contributions.

Stroll southeast along 14th St. and try to visualize this gritty, downtown street as a shady, tree–lined lane – bounded by irrigation canals and lined with the city's finest Victorian homes. Long before Cherry Hills Village, the Denver Country Club, or Grant Avenue, the city's elite built their mansions along 14th St., Denver's first "millionaire's row." Earlier we mentioned that Gov. John Evans lived and entertained guests at 14th & Arapahoe. David Moffat and W. B. Daniels were neighbors a block uptown along Curtis & 14th St..

One of Denver's more influential millionaires, and a U. S. senator, was the brilliant metallurgist, Nathaniel P. Hill, who solved the vexing problem of ore extraction and made a fortune in smelting. He lived at 14th & Welton, diagonally across from Governor John L. Routt, who guided Colorado into statehood. (The Routts lived on the corner occupied by the Convention Center.) Many early leaders located near Dr. Evans' Colorado Seminary on Arapahoe and St. Mary's Academy at 14th & California, offering the prospect of private education for their children. 14ᵗʰ Street's age of glory was short lived, however.

As the city grew and Henry Brown's Bluff (Capitol Hill) gained popularity with the local aristocracy, fewer nobs settled along 14ᵗʰ St. Certain older families remained through the century's end, but gradually the street commercialized. In 1911 the prestigious St. Mary's Academy relocated to Capitol Hill, next to one of its chief financial patrons, the unsinkable Molly Brown. Colorado Seminary, re–incarnated as Denver University, began moving its various schools to a new campus in University Park in the 1890s, although certain functions continued on 14ᵗʰ St. for many decades. Time took its toll however, and by the time of World War I, the street's heyday as a society enclave was just a faded memory.

45. Colorado Convention Center – 14th St. & Stout – Fentress / Bradburn Architects – **1990, 2004**   **Score: 2.3**

Meets the Street – 2	Scale – 1	Integrity – 3
Public Spaces – 4	Mass –1	Imagination – 2

Is it a bird, or a plane, or an airline terminal? This 2.2 million square foot Goliath is hard to ignore, and perhaps even harder to appreciate. Fentress / Bradburn took their original listless, but palatable design, doubled the building's size, and tried to give it

Currigan Hall (1967) received several engineering awards for its unique roof truss design, and won a supporting role in Woody Allen's movie, "Sleeper." Attempts to salvage it or move it to another site never materialized, and after a brief life span it was carted to the land-fill.

a smart, new look by applying a thin veneer of sleek, modern redundancy. Unfortunately, the 20th century throwback modernity creates precious little buzz in the 21st. Architect Curtis Fentress calls it one of "...a quartet of icons," rhapsodizing that, "Set in the heart of Denver's burgeoning cultural district, the expanded center brings further definition to the city's street–scape." The center falls short of the sales brochure imagery, however; swallowing several downtown streets, exterminating an award–winning landmark (Currigan Hall), and egregiously imposing its 7¹/₂ square block "Chinese wall" presence on the neighborhood.

Mr. Fentress explains how "four angular roof blades detail the center's varied facades along 14ᵗʰ St.... These blades also gesture out, toward downtown, in a sign of inclusivity and pride." The aluminum fins cantilever theatrically over the sidewalk, at awkward angles, like tail fins on a 1959 Chevy, mocking the "form must follow function" mantra dutifully murmured further down in the convention hall polemic. (*Denver Post – Dec.4, 2004*) The giant bat wings seem trite, at best, and further obfuscate the former mountain vistas on Stout.

The most insensitive features are the screens along Welton and Champa. Crudely detailed bands of corrugated metal undulate like an ocean of dirty dish–water, for blocks: a dull, lusterless pattern of gray monotony. The gritty, industrial image clashes violently with the glassy curtain walls adorning 14th St. and Speer Blvd. Consider that the structure contains nearly 3 times the cubic volume of downtown's largest office building, and perhaps gross impersonality becomes a given; all the more reason to clad it decently.

Why is such a gargantuan consumer of space built, essentially,

"Something new is a'bruin here!" Klondike can "barely" recognize the old convention hall digs. Nowadays, giant bat wings sprout high above Currigan's former roof line.

above the ground, given the opportunity to exploit the naturally sloping terrain? Planning-wise it calls to mind the brute impact of New York's infamous Pan Am (Met Life) Building that visually crushes Grand Central Station under its weight, while shutting out the sky from Park Avenue. Despite this hall's economic importance, it fails its civic obligations because no one really cared to think outside the box. The only thing outside this box is the 40' blue, polymer bear peeking through the front windows, apparently hoping for a subsidized handout.

Turn left along Stout, for one block. The parking garage jutting several stories above 15th & Stout occupies the site of old St. Mary's Cathedral. Father Joseph Projectus Machebeuf and his assistant, Father Jean Baptiste Raverdy, had arrived from Santa Fe on October 29, 1860. Their parish extended as far as the Canadian border on the north and Great Salt Lake on the west! An Express Company donated two lots near 15th & Stout where the French priests collected enough building materials to erect a modest 30' by 60' chapel. For $75 they also contracted for a lean–to shack on the back side to serve as living quarters. Recruiting volunteer labor, Machebeuf made sufficient progress to celebrate Christmas Eve Mass in the unfinished chapel on Dec. 24, 1860. It was the first brick church in the new city. By January, 1863, Masses by composers such as Mozart were being sung regularly in the little church.

The ambitious Father Joseph later purchased a two–story frame house from George W. Clayton, a block away, to initiate a parish school. He convinced three Sisters of Loretto, back in Santa Fe, to brave passage through Indian country, accompanied by Father Raverdy. His job was to assure them that they would not be scalped during that

Courtesy, Archdiocese of Denver

Old St. Mary's Cathedral looked tired on the eve of its demolition in 1900. A cyclist and curious bystanders congregate on the church steps, waiting for the photographer to snap their pose. Stout appears quiet and laid back. Only the proto-"light rail" tracks provide any sense of continuity with today's busy thoroughfare.

tense summer of 1864 when such a fate was a distinct possibility. All arrived safely however, and on June 27, 1864, St. Mary's Academy was born, much to the relief of Denver's pioneer families, regardless of beliefs, starved as they were for education.

Meanwhile, Father Machebeuf continued to expand his little brick church, raising a roof here, extending the nave there, adding aisles on either side. In 1868 it became a cathedral when the Denver parish was separated from the mother diocese of Santa Fe. Denver became its own diocese, and later an archdiocese, equal in stature to Santa Fe. Bishop Machebeuf, elevated to episcopal dignity, resided here until 1889, when he died at Mount St. Vincent's Orphanage in North Denver.

The new bishop, Nicholas Matz, began dreaming of a grander cathedral, to be built on Capitol Hill. In 1900, old St. Mary's Cathedral was sold to Winfield Scott Stratton, who demolished it for a commercial venture. By that time many new Catholic parishes had been established in Denver, and the strains of Mozart, Gounod, and Hayden no longer drifted out into the busy lanes of 15th St.

Neusteter Lofts sits several doors down from the site of old St. Mary's Cathedral.

46. Rio Grande Lofts – 1531 Stout – Harry W.J. Edbrooke –
1917   **Score: 6.1**

Meets the Street – 6	Scale – 7	Integrity – 6
Public Spaces – 5	Mass – 5	Imagination – 8

Back in 1908, Harry W.J. Edbrooke left a successful Chicago partnership, Atchison and Edbrooke, to join his uncle, Frank E. Edbrooke, in Denver. The influence of Louis Sullivan from those Chicago years is quite apparent in the glazed terra cotta adorning this six–story addition to the former A.T. Lewis department store. The building bears some resemblance to Edbrooke's Kistler Building on Champa. Both are mid–block, "single facade" structures, but this version boasts cleaner lines and feels more organized. The Sullivanesque ornamentals give it flair, despite its monochrome face. The highly expressive facade achieves a degree of harmony that exceeds most buildings of this vintage. The A.T. Lewis firm went bankrupt in 1933, and for a time, the building was owned by the Neusteter family – who sold it, in 1942, to the Rio Grande Railroad. Ever since then the historic Rio Grande name has been attached to it.

The Denver & Rio Grande Railroad, founded by General William Jackson Palmer, boasts its own tumultuous history. A gun–toting railroad war with the Santa Fe Railroad, settled in court, earned it westward access through Pueblo and the Royal Gorge to the rich mining camp of Leadville. The Rio Grande also tapped the rich mines of the San Juan Mountains and developed tourism around the state. After Palmer sold his successful little railroad to New York railroad magnate George Gould in 1901, it was merged with the Rio Grande Western, extending its reach to Salt Lake City. Gould then saddled the line with crushing debt in order to build another road called the Western Pacific, connecting Salt Lake and California.

At the same time, David Moffat was trying to push his Denver Northwestern & Pacific over the mountains, thereby giving Denver a direct connection to the west. His efforts earned him the enmity of George Gould and also Edward H. Harriman, who controlled the Union Pacific and Southern Pacific Railroads. Gould and Harriman not only sabotaged Moffat's dream, but in struggling against each other, Gould overextended, losing the Rio Grande to creditors in 1911, the same year as Moffat's tragic death. The new owners kept the line alive until the effects of depression and heavy debt forced it into bankruptcy in 1935. Pundits of the time scoffed that "D & RGW" stood for "Dangerous and Rapidly Growing Worse."

The Dotsero Cutoff had physically tied the two bankrupt lines (Moffat Road, now called the Denver & Salt Lake, and the Rio Grande) together in 1934, and under Federal bankruptcy protection they gradually grew stronger into the 1940s. Finally in 1947, they were joined together as one railroad and returned to private ownership under the presidency of John Evans, Sr., the son of "Tramway Bill" Evans, who had carried on Moffat's fight for a tunnel under the divide.

Interestingly, David Moffat had formerly served as president of the Rio Grande during the Palmer days, in the early 1890s. Furthermore, William Gray Evans had accompanied Moffat at the time of his death in New York City. His father, Gov. John Evans, and Moffat had built the original Denver Pacific, to Cheyenne, in 1870. The Evans clan and Moffat had always stood shoulder to shoulder, promoting Denver as a railway hub, so it was fitting that a third–generation Evans led the fabled Rio Grande Railroad into its most prosperous era – a tale of faith, gutsy tenacity, and Western endurance.

Denver Public Library, Western History Collection Z-310
General William Jackson Palmer (1836-1907), a Pennsylvania Quaker, founded the Rio Grande Railroad and the City of Colorado Springs.

Robert Roeschlaub's **A.T. Lewis Bldg.**, originally called Salomon's Bazaar (1890), at 800 16th St., is the parent structure of **Rio Grande Lofts**, which began as an annex to the Lewis department store. This modest commercial structure is only one of two surviving commercial structures by Roeschlaub, Denver's early architecture dean (along with his 1901 **Hover Warehouse** at 14th & Lawrence). **Trinity Church** (#70) remains his most distinctive landmark. The Lewis building is nonetheless, a credible design for its era.

The rounded arch windows on the top story provide a little sense of geometry and expectation, otherwise disappointed by an uneventful pressed tin parapet. Many of the more flamboyant excesses of the Victorian and Second Empire styles, which decorated Denver's early commercial blocks, are conspicuously absent in this restrained design (brick mullions were removed to open up the second–story windows at a later date, thus altering the building's original appearance). It exhibits some of Denver's earliest architectural terra cotta, featuring deep red acanthus foliage ornamenting the spandrels. The store was built in two phases, the older section being towards the alley. A seamless 1902 addition pushed it to Stout St.

Directly across 16th St., Walgreen's occupies the site of the historic **Barth Block**, a four–story building which helped pioneer the 16th St. retail corridor. Back in the early 1880s this uptown location was still a transitional residential district. Stout would have been considerably removed from the established emporiums along Lawrence and Larimer. William Barth, who obtained these four lots for a song, had been living here since 1869, when this was the extreme edge of settlement.

By 1885 the new **Albany Hotel**, a block away from Barth's house, pointed the way of urban expansion. The prescient German recognized that most of Denver's wealthy clientele was establishing itself to the southeast as they migrated towards Brown's Bluff, soon to become Denver's Quality Hill. Commerce naturally pulled in the same direction and Barth was eager to take advantage of the developing trend. The rough and tumble districts along Larimer and Market were assiduously avoided by the wives of the *nouveau riche* aristocracy, now drawn to the new, higher class establishments along 16th St, such as Daniels & Fisher and Joslins (where J.C. Penny once clerked). Within five years of its opening, in 1887, the Barth was surrounded by a great phalanx of important buildings, extending as far up as Broadway.

47. Neusteter Lofts – 720 16th St. – Fisher & Fisher – **1924** – **Score: 6.0**

| Meets the Street – 7 | Scale – 6 | Integrity – 6 |
| Public Spaces – 5 | Mass – 6 | Imagination – 6 |

Once again the versatile brothers, William and Arthur Addison Fisher, collaborated to produce a refined, elegant design. The Neusteter family catered to an elite women's clientele, and their new store was intended to exude class and style. A pressed copper cornice, trimmed in elaborate, Renaissance brackets, protrudes boldly over the sidewalk. The dressed

Neusteter Lofts (left center) occupies a prime position on the 16th St. Mall. The Denver Dry Bldg. is to its left; the University Bldg. stands above the crowd at Champa.

limestone facade features over-size, Chicago-style windows. The original entry on 16th St. featured a recessed portico, forming display islands surrounded by plate glass on five sides. In its day Neusteters brought a bit of 5th Avenue to Denver. Today a retail pharmacy extends the plate glass right up to the sidewalk, but the classical decorative relief still graces the checkout stands. It feels less resplendent surrounded by sale banners and merchandise. One can observe molding on the store's ceiling, marking the glass panes that once enclosed trendy mannequins, modeling the latest fashions.

The Neusteter Building remains stylish even now, because of the simplicity of the forthright design. A part of the building, near the street corner, actually dates back to the late 1880s, where a dry goods store called J.W. Smith occupied the three–story Hughes Bldg. That building was not demolished but incorporated into the Neusteter store when it was wrapped around the older building in 1924. The whole was then refaced as we see it today.

48. Hudson's Bay Center – 1600 Stout – Skidmore, Owings & Merrill – 1982   Score: 6.0

Meets the Street – 6	Scale – 6	Integrity – 5
Public Spaces – 6	Mass – 8	Imagination – 5

Hudson's Bay Center (far right) offers photogenic panoramas of 16th St., including Tabor Center, the D&F Tower, and the former Denver Tea Room atop the Denver Dry Bldg.

Just as 17th St. threatened to swamp the 16th St. retail district around 1980, submerging it in the shadows of endless high–rises, Hudson's Bay Center appeared, making an honest effort to strike a balance between civic and economic interests. Fortunately the office boom subsided as a glut of space flooded the market, preserving 16th St. as a retail spine.

This building still supports the variety of life along the mall by providing ground–level retail, which feeds naturally into the pedestrian flow. The tower creates a sense of intimacy despite its 20 stories and somber, charcoal hue. The cut–away sculpting of upper floors effectively sets it back from the street and its more diminutive neighbors. An interior "light court" gives the lobby area a surprising feeling of spaciousness, considering the miserly plot upon which the building sets. Adept design, combined with fortunate positioning on the north side of 16ᵗʰ St. prevents the center from casting long shadows onto the mall. The building emerges organically from the mall's gray granite pavers, producing a lively dialogue with the street and sidewalk.

16ᵗʰ Street Mall – Broadway to Union Station – I.M. Pei – 1982

Although we have already criss-crossed the 16ᵗʰ St. Mall several times, I have chosen the intersection with Stout St. to comment on it. This is the historical mid-point, and

16th St. Mall can be a magical promenade on balmy evenings, after the crush of office workers retire and hansom cabs venture out, prowling for "carriage trade."

might be considered the strategic center of downtown Denver. Not many downtown malls have succeeded as well as 16ᵗʰ St., which ties all the elements together in a naturally urban, people–friendly environment. The idea of creating a pedestrian mall along the city's prime retail corridor had been tossed around for years by planners, but it was really the success of the Nicollett Mall in Minneapolis that provided a functional prototype for Denver. 16ᵗʰ St. merchants and traffic engineers were uneasy about the elimination of vehicular traffic in front of their stores. Minneapolis proved that removing cars wouldn't necessarily kill the street, despite contrary evidence in towns such as Fresno and Chicago, which finally gave up the transit mall concept on State St.

Denver and Minneapolis have successfully bucked the "failed mall" trend thanks to superior design and committed civic involvement by the business community. The catalyst for the 16ᵗʰ St. Mall back in 1980 was the Regional Transportation District (RTD), a public agency responsible for mass transit. RTD came up with a sensible and workable concept, connecting two major bus terminals at either end of 16ᵗʰ St. The Market Street Station was constructed underground at 16th & Market, while the Civic Center Station burrowed into the slope at 16ᵗʰ & Broadway. The mall itself was conceived as a spine, joining the two stations. Unlike other malls, regular buses were excluded on 16ᵗʰ St,. but free shuttle buses run frequently between the two transit nodes, essentially a 14–block escalator.

RTD retained a world-class architect with an established reputation in Denver, I. M. Pei, to design the mall. By the end of 1982, a traffic-choked gasoline alley had been re-configured into a tree-lined pedestrian boulevard with enhanced sidewalks and attractive granite pavers. Two bus lanes provided movement and emergency vehicle access. More importantly, Pei provided islands and benches where people can linger, play a games of chess, or just rest for a moment. The design's only weakness proved to be the granite pavers, which require constant maintenance.

The other key element in the mall's success was the creation of a special business assessment district that provides for the continued promotion, upkeep, and monitoring of the 16th St. Mall. When the mall was dedicated in 1982, at least five major retailers lined 16th St. Today all five are gone, having either quit business or fled downtown altogether. Economically the 1980s were a very rough period for Denver, but that recession undoubtedly saved much of the street's threatened architecture. Through it all, business and civic leaders made mall maintenance a high priority, which in the end paid off.

Two large retail centers, the **Tabor Center (#30)**, and **Denver Pavilions (#68)** took up some of the slack left after the department stores exited. Restaurants and hotel construction also contributed to creating new street life. As downtown *morphed* into a 24–hour city, with the creation of thousands of new residential units, 16th St. again became a kind of "Main Street" for pedestrians. As a result, suburbanites now make a special point of coming downtown just to stroll or dine out. "Give them a reason and they will come," seems to be the motto of 16th St., the mall that refuses to die. What ultimately attracts people is neither stores nor free parking, but other people. 16th St. Mall today is Denver's people place, in part because I.M. Pei provided a great space for people to watch, and linger.

49. Equitable Bldg. – 730 17th St. – Andrews, Jacques, & Rantoul – **1892**   **Score: 6.9**

| Meets the Street – 7 | Scale – 6 | Integrity – 7 |
| Public Spaces – 8 | Mass – 7 | Imagination – 6 |

Today it may be hard to imagine, but this nine–story Italian Renaissance Revival structure was the crowning pinnacle of Denver's skyline for nearly two decades, before the advent of the D & F Tower. It also helped establish 17th St. as the Wall Street of the West, while serving an important political role as well – the governor's executive offices were located here before relocating in the granite Capitol Building in 1896. Even today, dwarfed by the younger upstarts surrounding it, the Equitable maintains a

Colorado's executive branch housed in the brand new Equitable Bldg. until the unfinished Capitol Bldg. was occupied in Nov., 1894. The lobby is a surviving remnant of Gilded Age opulence.

commanding street presence. Boston architects Andrews, Jacques, and Rantoul collaborated with the New York insurance company to create a statement of permanence and stability.

The architects certainly felt the influence of Henry Hobson Richardson, but here they opted to use a more refined approach than the typically heavy, rusticated stone blocks. The Italian Palazzo style is grandly adapted for commercial space. The plan, popular in the East at the time, features double light wells on both street and alley

sides, a generous layout which gave every office access to natural light. The Equitable seems to resist its natural verticality, emphasizing the horizontal lines instead by banding each floor. A strong cornice re–asserts this lateral flow and lends it extraordinary strength of character.

Equitable's exterior walls are actually solid bearing masonry, while only the interior framing is of iron and steel. The two–story base is pink Pikes Peak granite, neatly cut and arranged in the Romanesque tradition. Deep recesses at the seams add to the sculpted quality. The hodgepodge of ledges, apertures, and miscellaneous do-dads, like random balconies, are quaintly 19th century. As with the Boston Lofts, the deep-set windows give it strong shadows. The interior public lobby is a sumptuous example of the opulence Americans took for granted in the days before skimpy construction budgets.

Denver readily accepted the new standard of excellence set by this important business structure. Denver architects appraised it with interest, but the market crashed before it could exert any significant impact on the local design profession. The Equitable, as the culmination of that first boom era, was never duplicated – and remains today a well–loved architectural anomaly in Denver.

50. Magnolia Hotel / 1st Natl. Bank 1910 – 818 17th St. – Harry W. J.
Edbrooke / Weary & Alford – **1910**   **Score: 6.5**

Meets the Street – 7	Scale – 7	Integrity – 7
Public Spaces – 5	Mass – 7	Imagination – 6

This is the house that David Moffat built for his First National Bank, the largest banking institution in the state and second largest in the West at one time. That is only the sales brochure story, however. Behind the gala grand opening attended by an estimated 30,000 persons on January 3, 1911, there lay a darker tale. Bank president David Moffat was unable to attend the opening, and never set foot inside his brand new office. He had been in New York since the beginning of December, desperately trying to obtain new financing for his Denver & Northwestern Railroad. Moffat had sunk his entire fortune (estimated at $10,000,000) and a good chunk of the bank's assets into the Moffat Road. Stretched to the limit, he turned to Wall Street, working to salvage the empire he had built up over the past 50 years.

He had powerful enemies in the persons of Edward H. Harriman, who controlled the Union Pacific, and George J. Gould, whose railroad subsidiaries included the Rio Grande. Neither capitalist wanted Moffat to succeed, thus creating new competition. By mid–March Moffat had nearly secured financing when some dark horse stepped in and blocked the deal. Moffat was ruined, although it is likely no one knew save for his business partner on that extended trip, "Tramway Bill" Evans.

On Saturday morning, March 18, 1911, Moffat's lifeless body was found in his New

York hotel room on 49th St. Presumably, he died of a heart attack at age 71, but under the circumstances, the possibility of suicide has always haunted historians. Only quick action by bank attorney Gerald Hughes, who quietly organized a campaign of wealthy Denver businessmen to financially underpin the bank, prevented an enormous scandal that surely would have initiated the bank's collapse. Hughes undoubtedly saved Moffat's reputation for posterity, and his dream of a railroad tunnel under the Divide, giving Denver direct linkage with Salt Lake City.

The business of business was cold and impersonal. Millionaires and common workers alike were frequently caught in its capricious webs. A week to the day after David Moffat's mysterious death in New York City, that city's Triangle Shirtwaist Factory burned on Washington Square, claiming the lives of 141 young women who were trapped in the blazing inferno by locked escape doors. The guilty factory owners were never convicted for their part in the disaster. In the jaded eyes of capitalism, no actions that assured a profit were considered nefarious. If one millionaire or a hundred working girls were sacrificed for commercial gain, it made little difference. In time, such attitudes would soften, but only after the public outrage mobilized the reform politicians.

The building that David Moffat never saw completed boasts a classic Commercial facade in the tradition of McKim, Mead, and White. It was thoughtlessly buried in 1962, under a honeycombed concrete grillwork. (That grillwork can still be seen on the adjacent parking garage that was a part of the '62 reconstruction.) The original classical banking floor by Weary & Alford of Chicago was also obliterated. The structure was converted from office space to a hotel in the 1990s, and the offending grill stripped away. This permitted an extensive restoration of the original facade, one of 17th Street's more dignified as it turned out. True to the times, a distinct base, shaft, and capital can be clearly seen, concluding with a handsome, projected cornice. The conservative bank architecture of that period was a natural expression of the city's premier banking institution, the First National. In 1910, this building hovered paternalistically over 17th St. – a symbol of its financial pre–eminence over the fabled "Wall Street of the West."

Proceeding along Stout, we pass the **Bank Lofts** (opened 1921) and housing the U.S. National Bank and Guaranty Bank for most of its life. It narrowly escaped demolition in the early 80s by a developer who, nevertheless, stripped the original interior banking room of its finery. The bank lobby, less grand than before, has found new life as the main ballroom for the nearby Magnolia Hotel. The formal Commercial style imitates the old First National Bank across the street, though it is surely less vibrant.

Courtesy, Colorado Historical Society   F-7354
The first Albany Hotel, seen here, heralded the movement of the gentry and upscale firms to upper 17th St. The Albany pre-dated the Brown Palace by nearly seven years.

Across Stout, where the nondescript **J M Plaza** now hunkers, the **Albany Hotel** once reigned prominently for more than 90 years. The original Albany, a four–story Italianate contraption notable for protruding bay windows, opened in 1885. The Albany pre–dated both the Brown Palace and the Oxford, and began the transformation of upper 17th St. from a quiet residential quarter into a leading avenue of commerce. A major expansion doubled it in the 1920s; then, in 1937, the original section was replaced by a sleek, modern building designed by the gifted Burnham Hoyt, keeping it competitive with the city's finest hotels.

The new Albany had a streamlined modernity, undoubtedly influenced by the Constructivism of post World War I Europe. This seven–story structure featured rich, sensuous materials, like travertine, that amplified a boldly rounded corner doubling as a marquee. The extensive use of glass brick around the window openings gave it a heightened sense of transparency. The hotel was badly damaged by a fire on Sept. 2, 1962, after which it was carefully restored. By the mid 70s the ground under the Albany had become its most valuable asset and so one of Denver's most historic hotels fell victim to a land assemblage scheme.

At the corner of 18th St. we come to one of the more unusual specimens of Denver architectural lore, a little three–story Romanesque adaptation from 1889 called the **Ghost Bldg.** Designed by William Lang, better known for his many distinctive Capitol Hill mansions, the building's haunting name does not imply para–normal activity. It is named for its builder, an early Denver pioneer, Arthur H. Ghost. It was

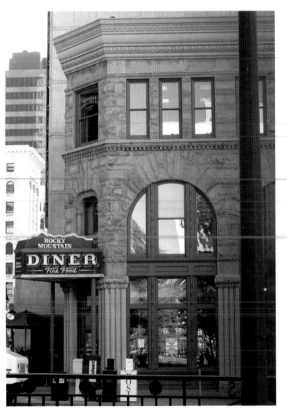

first situated at the corner of 15th St. and Glenarm Pl., but when that site was cleared, the North Dakota limestone blocks which faced it were carefully removed, cleaned, and stored. When developer Sandy Brown constructed a new building at 18th St. and Stout in 1985, he incorporated the old facade into the new structure so ingenuously that you would never guess that this Victorian–era pile is now a modern, steel-framed structure. The Ghost Building was thus resurrected and endowed with new life, an ironic coincidence in light of its unusual name, proving once again that you can't kill a ghost.

51. Byron White Federal Courthouse – 1823 Stout – Tracy, Swartwout, and Litchfield – 1910–16 Score: 8.7

Meets the Street – 8	Scale – 9	Integrity – 10
Public Spaces – 9	Mass – 8	Imagination – 8

The Byron White Courthouse is undoubtedly the finest Classical Revival edifice in the Centennial state. Three-story Ionic columns, carved from alabaster, Colorado Yule marble, address the street with an imposing dignity matched by few public buildings. The recessed colonnade along Stout encloses a long, raised portico ascended by a phalanx of marble steps. Smaller, protruding colonnades create dramatic end caps on the shorter, 18th and 19th St. facades. Two Rocky Mountain Bighorn sheep carved by Gladys Caldwell Fisher adorn the staircase on the southwest side. Inside, a sumptuous foyer runs the entire length of the building, where lucky patrons once waited to purchase stamps. It's worth a glimpse, but empty your pockets of metal objects first.

The building originally housed the Post Office as well as federal courts, neither of which had been very comfortable in the **Old Customs House** on 16th St. (see #26). This project dragged on for six long years, as Colorado Senator Simon

Byron White Courthouse was simply known as the Post Office for decades until postal functions moved elsewhere. It is possibly Denver's finest building, architecturally speaking. A full-block site gives it an imperial presence, distancing it from the mundane commercial environment.

Guggenheim fought for funding appropriations, but in the end, the delays were worth it. Denver finally had a first-class federal facility that bolstered its status as a governmental center for the region. Pueblo had seriously rivaled it since 1897 with a beautiful, Italian Renaissance Revival Courthouse and Denver wanted to re–assert its pre–eminence. This world-class structure left no doubt which city was the more important.

Postal functions were evicted in the early 90s. The building was given a complete facelift and re-named for Colorado's legendary football hero and U.S. Supreme Court justice, Byron "Whizzer" White. The Whizzer was a gridiron legend at C.U. in the 1930s. He was later appointed to the high court by President John F. Kennedy in 1962, where he deliberated for the next 31 years. Today the gleaming white marble contrasts starkly with the modern structures that encircle it, but the courthouse holds its own quite well. Three adjacent blocks have since been built up with various Federal courts and offices, creating an imposing "Federal Triangle" in the heart of downtown.

52. **U.S. Custom House** – 19th St. between California / Stout – James A. Wetmore – **1931**, expanded by G. Meredith Musick and Temple H. Buell – **1937**   **Score: 7.2**

| Meets the Street – 7 | Scale – 8 | Integrity – 7 |
| Public Spaces – 8 | Mass – 7 | Imagination – 6 |

The U.S. Custom House resides in the shadow of the Federal Office Building constructed in 1965. The four-block "Federal Triangle" now represents every phase of 20th century Federal architecture from Classicism to Modern Revival.

The original architect worked for the U.S. Dept. of the Treasury and came up with the Italian Renaissance Revival concept. Much of the building's elegance is a result of political pressure by the Colorado legislature, which demanded that the building be faced in Colorado Yule marble – as opposed to the specified limestone. The request made sense, in light of the deepening depression, as a means of supporting a Colorado industry, the stone quarry at Marble, Colorado. The net effect was well worth the effort and any added expense, however. The building glistens in the sun and, together with the Byron White Courthouse, gives this corner of downtown a stately scale and presence.

Prior to 1929, Denver's East Side High School stood here, a portly, Neo-Renaissance structure by Robert Roeschlaub. Inaugurated in 1881, but not finished

Denver Public Library, Western History Collection WHJ-10368 William Henry Jackson
City High School, where the U.S. Custom House now sits, became East Side High School as Denver expanded. Actor Douglas Fairbanks Jr. was a student here.

until 1889, it replaced the hopelessly overtaxed Arapahoe High School, the city's first. East became the city's finest high school as Denver spread out, serving the youth of "quality hill." The school building itself was a fussy, pompous edifice with a center section flanked by two wings – probably not Roeschlaub's best compositional effort.

Several famous luminaries were associated with East, including actor Douglas Fairbanks, Jr. and band leader Paul Whiteman, whose father, Wilberforce Whiteman, directed Denver's public school music programs for many years. Curiously, son Paul was responsible for commissioning a youthful George Gershwin to compose that quintessential American musical tribute, *Rhapsody in Blue*, in 1924.

53. **Holy Ghost R.C. Church** – 1900 California – Jacques J. Benedict & John K. Monroe – **1924, 1943**   **Score: 7.4**

| Meets the Street – 7 | Scale – 7 | Integrity – 7 |
| Public Spaces – 8 | Mass – 7 | Imagination – 8 |

Holy Ghost is arguably Renaissance Revival with certain Gothic features, but the Lombard shell and Romanesque tendencies, like Norman columns, are thoughtfully blended. Eclectic as it is, this has often been called Denver's most beautiful church interior – not without good reasons. Jacques Benedict was a master of the *Beaux Arts*, apparent from the way he deftly mixes so many different elements. He ties it seamlessly together with a salmon-colored travertine, giving the interior organic stability. Refined taste and compositional balance are the foundation of all Benedict's works, of which many survive, scattered around Denver and Littleton, where Benedict resided.

Holy Ghost is the church that Denver Post heiress, Helen Bonfils, built to honor her deceased parents. More amazingly, she had the clout to get it built smack in the middle of World War II, when everything from materials to skilled labor was either restricted or in scant supply. The church was dedicated in June, 1943, and it has been a downtown landmark and center of worship ever since.

Many colorful characters have been associated with the parish since its founding in 1905 by pioneer priest Fr. Frederick Bender. They include Fr. John Mulroy, founder of

Catholic Charities, and Fr. Charles B. Woodrich, Denver's legendary friend of the poor, and co-founder of the Samaritan Shelter. "Fr. Woody" instituted the shelter by opening the church to homeless street people, one freezing night in 1982. He also engineered the deal that made possible the construction of Holy Ghost's conspicuous neighbor, the towering **1999 Broadway**, providing a sensational backdrop to the church. Holy Ghost has a long history of attracting the movers and shakers, without neglecting the ordinary office worker and the indigent. Great architecture, music, and a rich history make it a premier downtown landmark.

Courtesy, Archdiocese of Denver

In early 1984, Holy Ghost Church was being engulfed by the tides of... mammon? In the end, God and commerce were able to co-exist quite peacefully. The juxtaposition of the church and lofty high-rise is mostly serene, but on blustery days the connecting plaza becomes exceedingly wind-blown.

54. 1999 Broadway – 1999 Broadway – Curtis W. Fentress & Assoc. –
1984 **Score: 7.8**

Meets the Street – 7	Scale – 7	Integrity – 8
Public Spaces – 8	Mass – 9	Imagination – 8

Somebody, at least, understands how to build a skyscraper that fulfills our expectations! 1999 Broadway marked the end of the 30–year boom cycle that redefined downtown Denver. Though the initial lack of tenants forced the development into receivership, the 19th St. location, while financially risky, was aesthetically rewarding. To this day 1999 remains un–hemmed by tall neighbors, allowing it to soar, unfettered, into the heavens. And soar it does, pointed aerodynamically down Broadway like the prow of a great ship.

The building site is actually a triangular block, further complicated by a large bite taken out by the **Church of the Holy Ghost (#53)**, around which the office tower was designed. Despite the apparent incongruities of style and scale, the two structures pair off amazingly well. 1999's floor plan is roughly shaped like a battery clamp, the two handles, or arms in this case, wrap protectively around the brick and terra cotta church. The concave arc thus formed rises 43 stories, dramatically enveloping the church in a curtain of green reflective glass, trimmed in stainless steel mullions. The faces along 19th St. and Broadway feature bands of smooth limestone, while cylindrical pylons support the tower base. A two-story glass atrium invites the outdoor plaza inside, right up to the elevator banks, trimmed in green marble.

I consider this Denver's proudest skyscraper for several reasons. It stands out prominently on the skyline and possesses strength, confidence, and elegance. The form is distinctive, the coloration is tasteful and yet bold. Furthermore, it respects the Renaissance Revival **U.S. Custom House (#52)** and **Holy Ghost Church (#53)**, striking a delicate balance with its historic neighbors without sacrificing its own mission. The extensive use of glass around the church was Fentress' solution to positioning the enormous mass of 1999 without overpowering the church's human scale.

The architect's choice of materials complements the yellow brick, terra cotta, and green tile roof of the church which are reflected handily in the green-glazed and limestone tower. The gray–green granite used to pave the plaza further ties the two buildings together, proving that God and mammon can co-exist in some degree of architectural harmony. 1999 Broadway does well what all great skyscrapers manage to do: create a sense of awe without bludgeoning the senses. It teases us by presenting different facets of its personality from various perspectives, like an intriguing woman whom we appreciate more with the passage of time.

Curtis Fentress is an enigmatic designer. A principal in the Fentress / Bradburn firm, he originally worked in New York for I. M. Pei (see #72 also #74) and later moved to Kohn, Pederson, Fox, where he helped design Denver's **1675 Broadway (#75)**. Both 1675 and 1999 Broadway rank among Denver's finer office towers, but the project which became his signature piece is Denver International Airport. In my opinion, 1999 Broadway is his most edifying work; good enough, in fact, to help us wink at his less successful Colorado Convention Center (#45). Nobody bats 1.000, not even architects.

55. 1801 California (Qwest) – 1801 California – Metz, Train, Youngren – 1983

Score: 5.6

| Meets the Street – 5 | Scale – 3 | Integrity – 5 |
| Public Spaces – 7 | Mass – 7 | Imagination – 6 |

One of the skyline's "Big Three," 1801 California is a hugely–scaled office building, soaring 52 floors and 708' into the atmosphere. Such heady figures stir a certain ambivalence. It strikes me as unnecessarily ponderous, considering its sensitive, full block location, facing the Neo-Classical **Byron White Courthouse (#51)** and refined **U.S. Customs House (#52)**. Fifty-two floors don't relate cogently with all that white, wedding–cake marble. The big parking garage is a real downer along 19th St., a triumph of functionality over aesthetics. Decidedly, the design is far better than the big, beer gut **Marriott / MCI Tower** across the street. It also provides a pleasing entry plaza. Adept sculpting of the tower's mass by way of setbacks, and the orientation, turned deftly at 45 degrees, offers relief from the rigid downtown grid.

The tower portion consists of two interlocking octagons playing off against one another. The warm, chocolate aggregate is palatable, but hardly daring. Granite clads the two-story base, lending character to the whole and keeping the cheaper aggregate at a safe distance. The taller shaft terminates abruptly, though I suspect the temptation to give it a crown was a strong one. Perhaps, one day, they will cap it with a New York–style pyramid, which will at least give it a sense of distinction as well as making it the epicenter of the Denver skyline. Its colossal scale is already a done deal so, short of shrinking it down by 30%, giving it a schmaltzy hat could be the best way to rationalize its unsettling magnitude.

Proceeding along California we pass through the **City Center Group**, four large towers attributed to various architects between 1959 and 1981. Their names will not be mentioned here, but it's hard to imagine a more dis-engaged group of misfits. What ties them together are two open-air plazas straddling California. These combine to define (loosely) a kind of town square at the very heart of the city. Union Square it's not, thanks largely to the surrounding melange of architectural claptrap. Mies van der Rohe was once quoted as saying, "I am, in fact, completely opposed to the idea that a specific building should have an individual character," a point well-illustrated by these four, soulless monoliths.

The smaller plaza, tastelessly reworked only recently, came first – followed by the lush, big space across California, actually the rooftop of the Marriott's underground banquet facilities. The raised planters and (thankfully) large trees soften the nasty bulkiness of **J M Plaza** and the "fat lady," a combination hotel and office tower. The latter is a brawny, bulging edifice; dark, foreboding, and... pregnant? It bevels out about 20 floors up to accommodate enlarged office floor-plates, thus reversing the whole rationale of setbacks to hideous effect. The architects might have mitigated its discomforting girth somewhat by lightening the building's skin, but they apparently wanted us to experience the "full treatment" which is, painfully, what we get. The public benefits primarily from some much-needed open space in a perfect location, but at what a price to our sensibilities!

56. Matrix Capital Bank – 700 17th St. – Raymond Harry Ervin –
**   1962**   **Score: 6.8**

Meets the Street – 7   Scale – 7   Integrity – 8
Public Spaces – 5   Mass – 8   Imagination – 6

After several unsuccessful attempts at adapting Modernism to local tastes, architect Raymond Harry Ervin finally produced a gem. Matrix Capital Bank (originally Western Federal Savings) is an International Style building, done in a regional vernacular, that belies its 40–some years. A remodeling a few years back removed the original awning and concrete latticework on the four story podium facing California, wrapping beams and columns in stainless steel. The 17th St. facade is basically unchanged however, manifesting clean, functional lines that make this building appealing. Above the base, a sleek 20–story tower soars, vertically reinforced by stainless mullions and white pre–cast pilasters that lend the design a regional, "Western" flavor, without spoiling the overall Modern effect. The edifice is crowned by a cooling tower / billboard worn like a big stetson. The tripartite form: base, shaft, and capital (albeit a clumsy one) rises 354' on the meager (12,500 sq. ft.) lot, mandating economy–sized floors that really let it soar.

By contrast, the stout, solid **Equitable Bldg. (# 49)** just across the alley, provides a weighty mass that visually grounds the airy lightness of Matrix Capital. The two buildings, irreconcilable as they might appear, actually manage to show deference to

Courtesy, David Eitemiller.

In its original manifestation as the Western Federal Savings Bldg., the "Big W" was a highly visible logo. Today the tower is more hemmed-in and hard to spot from a distance.

one another and the street. This building is undoubtedly fussy in some senses, notably the dull, cubical hatbox on the roof, but it is scaled ideally to its compact site and soars lightly without intimidating or casting long shadows. It is an underrated skyscraper whose proportioned massing and vertical, linear form quietly commands attention without having to shout.

The slender, **California Building** (circa 1892) by Frank E. Edbrooke filled this corner for 70 years. The six-story, Richardsonian brick and stone edifice was possibly his purest, commercial composition. Standing across California St. was a slim, 12-story tower, the 1927 vintage **Security Building** (see photo, chapter 2) by Fisher & Fisher. Its vertical, jazz–age lines, green terra cotta facing, and crenelated roof-line made it one of 17th St's. more exotic structures.

57. Colorado Bldg. – 1615 California – J. Roberts / F. Edbrooke –
1891 / 1909, Jacques J. Benedict – **1935**   **Score: 5.8**
Meets the Street – 6   Scale – 6   Integrity – 5
Public Spaces – 4   Mass – 7   Imagination – 7

Denver's holdover from the jazz age is served up by the irascible, yet gifted Jacques Benedict, better known for his *Beaux Arts* masterpieces. His contribution here was the Art Deco facade, which effectively gave the building a new face. The structure is totally hybrid. The original five-story Victorian commercial edifice was later topped by two additional floors (shorter than the originals) designed by Frank Edbrooke in 1909.

In an effort to unify the warring elements in this confused assortment of architectural bric-a-brac, and modernize its appearance, Benedict removed Edbrooke's cornice and wrapped the columns in sleek terra cotta. He added a jazzy, rooftop profile surmounted by creamy, soaring finials (vertical masonry posts), thus permitting the building, at only seven stories, to seemingly scrape the sky – a clever optical illusion. A decorative terra cotta string-course wraps around just above the retail windows and provides a base for the columns. The Depression was in full swing, so the original 1891 floral patterns ornamenting the spandrels were merely repainted.

Today, the Colorado Bldg. must be appreciated in the mind's eye, due to many years of neglect. Taking a squat, undistinguished business block with no great height or distinction, Jacques Benedict ingeniously endowed it with a surprising sense of verticality. This neglected gem is an ugly duckling, waiting to be restored to its original luster by just the right owner.

58. Denver Dry Bldg. – 700 16ᵗʰ St. – Frank E. Edbrooke, et al –

1889, 1898, 1906, 1924   **Score: 6.1**

| Meets the Street – 7 | Scale – 7 | Integrity – 6 |
| Public Spaces – 6 | Mass – 5 | Imagination – 5 |

The Denver Dry struggles to synthesize its various stylistic components. This block-long structure has a rich history, accounting for its disparities, being constructed in four separate phases. Originally this was the site of a popular skating venue called Mammoth Rink. As fashionable business moved uptown, the rink was removed to make way for the McNamara Department Store, which accounts for the first three floors along 16th St. The cornice from that original construction still projects, rather incongruously, between the third and fourth stories.

The Panic of '93 forced a reorganization of McNamara, and in 1894 the Denver Dry Goods Co. was formed under the direction of banker Dennis Sheedy, wealthy proprietor of the Globe

The terra cotta Colorado Bldg. (right) and former Denver Dry Goods square off with one another at 16th & California. The "Denver" once boasted the world's longest department store aisle, some 400 feet.

Smelter. By 1898, business had recovered enough that the architect, Frank Edbrooke, was brought back to add a fourth story, featuring round–head windows, grouped in threes, all capped by a bracketed cornice. This Italianate Revival addition accommodated business for a short eight years.

By 1906 the store was again bursting at the seams; additional lots were acquired and Mr. Edbrooke was once again retained to double the building's capacity. This six-story addition extended the store all the way to 15ᵗʰ St., allowing the Denver Dry to boast the longest department store aisle in the country, 400' in all. The aesthetic merits

Cornice detail of the Denver Dry Bldg

of this new addition are debatable, although it reflects the straightforward commercial style that differentiated the 20th century from 19th century revivalism. Ironically the fourth, and final, phase of building, in 1924, reverted to the old style, crowning the original section with a two-story, Renaissance Revival penthouse, resembling a layered wedding cake.

When a 1980s corporate merger forced the closure of the store, the landmark sat empty for several years, until the Denver Urban Renewal Authority put together a deal to restore it. Loft apartments were carved from the upper floors, underpinned by three levels of renovated commercial space.

Across California, next to the Light Rail kiosk, we see the **McClintock Bldg.** by Willison & Fallis – 1910. This was actually the second McClintock building erected by early Denver pioneer, Washington McClintock, whose first McClintock Bldg. (1875) at 16th & Larimer housed David Moffat's First National Bank. This version fortunately survived the bulldozers. It is an exotic, vernacular structure featuring flattened ogee arches over the second story windows, and rich ornamentation projecting from the upper cornices. Continuing along California we fall under the shadow cast by Denver's newest, and tallest hotel.

The fantastically creative McClintock Bldg. sits under the watchful gaze of the old Denver Tea Room, patronized by generations of proper Denverites.

59. Hyatt Denver Convention Center – 15th St. & California – Klipp Colussy Jenks DuBois / Brennan Baer Gorman – 2005 Score: 5.9

Meets the Street – 5	Scale – 6	Integrity – 6
Public Spaces – 5	Mass – 7	Imagination – 7

For years, the *Denver Post* called this site home and, as a kid, I remember the fascination of peering into the press room through the large plate glass windows along California. Grimy pressmen would grin right back, wearing their distinctive caps, folded from newsprint. The hatch-like windows were equally intriguing to a ten–year–old, conjuring up images of Captain Nemo's *Nautilus*. Even today, when I think of the *Post*, those windows come to mind.

Long before the newspaper took over the property in the late 1940s, this had been the location of the very first Catholic school in Denver, St. Mary's Academy. The school is still in business today, but in far–off Cherry Hills. Come to think of it, this was also far removed from the center of town, in 1864, when Bishop Joseph P. Machbeuf purchased the home of pioneer George W. Clayton for a new

Courtesy, Archdiocese of Denver

Denver's first Catholic bishop, Joseph Projectus Machebeuf, started St. Mary's Academy, in 1864, where the Hyatt Denver Convention Center Hotel sits. Machebeuf lived a block away, next to St. Mary's Cathedral on Stout.

school. The house also included all the land between 14th and 15th St. along California.

Today the new Hyatt Convention Center Hotel rises where impish boys once dipped schoolgirls' pigtails into inkwells. At 37 floors, this is the first building to punch a recognizable hole in the Denver skyline in over 20 years. The building makes a lot of interesting statements but lacks a unifying theme, the sort of motif that Eero Saarinen called a "strong, unified concept." On one corner it mirrors the convention hall's glass curtain wall, on another, it resorts to limestone to give it a grounded feeling. The architects worked hard to break up the inevitable monotony of such a monolithic structure, but the results don't necessarily feel unified.

The hotel rooms straddle a five-story podium. Two towers of varying heights join at the service core, offset like pinwheel armatures. Three distinct patterns embellish the facade, featuring lots of glass, limestone, granite, and titanium. The project is not particularly kind to Welton and 15th St. where killer cabs pull in front of pedestrians. Whatever happened to the more civilized pull-up lanes that preserve the autonomy of sidewalks? Overall, the hotel's perpendicular shafts are pleasing, culminating in a semi–transparent mast that vaguely echoes the Art Deco skyscrapers of the 30s. The Hyatt's articulation of verticality is decent, not soaring, but poised. It's a respectable structure that engages us, but could also project a little more passion and conviction.

The Hyatt Convention Center forges an important urban link between the convention hall and the rest of downtown, especially the 16th St. Mall, generating a steady flow of pedestrian traffic along California. It fills a desolate hole in the city's fabric, where the *Denver Post* once hummed. As a historical reminder, a pair of those *Nautilus* windows from the old **Denver Post Bldg.** are set into the corner, at 15th & Welton. Peer in, but you'll have to imagine your own gritty pressmen wearing newsprint caps, eating lunch on the other side.

60. Public Service Bldg. (Xcel) – 550 15th St. – Baume & Polivnick – 1962

Score: 6.2

| Meets the Street – 7 | Scale – 6 | Integrity – 7 |
| Public Spaces – 6 | Mass – 6 | Imagination – 5 |

Back in 1962, this structure was a real statement of faith in the future of 15th St., downtown's perennial poor cousin. 15th struggled to match the respectability of 16th and 17th Sts. By 1960 it contained a motley assortment of bookstores, gin mills, and grimy residence hotels. It had few friends apart from the *Denver Post* and Public Service Company, its sole corporate sponsors. The Denver Dry Goods and May D&F maintained "back door" store entrances as a courtesy to their bus patrons, who boarded the coaches along 15th St.

The Public Service Bldg. towered over 15th St. in 1962. Floodlights, constantly changing color, bathed the building's "hat" every night.

Photo by J. J. Karius,

The brand new quartz-colored tower that Public Service constructed at 15th & Welton in 1962, towered over the two–and three–story neighbors. The building is pleasantly Modern without obsessing over profusions of glass. Spartan windowpanes set flush with the rosy aggregate that gives the building its distinctive cast. Stainless steel highlights the columns, terminating in a wide stainless band across the parapet. Narrower bands of steel demarcate each floor. A recessed portico fronting 15th St. makes for a civilized entryway. The mechanical tower sets back on the roof, simple, yet effectively balanced against the overall structure as a "hat." The building, neither stunning nor bland, articulates its form clearly, honestly and interacts humanely with the street.

From 15th & Welton, walk towards 16th St. for one block, past the **Denver Pavilions (#67)**.

61. Masonic Bldg. – 535 16th St. – Frank E. Edbrooke – 1889

Fentress & Assoc. – **1985**		**Score: 6.0**
Meets the Street – 6	Scale – 7	Integrity – 6
Public Spaces – 6	Mass – 6	Imagination – 5

The Masonic sits back to back with the **Kittredge Bldg. (#67)**, a pair of well- scaled structures that define the block clearly. Masonic is one of Edbrooke's less articulate designs, however. It lacks the more cohesive detailing of his Brown Palace Hotel, despite its solid appearance. The Neo-Renaissance elements feel muddled, not crafted. H.H. Richardson's Marshall Field Warehouse is oft-quoted here in a fragmented sense.

The structure's most interesting element is undoubtedly the main entry arch on Welton lifted almost verbatim from Louis Sullivan's Midwest Stock Exchange Bldg. Edbrooke chose to set it to one side rather than centering it, however. A smaller arch adorns the 16th St. side, illustrating the Chicago influence on Edbrooke, who was trained there under his father, Robert J. Edbrooke, and brother, Willoughby J. Edbrooke.

The building you see is virtually new; only the facade belongs to Frank Edbrooke. A sensational fire gutted the structure in 1984, so after the external walls were stabilized, a new, steel-framed structure was built behind them. The recessed penthouse floors, above the parapet, are the only apparent evidence of that difficult reconstruction.

62. 600 17th St. (Dominion Plaza) – WZMH Habib, Inc. –
1982   **Score: 6.3**

Meets the Street – 6 | Scale – 7 | Integrity – 5
Public Spaces – 6 | Mass – 7 | Imagination – 7

Originally called **Dominion Plaza**, this imaginative tower suffers mainly from its context, and the slap-dash pre-cast panels. The double-octagon floor plan and rose-colored aggregate highlighted by powder blue mullions give it a bit of schmaltz. Stair-stepped setbacks begin on the lower tower facing 17th St. and rise to the summit of the upper tower, adding a playful touch of geometry amid the grim environs along Welton. Unfortunately, the windows were not carried all the way around, interposing a hot, blank wall over 16th St. Pylons allow for recessed entryways and release a generous amount of open space at ground level, giving the towers buoyancy and spaciousness. Although I generally dislike buildings balanced on stilts, 600 17th St. is a happy exception, no doubt a result of its cheerful, sanguine personality.

600 17th St. attempts to spice up the disjunct urban hodgepodge around Welton.

This tour ends almost exactly where the next one, "Broadway & Brown's Bluff" begins. Turn a half block down 17th St. to the base of the tall, glass tower hovering overhead known as **555 17th St.**, originally dubbed the **Anaconda Tower**. Strange to live at a time when public buildings all seem to bear corporate titles (e.g., the Pepsi Center, Coors Field, etc.) while private buildings are shedding corporate identities for banal street addresses.

TOUR 4: BROADWAY & BROWN'S BLUFF

Tour 4. Broadway & Brown's Bluff

Tour 4. *length 1.2 miles.*   Begins at 16th St. & Glenarm Pl.
Ends at 16th Ave. & Sherman St.

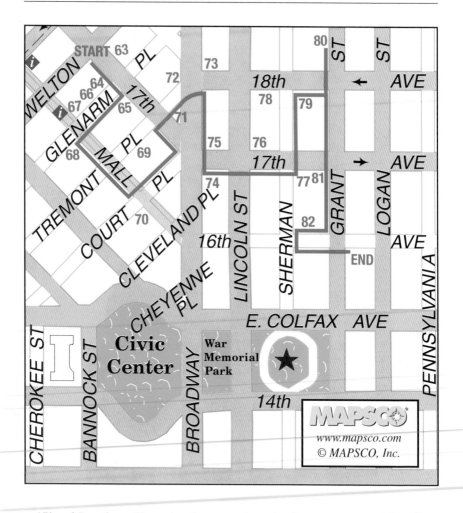

17th and Broadway. Five points intersect where the downtown street grid re-aligns itself to the rest of the city, akin to San Francisco's Market St. The result here is visually more archaic than the "City on the Bay," however. The ubiquitous cloud-scrapers are anchored by the venerable Brown Palace Hotel, nine stories of reddish, Arizona sandstone, wedged on a triangular block where Henry Brown used to graze cows.

The story of Henry C. Brown, and the hill he "pre-empted" in the early spring of 1864, plays large in Denver's development. The elevated landscape east of Broadway is now referred to as Capitol Hill. A century ago it was known as Brown's Bluff, after the visionary homesteader. Brown, an Ohio-born carpenter, took a gamble when he filed a claim on four, forty-acre parcels strung along Broadway, between present day 11th and 20th Avenues.

Henry Brown had drifted about California and Oregon during the gold rush before ending up in Denver. He apparently liked what he saw, and on April 15, 1864, he entered a patent claim on a 160-acre homestead east of town. By May, he was busy constructing himself a small frame house on this high ground, near present day 12th & Sherman St., after his first cabin got washed away in the big Cherry Creek flood that very same month. The Denver Town Company was offended by his enterprise since it, too, considered (illegally) the bluff to be part of the town-site. In reality, it stood outside of the official Congressional grant that had legalized Denver, *ipso facto*. Town Company president, Dick Whitsitt, dutifully rode out onto the dusty prairie to confront the erstwhile homesteader, busily engaged in his carpentry, and demanded to know what he was doing here. Brown looked up at Whitsitt – a steely glint in his eye; carpenter's ax in hand – and firmly explained that he was building himself a habitation, which was no concern of Whitsitt or anyone else. Brown's bluff worked. Dick took the hint and rode back into town. Thereafter, nobody dared question Henry Brown's claim to this high patch of earth.

According to the Homestead Law, Brown was entitled to purchase the land outright from the government, after making certain improvements and dwelling on it for six months. Paying it off in cash reduced the price from $2.50 per acre to $1.25 per acre, which is what Henry C. did on Dec. 1, 1865, paying $200 cash for the entire claim, to become its the rightful owner. He was quite alone out there, a good mile from the nearest edge of the fledgling city. Some time later a gentleman offered him a whopping $500 for his 160 acres. Brown was tempted, but after much thought declined the offer, to which the first party exclaimed that it didn't matter because the city would never reach that far out anyway.

Henry Brown eventually tired of living so far from civilization and moved his frame house to the extreme western edge of the property, resettling it where the 1700 Broadway Bldg. now sits. He had one neighbor, Alfred Clements, who wisely pre-empted an adjoining "quarter section" (160 acres) just north and east of Brown's. Clements hired Brown to build him a frame cottage for the princely sum of $100, the beginning of what became known as Clements' Addition. The subdivision business moved slowly at first, so Henry busied himself by contracting out his building skills in town. He apparently prospered because in 1868, he built a three-story business block on the east corner of 16th & Market, the first brick building facing 16th St.

Brown held onto his high ground in the meantime, and when the territorial legislature voted on Dec. 9, 1867, to make Denver, not Golden, the permanent capital, Henry C. sweetened the pot by donating ten acres atop Brown's Bluff for a new capitol building. The legislature enthusiastically approved this largess, although another 20 years, and several lawsuits, transpired before construction on the capitol building actually began. By 1875, Brown was prosperous enough to build himself a large, new residence where the old house dwelt, on Broadway, still out in the boondocks.

The city was booming by then, and within four years Brown sold his house, along with the entire block, for the unimaginable sum of $40,000. The purchaser was a newcomer to town — a precocious millionaire just arrived from Leadville named Horace Austin Warner Tabor, and his parsimonious wife, Augusta. The Tabors moved in on Jan. 1, 1879, and Brown smiled all the way to the bank. As yet, only a handful of homes peppered his promising bluff, but the generous, likable Tabor, brimming

*The Tabor Residence,
built by Henry C.
Brown, spurred an
exodus of wealthy
patrons to Brown's
incline, east of
Broadway. After her
divorce from H.A.W.,
Mrs. Augusta Tabor
stayed on here for
some years before
retiring to a suite in
the Brown Palace.*

with optimism and new found millions, shortly changed the destiny of the neophyte city. Within two years his sensational opera house on Curtis and magnificent Tabor Block at 16th & Larimer wowed the locals, lending the city a more permanent, if not pretentious, air. Society naturally followed the affable Tabor, and Brown's Bluff began to fill up with new mansions for the city's finest.

The decade of the 80s poured tremendous wealth into the emerging metropolis, both from the mountain mining camps and burgeoning plains agriculture. Brown's Bluff became the place to show off all that wealth, especially Grant Avenue, Denver's answer to Fifth Avenue, where millionaires competed to display their wealth. Brown's gamble was now paying handsome dividends to the patient carpenter who carved it into estates for the cream of Denver society. Boettcher, Kountze, Palmer, Moffat, Byers, and Sheedy all flocked to his $200 homestead, disproving the early nay-sayers who predicted that it would never amount to a thing.

Brown's Bluff succeeded beyond anybody's grandest expectations, becoming Denver's undisputed Quality Hill and making its owner a wealthy man. Ironically, Brown and Tabor both died poor men, beset by financial woes in the 1890s, but their enormous contributions to the emerging city of Denver can never be overestimated.

Surveying the patchwork of offices and parking lots today, one could hardly guess at the hill's elegant past. Broadway, which once held such promise, struggles to assert its identity. The Brown Palace closed off its Broadway entrance years ago, a statement of that boulevard's deteriorating prestige. Gaping holes on either side of historic Trinity Church. Irregular setbacks and cornice lines deprive the street of definition. The wanton destruction of the Cosmopolitan Hotel in the early 80s hastened the visual disintegration of this once fine street. New constructions also failed to reinforce the street line, thus abetting the visual clutter. A half block to the west, the insensitive bulk of Republic Plaza weighs heavily on the hapless street-scape, although it did contribute a welcome pocket park as partial restitution.

The compaction of hotels and office towers within these few square blocks is unrivaled anywhere in the Rocky Mountains. 17th St. once called itself the "Wall Street of the West" because financial firms were so concentrated here. Today many banks and insurance companies have merged or relocated to "edge cities" such as the Denver

Tech Center. Nevertheless, an impressive array of financial firms, oil companies, and the like still do business near Broadway and 17th. The architecture is generally 20th century corporate, but a few survivors from bygone eras cluster immediately around the Brown Palace, which seems to shelter them in its maternal penumbra.

The tour begins along 17th St., just west of Glenarm Pl., where the mid-block entrance pavilion of **555 17th St.** beckons us to sample the Pinnacle Restaurant, 37 floors above the street, where oil moguls once consummated million dollar deals on a handshake. The Petroleum Club is no more, but for nearly 40 years (starting at 16th & Broadway) it was a force to be reckoned with in Denver's business community. Like the Mining Exchange, from an earlier era, the Petroleum Club represented a key industry that contributed substantially to the city's development and prosperity.

63. 555 17th St. – 555 17th St. – Skidmore, Owings & Merrill – 1978   Score: 6.0

Meets the Street – 7	Scale – 5	Integrity – 6
Public Spaces – 7	Mass – 5	Imagination – 5

The sober profile of this 38-story, Late Modern tower blends like a dark suit into the financial district. It notably outshines its deadly dull companions, a hotel and parking garage. The simple, rectangular tower was Denver's first building to break the 500' height barrier, a barometer of Denver's energy boom in the 70s. Despite considerable bulk and ungainly proportions, it assumes a dignity commensurate with S.O.M.'s ability to wrap boxes stylishly.

The facade is effectively divided into zones, marked by recesses in the smooth glass skin at the 13th mechanical floor, and the 38th floor, where the Petroleum Club, now a restaurant, once reigned. The first two floors are likewise differentiated, clad in black aluminum. The use of clear glass on these floors, and floor 38, permits visual penetration, whereas the office floors feature a silvery, reflective glass that changes the building's appearance with every caprice of Denver's weather. On cloudy days, the building broods, somber and gray, but on crisp afternoons it can turn sky blue, and at sunset, blaze like amber. While its form is less

The reflective 555 17th St. and Denver Club Bldg. (lower center) typify the contrast between late and early Modernist trends in the Mile High City.

spectacular than the IDS Center in Minneapolis, it evokes the same feeling of transparency. It's a sensible building, which naturally welcomes the sidewalk and raises its crown in a dignified manner.

The block itself contained a wealth of fascinating buildings at one time, including the six-story **McPhee Block** by Frank Edbrooke (circa 1889). The McPhee was perhaps Edbrooke's most sober statement, featuring a deep light well along 17th St. Poised behind the alley from this was the ten-story **Patterson Bldg.**, named for Sen. Thomas Patterson, whose home previously occupied the site.

Patterson, a Democrat reformer, published the *Rocky Mountain News* and earned the enmity of both Robert W. Speer and rival *Denver Post* owner Fred Bonfils, who once viciously attacked the elderly Patterson with a walking stick. For many years, the *Rocky Mountain News'* offices were located on Welton, right next door to the Patterson Bldg. Thomas Patterson also holds distinction as Colorado's first congressman, elected to the House in the first statewide election, in 1876. Later he also served Colorado in the Senate from 1901-1907.

One of Denver's finer buildings, sadly reduced to rubble, was the **Continental Oil Bldg.**, occupying the corner of 18th St. & Glenarm Pl., where automobiles now disgorge from an abysmal parking structure. The building stood 10 stories tall, clad in creamy terra cotta facing. An illuminated, red "CONOCO" logo added another six stories above the roof-line, making this one of downtown's most visible buildings at night. The elegant structure's demise left 18th St. stripped, aesthetically.

64. Denver Club Bldg. – 4 17th St. – Raymond Harry Ervin –

1954		Score 4.9
Meets the Street – 6	Scale – 5	Integrity – 4
Public Spaces – 4	Mass – 6	Imagination – 4

Mention should be made of the wonderful, Richardsonian mass that was the first **Denver Club Building**, built on this site in 1889. The architects were Ernest Varian and Frederick Sterner, whose **Denver**

The old Denver Club at 17th & Glenarm Pl. possessed the ambiance of a true gentlemen's club.

Denver Public Library, Western History Collection X-18859

Athletic Club at 1325 Glenarm Pl. is still extant, though nothing like the old Denver Club.

Heavy massing and poly-chrome stonework gave the Denver Club a distinctive presence on 17th St. The arbitrary window placement and a weighty Richardsonian archway, set off-center, emphasized the building's eccentricity. Its 4 ½-story mass was pleasing and carefully sculpted, surmounted by several rectangular chimneys and a hip roof that made it feel domestic. Varian and Sterner's juxtaposition of formal symmetry with asymmetrical fenestration produced lively dialogue with the street. This and the **Mining Exchange Bldg.** were Denver's finest tributes to the genius of Henry Hobson Richardson.

The present Denver Club Building signaled a post-war building boom that completely transformed Denver's skyline. The Denver Club actually required special legislation in order for the project to proceed. The club owns the top six floors, while the lower 16 stories are private offices. This arrangement led to the state's first condominium law, allowing separate parties to own different parts of the "air space" comprising a building's bulk. The building itself is a marginally rendered 1950s interpretation of Modernism; one of the very few tall buildings downtown to utilize New York-style setbacks, probably rescuing it from terminal dullness. It has achieved a certain "period respectability," and the greenish terrazzo and glass give it a distinctive flavor.

Photo by J. J. Karius,

1953 marked the beginning of Denver's new sky-scraping profile with I. M. Pei's Mile High Center at 17th & Broadway, and Raymond Harry Ervin's new Denver Club Bldg. (right) as both towers climbed skyward above 17th St.

The Denver Club came out of the ground at exactly the same moment as I.M. Pei's **Mile High Center**, a few blocks away at 17th & Broadway, which outclassed it entirely. Both buildings were historic in another respect, as they were the first towers to puncture the skyline after the old Denver ordinance holding downtown buildings to 12 stories was repealed. From that moment, a new era in downtown's development began, allowing developers, such as New York's William Zeckendorf and Clint Murchison of Texas, to re-sculpt the cityscape.

65. Midland Lofts (Midland Savings Bldg.) – 444 17th St. – Fisher & Fisher – 1926   Score: 7.8

Meets the Street – 7   Scale – 8   Integrity – 9
Public Spaces – 7   Mass – 8   Imagination – 8

Nestled in the bustling cavern of 17th St., it's easy to overlook this 10-story Sullivanesque gem, but don't. How many Denver buildings can boast a company of fearsome gargoyles standing sentry on the roof? Though not immediately apparent, set back on the tile-roofed penthouse, their menacing grimaces can be viewed from a short distance up Glenarm Pl., where the angle is better.

The **Midland Savings** and the **University Bldg. (#41)** are undoubtedly two of the best early 20th c. period pieces around: both demonstrate the remarkable subtlety and originality of Fisher and Fisher, who were equally expressive with any number of styles. Their best work was done in brick and terra cotta, however. Pencil thin, terra cotta pilasters swirl unbroken for eight stories above the limestone base. The richly textured fenestration is enhanced by horizontal bands of amber-colored brick. Orange and burnt sienna earth-tones play off sympathetically with the nearby **Brown Palace Hotel (#71)**, the only two masonry structures

offering relief from the overwhelming modernity along upper 17th St. Warm brick, tiled hip roof, and horizontal string courses are faintly evocative of the Prairie School style.

This building exudes the smooth, formal quality and orderly symmetry of Louis Sullivan. It almost seems too graceful for the rectangular geometry hemming it in – crying out for a park-like setting. Midland is another outstanding example of this prolific architectural firm that practically defined Denver's regional Expressionism.

Fisher & Fisher produced a remarkably distinctive structure in the Expressionist vernacular for the Midland Savings Bank.

Courtesy, David Eitemiller

66. Paramount Theater – 1631 Glenarm Pl. – Temple Hoyne Buell –
1930   **Score: 5.7**

Meets the Street – 6   Scale – 5   Integrity – 5
Public Spaces – 6   Mass – 6   Imagination – 6

The grand opening of downtown Denver's only surviving movie palace drew 20,000 people on Aug. 29, 1930. The silver screen was fast becoming the new mass entertainment medium, and no expense was spared to create illusion, even in the architecture. Temple Buell, a part of the C.W. & George Rapp design firm at the time, designed this 2,100-seat, Art Deco movie palace, sadly the only survivor out of more than a dozen downtown theaters. It features a classic Wurlitzer theater organ, capable of filling the house with an abundance of rich sounds. Although the shallow stage made live productions difficult, a recent restoration of the theater made substantial backstage improvements – making the Paramount a popular live entertainment venue today.

Its chief competitor, the **Denver Theater**, was situated directly across 16th St. where the **Denver Pavilions (#68)** currently sits. The Denver Theater opened in 1927 with a spectacular price tag of $2,000,000 and sat 3,000 patrons comfortably. Its stage was equipped to handle full-stage productions, so it was more versatile than a mere movie palace. An emerald chandelier hung grandly from the auditorium ceiling and two grand staircases mounted to the mezzanine promenade. In 1982, it was scraped for a 57-story office tower that never got off the ground – a victim of the evolving movie industry and a hyper-ventilated real estate market.

67. Kittredge Bldg. – 511 16th St. – A. Morris Stuckert –
1891   **Score: 7.1**

Meets the Street – 7   Scale – 7   Integrity – 8
Public Spaces – 6   Mass – 8   Imagination – 7

Romanesque warmth and splendor emanates from the Kittredge, and spills out onto the 16th St. Mall as effusively as its restaurant patrons. Developer Charles M. Kittredge collaborated with architect A. Morris Stuckert to produce the city's best surviving example of Richardson Romanesque. The granite base is from Pikes Peak, supporting several floors of rosy, Castle Rock rhyolite. All that rusticated Front Range stone gives the building a strongly local flavor. Carved turrets crown the parapet, while Roman arches, on the sixth floor, harmonize sympathetically with the **Masonic Bldg. (#61)** to the west. A pitched pediment, up top, calls attention to the center entry bay.

The Paramount, downtown's sole surviving movie palace, is tucked neatly behind the Romanesque Kittredge Bldg. with its medieval turrets. Denver Pavilions offers a Post-Modern counterpoint.

For decades the neighboring **Paramount Theater (#66)** rented space in the Kittredge for its box office, marquee, and main concourse, thus giving the theater a grand presence on 16th St. Today the big "PARAMOUNT" sign is gone, but its smaller cousin can be seen around the corner on Glenarm Pl., over the current box office. The Kittredge was carefully restored in the 1980s.

The Paramount Theater's former foyer and box office is now celebrated as the Paramount Cafe, on the lively 16th St. Mall.

68. Denver Pavilions – 500 16th St. – ELS Architecture & Urban Design – 1999

		Score: 5.9
Meets the Street – 7	Scale – 6	Integrity – 4
Public Spaces – 6	Mass – 7	Imagination – 5

Even non-stop talkers, if they talk long enough, eventually say something, which sums up the Denver Pavilions. There's a lot of dialogue going on here, but one wonders how much it really adds up to. It's an agreeable enough place and honestly performs its function, which is to hawk merchandise, but like many talkative people, it projects shallowness. Plenty of festive, eye-catching baubles attract legions of shoppers, thus benefiting 16th St. and creating the bazaar atmosphere all exciting cities need. Underneath the

"cartoon architecture" veneer, however, Pavilions is basically a suburban, shopping theme-park, re-packaged for its downtown location. There is enough allusion to the language of architecture to suggest personality, but its soul is two-dimensional, cardboard *pastiche.*

In terms of adding life to the street and making this end of downtown hum after hours, Pavilions has been a welcome success. It also revived the downtown movie-going experience, after a long hiatus, and plugged an ugly, two-block scar left over from the 1980s speculative bubble that erased several important buildings - like the **Lawyers' Title**, and **Empire Bldgs.** The Denver Pavilions essentially re-vitalized this end of 16th St. by restoring the retail momentum lost when the May D & F anchor store retreated to Cherry Creek.

69. Republic Plaza – 370 17th St. – Skidmore, Owings & Merrill – 1983   Score: 4.4

| Meets the Street – 5 | Scale – 2 | Integrity – 6 |
| Public Spaces – 7 | Mass – 2 | Imagination – 3 |

This hulking, light gray slab of office space is Denver's monument, *par excellence*, to the grossly inflated land values in the early 80s. Fortunately S.O.M. used light, semi-reflective materials (a big black box at this scale would feel crushing), but these hardly compensate for the intimidating proportions. Awkward massing and squat, oversize windows further intensify the discomforting bulkiness of this un-sculpted behemoth. Could a pair of stair stepped towers have served just as well?

The street level features a formal, elevated plaza on 17th St. that buffers the Brown Palace Hotel from its lanky neighbor. A larger, bi-level, retail plaza interfaces with the 16th St. Mall, removing the 56-story monolith to a palatable, if not a comforting, distance. The tower's presence on Tremont Pl. is abysmal, however, casting a sinister shadow over the human ants who must brave its cold, deserted sidewalks. The use of high-class materials and intelligent open spaces mitigates the tower's chilliness. One wonders if S.O.M. had spent the same amount of creative energy on the actual box that they obviously expended wrapping and landscaping it, what improvements might have resulted.

I have been to the top floors of Republic Plaza, and the views are absolutely stunning. Thanks to geography, Denver enjoys great vistas. The best part of this particular view is that Republic's blank outline isn't a part of it. In its defense, the tower can possess a surprising reflective quality in just the right light and climatic conditions. From Civic Center however, its disagreeable bulk hovers over a beautiful civic space like a fat ballerina. Republic's greatest failing is that, within a certain wide radius, you can't escape its dominating presence.

Photo by Francis J. Pierson

Yesterday's 16th St. Alas, the Metropolitan Bldg. (far right), Republic Bldg. (center), and Centre Theater, whose marquee just peeks into the frame, are no more. This 1973 photo profiles the pre-mall thoroughfare, bustling with automobiles headed towards North Denver.

A historical footnote: Denver's best loved medical arts building, the **Republic Building** by G. Meredith Musick, 1928, was unceremoniously scraped to make way for its ungainly namesake. The medical arts have never regained the footing they once enjoyed downtown, since that untimely removal. The old Republic Bldg. boasted Denver's first underground parking garage, two complete floors. City fathers initially scoffed at the idea. Finished in light cream brick and terra cotta, Republic raised its cheerful head a proud 12 stories. The double wing arrangement, alternating with two, deep light-wells, was asymmetrical, but one never noticed from the street. The main lobby was forever bustling with people and the brass trimmed elevator cages were manually operated until the day this grand building died, prematurely.

Every time I walk down Tremont Place, I still recall the sonorous clap of a brass bell, followed immediately by the operator's sing-song cry, "Going Up!" One definition of an old timer in Denver is someone who remembers riding the polished brass elevators in the Republic Building, as the floors were announced like a train passing through stations.

70 . Adams Mark (Hilton) Hotel – 1550 Court Pl. – I.M. Pei Partners –
1956, 1960 *Scores refer to original Hilton* **Score: 6.6**

Meets the Street – 5	Scale – 7	Integrity – 6
Public Spaces – 7	Mass – 8	Imagination – 7

The Adams Mark covers nearly two square blocks, Denver's largest convention hotel, containing over 1,200 rooms. It consists of two buildings connected by a bridge over Court Pl. Flamboyant New York developer William Zeckendorf developed Courthouse Square – now the Adams Mark – back in the mid 1950s, some time before his real estate empire crumbled in the 1960s. The squat hat box opened first, in 1956, as the May D&F Department Store.

The original design was shockingly modern by Denver standards. A hyperbolic paraboloid structure gave the store an iconic face, and display windows on 16th St. It also helped

Photo by J. J. Karius

Remember skating on Zeckendorf Plaza? If so, you qualify as a bona-fide old timer. May D&F is tucked in under the Hilton's towering mass, around 1961.

contain Zeckendorf Plaza, a sunken space that remotely conjured images of Rockefeller Center. In winter months it functioned as a popular public skating rink. Both the plaza and paraboloid were demolished in 1996 to create the current hotel entry.

Two famous retailing entities were merged to create May D&F. The May Company, founded in Leadville by David May in 1877, was destined to become one of the country's largest department store chains. The fabled Daniels & Fisher grew up in Denver, down at 16th & Lawrence. William Cooke Daniels, son of W.B. Daniels, who began the store in 1864, built the distinctive D&F Tower that still identifies the city of Denver. In 1956, the combined entities opened shop in the glittering Courthouse Square store that re-incarnated, a mere 40 years later, as the frumpy, corporate hostelry we see today.

The name alludes to the grandiose Arapahoe County Courthouse that occupied the site until 1936, shortly after city and county functions were consolidated in the new **City & County Bldg. (#93)** on Civic Center. Denver was the seat of Arapahoe County, until Denver County became a distinct entity in 1904. (Adams County was also carved out of the original county.) After demolition of the old courthouse, the block functioned as a public park, for a number of years, until the city sold the property to Zeckendorf for the new development. This was a curious decision, considering the absolute paucity of public open space in the crowded downtown of that time. Nonetheless, a huge excavation, four stories deep, commenced under Court Pl. and its adjacent blocks, creating the largest underground garage the city had ever seen. The other half of Courthouse Square, east of Court Pl., opened in 1960 as the Hilton Hotel.

The same scene today, absent the public amenities and daring architecture that made Zeckendorf Plaza a special place.

The Hilton was a close collaboration between I.M. Pei and chief designer, Araldo Cossutta, who produced one of the better International Style buildings west of the Mississippi. The influence of the famed architect, Le Corbusier, is immediately apparent in the deep-set windows and articulate grill work on the lower floors. Going one step beyond Le Corbusier's bare concrete approach however, Pei elected to use a concrete aggregate mixed from gravel excavated at the site. The brown, pre-cast panels made from this material give it the natural, organic color and texture that is so appealing. The building's other notable feature is a long, slender form, traversing an entire block like a great, man-made cliff.

Few Modern buildings have achieved the dramatic intensity that this soaring palisade affords. An insensitive canopy, constructed for the Adams Mark in 1996, mars the linear continuity of Pei's "great wall," but thankfully the original curtain wall is intact.

I.M. Pei, no stranger to Denver, went on to international fame in the world of architecture after his early works here. His designs in Boston, Hong Kong, and at the Louvre in Paris are recognized world-wide. Pei himself was a modest, polite, and diminutive man. One would never have guessed, upon meeting him, that this was one of the superstars of the design world. Coincidentally, his other Colorado projects include the **Mile High Center (#75),** the acclaimed **National Center for Atmospheric Research** on Boulder's Table Mesa, and the 16th St. Mall.

71. Brown Palace Hotel – 17th St. & Tremont Pl. – Frank E. Edbrooke –
1892   **Score: 7.7**

Meets the Street – 7	Scale – 8	Integrity – 6
Public Spaces – 9	Mass – 9	Imagination – 7

Only a sliver of the lot, occupied by this grand hotel, was a part of Henry C. Brown's original homestead patent. When government surveyors laid out the line that became Broadway back in 1863, it sliced diagonally through a series of lots that the Denver Town Company had already established. Those partial lots were grandfathered by the 1864 Congressional Grant, but they had marginal value at the time because of their remoteness and fractioning. Henry Brown astutely bought them up, over a period of time, to assemble the triangular cow pasture that he used for grazing over the next 25 years.

Today, that cow pasture is a great hotel in a class by itself. How many hotels can claim their own artesian well in the basement, or a secret tunnel to spirit important guests, unseen, across the street for an amorous rendezvous or a spin of the roulette wheel? These are only a few of the reasons why the Brown Palace is the fabled hotel of the West. The "Brown" (as locals call it) boasts architectural as well as historic significance.

After a failed start, resulting in a huge excavation and a few walls, landowner Henry C. Brown hired Frank Edbrooke to re-design the grand hotel. Edbrooke took a cue from Billy Ralston's sensational Palace Hotel, in San Francisco, completed in 1875, and destroyed in the great earthquake and fire of 1906. The Palace featured a soaring, covered atrium large enough for carriages to pull completely into the building and turn around. It was the finest hotel in the West, so Henry Brown no doubt felt obliged to match its opulence, thus proving that Denver was

Denver Public Library, Western History Collection H-15 Rose & Hopkins

Dogged character is written in the face of Henry C. Brown, an intrepid pioneer, known for persistence and hard-headed determination.

no second-rate town. His architect created a soaring, nine-story atrium, enclosed

by stained glass – basically a square, 56' on a side and sliced along the hypotenuse (Broadway) of a block-sized triangle. The result is one of the most exciting interior spaces ever created. Profusions of marble, dark onyx, and brass lend it the elegance of a bygone age.

The exterior, though less dramatic, is still formidable. Its Neo-Renaissance form seems distantly related to Richardson's famous Marshall Field Warehouse in Chicago. Edbrooke exploited his unusual site masterfully, rounding the building's three corners, so that it resembles the prow of a great ocean liner from either end of Broadway. (This rounded motif was successfully emulated in the silvery **1670 Broadway (#74)**, diagonally across the street.) A sturdy granite base is topped by eight floors of brown Arizona sandstone

The glowing atrium of the Brown Palace Hotel left President Taft speechless when he first entered it. It always managed to convey a sense of warmth and friendliness, regardless of its opulence.

which has weathered poorly during its first century, requiring the shaving off of much of the original molding. Unlike the **Boston Lofts (#38)**, this has not improved the building's appearance. Nevertheless, it still exerts a forceful presence on the street. One could muse that the Brown's interior inspiration came from San Francisco, and its exterior from Chicago – making it a true western-American hybrid. It is undoubtedly Frank Edbrooke's masterpiece.

As fascinating as the architecture may be, the Brown's history is equally rich. Like so many others, Henry C. Brown lost his fortune and his hotel in the Panic of 1893. In a parallel twist of fate, the builder of the Palace Hotel, Billy Ralston, whose Bank of California had made him one of the West's richest men, also lost everything in the end. A mining stock panic in 1875, partly engineered by Ralston's unscrupulous partner, ruined Ralston, but only after the partner had acquired Ralston's interest in the Palace Hotel.

In Henry Brown's case – various legends still circulate about the details. Cripple Creek millionaire Winfield Scott Stratton ended up holding the mortgage, and the deed, to the Brown Palace. Oddly enough, Stratton and Brown were both carpenters by trade. His humble beginnings probably made Stratton a down-to-earth gentleman. It was he who took pity on his old friend H.A.W. Tabor a few years later when the broken silver king appealed to Stratton right here, in the bar of the Brown. Stratton helped put Tabor back on his feet.

Tabor's son, Maxcy, and business partner William Bush, invested early in the Brown Palace and they subsequently managed the hotel. After its completion, Augusta Tabor (Maxcy's mother and Tabor's first wife) moved into the Brown from her mansion across the street. Unlike Horace, Augusta was a shrewd New England type who invested her divorce settlement carefully, and died a millionaire. Tabor himself died poor, at the Windsor, shortly after regaining some respectability as the Denver Postmaster, thanks to Senator Ed Wolcott's intervention.

Stratton eventually sold the hotel to an Eastern syndicate, in 1912, who then sold it to Horace Bennett a decade later. It was during this period that a sensational double murder in the hotel's bar unleashed a scandal of epic proportions. The killer, Frank Henwood, shot down his rival, the socially prominent Louis von Puhl, and an innocent bystander, in a crime of passion. The object of both men's love (Henwood and von Puhl) was a beautiful, young (and married) society matron, Isabelle Springer, who had been playing her two lovers against one another. The lurid trial that ensued ruined Isabelle's marriage and reputation. She died a decade or so later – in a cheap New York hotel room, drug addicted, alone, and forgotten.

As the Great Depression strained the hotel's profits, the Brown was acquired in the late 1930s by Colorado's most successful industrial tycoons, Charles Boettcher and his son, Claude K. Boettcher. The Boettchers invested new money in the Brown, operating it as a first-rate, continental hotel. Shortly after World War II, another double murder occurred when a deranged veteran went berserk inside.

Over the years the Brown also hosted prize livestock during the National Western Stock Show, corralling various Grand Champion steers in the hotel's spacious lobby. The Brown has entertained virtually every president since Teddy Roosevelt and became the summer White House during the Eisenhower era. First lady Mamie Doud Eisenhower hailed from Denver. The Eisenhowers frequently spent time here, visiting Mamie's mother on Lafayette St.

Few places with a history of little more than a century could match the Brown Palace for legends and stories. Today, it is as central to the city of Denver, socially and economically, as it was when it first opened. The best time to wander into its marvelous lobby is at Christmas, when decorations turn the stunning space into an ethereal fantasy land of lights, shapes, and colors. The Brown is more than a great hotel, it's an institution that has become synonymous with the city of Denver.

72. Trinity Place – 1801 Broadway – Clothier, Weber & Assoc. –
1981   **Score: 6.6**
Meets the Street – 6   Scale – 7   Integrity – 8
Public Spaces – 6   Mass – 7   Imagination – 6

A very sensitive design in a key location, surrounded by historic structures, Trinity Place functions as an important character building. Much of its urban context was lost shortly after its completion by the heedless "imploding" of the refined Cosmopolitan Hotel, leaving an eyesore parking lot in its place for over 20 years now. Nonetheless, this handsome building, whose amber brick successfully complements the surrounding architecture, borrows its name from the landmark **Trinity Church (#73)**, just across Broadway. Modesty is often a real virtue in a building, which is one reason Trinity Place is so appealing.

The naughty Navarre now leads a quieter, secluded existence, hidden away among 17th Street's corporate giants.

Tucked in between Trinity Place and Comfort Inn, the restored Victorian face of The Navarre (1727 Tremont Pl.) peeks innocently onto the sidewalk. This schoolgirl patina belies the true character of the Navarre's naughty history. It was possibly designed by Frank Edbrooke, around 1880, for an academy called the Brinker Institute.

After Prof. Brinker passed on in 1886, the place eventually fell into the hands of gambling kingpins Ed Chase and Vaso Chuckovich, a political figure with underworld connections. Chuckovich, who was closely allied with Mayor Speer, lived in the little brownstone that still stands in a sea of parking at 1439 Court Pl. Together with Chase, he ran the city's finest gambling establishment, for gentlemen only, right across from the swanky Brown Palace. Legend has always been that a submerged tunnel joined the Brown and Navarre, allowing wealthy clients to enter the scandalous Navarre unseen. Discretion was management's policy in such affairs. Private rooms were available for the gentleman and his lady, where they might dine, sip on champagne, or place a wager with the house, among other activities. The main bar and dining room, on the second floor, were plushly decorated with fine art pieces that hung on the wall.

After Mayor Speer finally shut down the gambling salons, the Navarre became a fine restaurant for many decades, until the building was gutted and restored as an art gallery in the early 80s. Its scarlet reputation has always lingered, however, giving it an air of awe and mystery.

73. Trinity Methodist Church – 1820 Broadway – Robert Roeschlaub –
1888   **Score: 7.2**

Meets the Street – 6	Scale – 8	Integrity – 8
Public Spaces – 6	Mass – 9	Imagination – 7

The towering mass of Trinity Church is eloquent testimony to the migration of Denver's upper crust towards Brown's Bluff, now Capitol Hill, in the 1880s. The structure further characterizes the wealth and influence that Trinity's early parishioners certainly possessed. This Gothic-Revival church, executed in rhyolite stone, is situated commandingly at one of Denver's "five point" intersections. Later modern developments have been rather unkind to it, however. A 1954 annex for the neighboring Brown Palace included an elevated bridge over Tremont Pl. that mars the dramatic vista of the church from Tremont. Since then, it has been visually assaulted by urban clutter and ugly parking lots.

Today Trinity looks like a beached whale from certain angles. The church directors abetted this visual isolation by a decision to demolish the adjoining but stylistically compatible 2 ½ story education building on Broadway, which was replaced by a sunken plaza and subterranean offices. A large developer had visions of wrapping two huge office towers around the church, but that scheme never materialized. Now the area is an asphalt "no man's land", depriving a historic building of context.

Trinity's one shortcoming is that it squeezes the site while rumbling traffic on 18th Ave. practically occupies the sanctuary. The city further compounded problems by shoving too many traffic lanes into a tight roadway. At the very least, a parking lane next to the church would alleviate some of the claustrophobia. A better solution would be to widen the sidewalk by 8 feet. Any landmark as important as Trinity Church certainly deserves that much consideration.

Trinity Church predates the imposing **Brown Palace Hotel** just across the street. The two landmarks play off in a friendly joust with one another. The light, rusticated stone of the church sings a lyrical counterpoint to the smooth, rounded sandstone comprising the Brown. Richardson's influence is unmistakable in Trinity, yet for all its weight, the structure soars effortlessly: a stony mass culminating in a slender spire soaring some 182' above the pavement. The compact massing, independence of elements, and a firm visual grounding are hallmarks of Roeshlaub's style, but at Trinity he fuses those elements more effortlessly than in his other works (e.g., Central City Opera House and University Hall at D.U.) The eye is surprised, regardless of where it is drawn – whether to decorative finials, rectangular corner towers (all different), or the horizontal bands of stone, which subdivide the steeple into three parts, no doubt symbolizing the Holy Trinity. The interior auditorium is equally breathtaking. Roeschlaub's concern was not symmetry, but the organization of elements.

Robert Roeshlaub was the dean of early Denver architects. He served for 20 years as president of the Colorado chapter of the American Institute of Architects, from its inception in 1891. While certainly influenced by Henry Hobson Richardson, he successfully managed to translate those ideas into his own vernacular interpretation. Denver's Trinity Church is stylistically unique; quite independent of Richardson's more famous Trinity Church in Boston.

The Cosmopolitan Hotel typified the prosperity of the late 1920s, at least for some. Its wanton execution in 1982 left a gaping hole in the city's heart... still waiting to be healed.
Denver Public Library, Western History CollectionMCC-2831
Louis McClure

One of the city's more savage scars remains the empty parking lot at 18th & Broadway, where the elegant **Cosmopolitan Hotel** existed sedately from June, 1926, until May 20, 1984, when it was spectacularly imploded. At the time Denver's office market was beginning to reel from the contraction of oil and gas companies. Shortly after perpetrating this act of vandalism, the big, out-of-town developers disappeared, never making good on the promise to redevelop this highly visible site.

Along with that same destructive act, the neighboring **Hotel Metropole** was erased. The Metropole, designed by Frank Edbrooke, pre-dated the **Brown Palace (#71)** and included William Bush's **Broadway Theater**. When the Broadway, with its exotic Moorish theme, came onto the Denver theater scene in 1890, it rivaled Horace Tabor's Grand Opera House down on Curtis. William Bush, owner of the Windsor Farm Dairy that supplied the Brown and Metropole Hotels, was closely allied to the Tabors. It was Bush who first introduced Horace Tabor to Baby Doe in Leadville, in the spring of 1880. He later built the Broadway Theater, eventually managing that and the **Tabor Grand Opera House**. He also was a partner in the Brown Palace Hotel, which he and Maxcy Tabor managed.

74. 1670 Broadway – 1670 Broadway – Kohn, Pederson, Fox –
    1980   **Score: 6.5**
Meets the Street – 6   Scale – 6   Integrity – 6
Public Spaces – 7   Mass – 8   Imagination – 6

At the height of the oil and gas boom, Amoco Petroleum was one of the more active producers in the Rocky Mountain region, maintaining a huge Denver exploration office. This building, originally called the Amoco Tower after its largest tenant, went up literally at the peak of a bull market, when new office buildings were being announced almost weekly. **1670 Broadway** certainly boasts one of the most visually exciting sites downtown, at the very head of 17th St. The tower points like a great ocean liner dramatically up 17th. Architecturally, it is one of the fresher designs to come out of the late 1970s. Its carefully sculpted form is enhanced by the gentle rounding at the tower's two extremities.

Setting the tower at an angle on the plot allows it ample breathing space and keeps the 35-story bulk from overpowering Broadway, or the Brown Palace. The Broadway frontage is set back the same as its classic neighbor, **1700 Broadway**, an I.M. Pei gem. A three-story podium / atrium on Broadway holds the street line, while reconciling the oblique tower logically with its site. The elongated hexagonal shaft is a natural expression of the two intersecting street grids. Too bad, the building is hemmed in by trite neighbors. 1670 Broadway proves that Late Modernism was not totally bankrupt, just rarely well done.

The Shirley-Savoy Hotel, a favorite of stockmen, peered modestly down 17th St. Today, the 1675 Broadway Bldg. occupies the site.

Courtesy, Sanborn Ltd.

Cheesman Realty Company was the local entity that helped spearhead the development of 1670 Broadway back in 1978. Cheesman's president, John Evans III (a.k.a., "Jr."), was the great-grandson of Dr. John Evans, who figured so prominently in Denver's early history. John III, a decorated WWII paratrooper, who dropped out of college (sic.), still managed to carry on the Evans' tradition of building up Denver.

The corner of 17th & Broadway was the longtime home of the **Shirley-Savoy Hotel**, which consisted of three, distinct six-story buildings, (the last one designed by G. Meredith Musick in 1936), extending clear to Lincoln St. The Shirley opened in 1903, the Savoy in 1904, right next door – and the two merged in 1919. The combined Shirley-Savoy was popular with stockmen, ranchers, and traveling salesman, according to Musick. It was a reasonably-priced alternative to the Brown, appealing to budget-conscious businessmen who still wanted a decent hostelry. The hotel came down in 1970, in anticipation of Columbia Plaza, a 50-story development that was fortunately stillborn. Its later incarnation (as the Amoco Tower) turned out to be a much friendlier design

Across Broadway the twin **World Trade Center** buildings at 1625 and 1675 Broadway, by Skidmore, Owings & Merrill, mimic their older brother at **555 17th St. (#63)** but only succeed in annoying the senses. S.O.M. tried to exploit a provocative site, but they failed. The excessive geometry becomes a jumble of disjunct triangles, octagons, etc., because: 1. The street grid is already confusing in this part of Denver. 2. The street lines need to be re-enforced, not finessed. 3. Surrounding buildings tend to be competitive, not harmonious, so why insist on reflective glass that only compounds this problem?

75. 1700 Broadway (Mile High Center) – I.M. Pei & Partners –
1954   Score: 6.4

Meets the Street – 6	Scale – 7	Integrity – 6
Public Spaces – 5	Mass – 7	Imagination – 8

It's a pity when architects vandalize the good works of other architects. It is hard to imagine that Philip Johnson really felt that I. M. Pei's textbook Modern Mile High Center of 1954 required such drastic reconfiguring. This meant the destruction of a lovely, urbane fountain and plaza building which gave grace and balance to the whole. Pei's 22-story office tower survived Johnson's "improvements," though heedlessly marred by the attachment of a vaulted glass lean-to, stacked half-way up two sides. This feeble attempt to recreate the ambiance of his successful Crystal Court in Minneapolis falls utterly flat here, compromising the integrity of the original, free standing tower. The vaulted glass theme carries over Lincoln St. (**Wells Fargo Center #76**), and quickly tires the senses. Considering the hillside topography, a pedestrian bridge thrown in the air seems all the more senseless. More logically, the two buildings might have been connected by a tunnel under Lincoln St., thus respecting Pei's original, sensitive layout.

What survives of Pei's design, namely the office tower itself, is still a pearl of the International Style. This was the project that brought Pei out of the classrooms at Harvard and into the trenches, so to speak. The intricate, gray and white basket-weave pattern produces a visually engaging, almost three-dimensional effect. The base is mostly open space, creating a deep arcade

The Mile High Center before its defacement by Philip Johnson. To the left, a slice of Frank Edbrooke's bizarre Majestic Bldg. is visible, shortly before its demise about 1977.

around the tower's perimeter. The cooling tower on top sets back from the parapet, forming a simple but correctly proportioned hat.

Pei would go on to greater things, but this early work represents an important milestone in his career – and Denver's. In fact, the old height ordinance had to be modified by Mayor Quigg Newton in order to build Mile High Center, Denver's first "modern" skyscraper. The new rules abolished height restrictions in return for a 25' setback along Broadway; opening the door for the subsequent skyscraper sweepstakes that would forever alter the face of Denver.

According to Pei's Denver associate on the project, G. Meredith Musick, developer William Zeckendorf insisted on using his New York contractor George Fuller. Musick, overseeing the actual construction, was appalled by what he considered to be the shoddy practices of the out-of-towners. He vouched for the structural integrity of the building, but otherwise was unimpressed by Fuller's workmanship. Nonetheless, the building has functioned well for the past 50 years, and remains a Denver landmark, even in its altered state.

76. Wells Fargo Center – 1700 Lincoln St. – Philip Johnson / John Burgee – 1983   Score: 5.0

| Meets the Street – 3 | Scale – 3 | Integrity – 7 |
| Public Spaces – 6 | Mass – 6 | Imagination – 5 |

It soars distinctively into the sky, but it slams to the ground like a skydiver whose chute failed to open. The Wells Fargo Center by Philip Johnson.

It's certainly the most distinctive silhouette on the Denver skyline, but it is frightfully crude where it actually meets the street. Philip Johnson's iconic Wells Fargo Center (originally United Bank), referred to locally as the "cash register," is easily reviled and praised, almost in the same breath. Mild controversy surrounds this Post Modern building. Johnson himself reminisced about the developer, Gerald Hines, thus, "He only gave me one cheap building, in Denver. It was a success all right, but I was never pleased with it." (Philip Johnson, the Architect in His Own Words, 1994). Mr. Johnson pretty much sums up our own disappointment regarding it.

The truncated, barrel-vault motif, which creates that recognizable profile, is awkwardly restated at the building's main entries. Furthermore, the 52-story tower assiduously ignores the problem of making a logical connection to the street. It slams into the sidewalk like a skydiver whose chute failed to open. The steep gradient along 17th Ave. greatly reinforces this sense of discomfort. Only the Sherman St. entry, on the high end of the site, is reasonably agreeable, perhaps because it is also understated. Johnson ignored the possibilities of topography, treating it as an annoyance rather than an opportunity to create an imaginative base.

The rather intricate facade consists of rose-colored Swedish granite and reflective gray window panes, trimmed in white metal. Smaller panels of polished red granite add complexity and interest to the pattern. A handsome two-story lobby is warmly detailed with stylized Romanesque archways and a beautifully articulated ceiling - creating a handsome foyer. Try to enter from Sherman St., avoiding the Lincoln entrance, which has the feel of an oversize mud room. Philip Johnson's own dissatisfaction with this project may be that it fails to achieve its full potential. It is undoubtedly a high profile, landmark structure that "could have been a contender!" in the words of Marlon Brando. Instead, it disappoints close up, even as it teases our senses from a distance, the fatal weakness of too many skyscrapers.

The glassy entry bubble on Lincoln St. marks the third Denver home of pioneer banker and railroad baron, David H. Moffat. Sometime in the early 1880s, Brown's Bluff began to look more fashionable to the Moffats than 14th St., which had been the early city's prime residential promenade. They dutifully built a stylish, modern Queen Anne mansion at 1706 Lincoln, which remained the family's principal residence for the next quarter century. The gangly Moffat enjoyed a brisk, seven-minute walk to his First National Bank, located after 1892, in the **Equitable Bldg. (#49)** on Stout. Moffat rose to the pinnacle of success and wealth while living on this corner.

Only at the very end of his life, when business troubles were weighing heavily on him, did he build the palatial mansion at 8th & Grant, perhaps as a gesture of confidence to the outside world. Some say he never got the chance to entertain in that monumental house, before he died in New York City in 1911. His death culminated the end of the pioneer era. John Evans, William Jackson Palmer, Walter Cheesman, and William Byers had all preceded him. Not long after Moffat's death, his widow moved back here until her passing, probably because it had more memories of their family and life together.

77. Central Presbyterian Church – 17th Ave. & Sherman St. –

Frank E. Edbrooke – **1890**   **Score: 7.0**

| Meets the Street – 7 | Scale – 7 | Integrity – 7 |
| Public Spaces – 6 | Mass – 8 | Imagination – 7 |

Another of Frank Edbrooke's masterpieces, Central Presbyterian is characteristically Richardsonian, but uniquely Edbrooke. The massing is masterful; the tower is its crowning achievement, more floating and shapely than anything Richardson ever conceived. The soaring finials have been truncated over the years, undoubtedly for safety reasons related to the native sandstone, which tends to weather unevenly. The structure occupies its corner lot solidly and manages, even today, to hold its place amidst larger, bulkier neighbors that unsuccessfully compete with its easy-going splendor. Unfortunately, a banal annex, conceived in the 1950s, does more to tarnish its image than any surrounding structures. Brown brick is not the same thing as sandstone block, a cheap effect compounded by metal window frames completely out of character with the main church. Otherwise, few church exteriors in Denver are as powerful, or as well-composed as this one.

Central Presbyterian Church by Frank Edbrooke boasts an elegant spire. A thoughtless addition mars the integrity of the whole, however.

Walking north on Sherman St., we pass the tackiest parking garage enclosure ever attempted, designed as a part of the Wells Fargo banking complex that spans three blocks. This mass of tin, resting on a granite clad base, is the tombstone of one of the hill's more colorful early mansions. Longtime residents will remember it as the Democratic Club, at 1712 Sherman St. For a good half century the Democratic Party had its headquarters here.

Originally it was the Richard Pearce Residence, a gloriously inventive Queen Anne structure. It earned the nickname "house of heartbreak" after its owner, Richard Pearce, lost his wife and daughters while living here. Eventually he moved away, too grieved by their memories to remain in that sad place. No doubt, 1712 Sherman later continued the tradition of heartbreak on many a November election night when a Republican candidate might beat out the Democratic rival: but how many more nights of victorious revelry were there? We may never know.

78. Denver Financial Center – 1775 Sherman St. – Skidmore, Owings & Merrill – 1984

Score: 6.7

Meets the Street - 6   Scale – 7   –Integrity – 5
Public Spaces – 7   Mass – 7   Imagination – 8

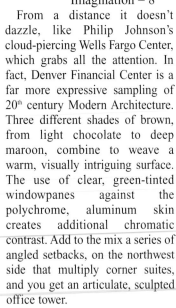

From a distance it doesn't dazzle, like Philip Johnson's cloud-piercing Wells Fargo Center, which grabs all the attention. In fact, Denver Financial Center is a far more expressive sampling of 20th century Modern Architecture. Three different shades of brown, from light chocolate to deep maroon, combine to weave a warm, visually intriguing surface. The use of clear, green-tinted windowpanes against the polychrome, aluminum skin creates additional chromatic contrast. Add to the mix a series of angled setbacks, on the northwest side that multiply corner suites, and you get an articulate, sculpted office tower.

A smaller companion structure sits at the Lincoln St. base of this sloping site, neatly accentuating the topographical possibilities, in stark contrast to the **Wells Fargo Center**, a block hence, that seems completely befuddled by the very idea of a hill. The smaller and larger buildings are tied together by an internal, terraced concourse connecting Lincoln and Sherman Streets. Denver Financial Center is a breath of fresh air in an "edge" locale, possibly S.O.M.'s most articulate downtown design, witty and urbane.

A block north, at the corner of 19th Ave. & Lincoln, the early railroad man and town builder, General William Jackson Palmer, maintained his Denver residence. The house was modest in scale, but elaborately Second Empire in style. Palmer, a Pennsylvania Quaker, brought the Kansas Pacific into Denver in 1870, then stayed on to build his Rio Grande narrow gauge line, founded the city of Colorado Springs, and developed the Colorado Fuel & Iron steel mills, in Pueblo.

Palmer's main residence was outside of Colorado Springs, at Glen Eyrie, near the Garden of the Gods. Palmer probably gets as much credit for Denver's early development as any local booster. He brought inestimable amounts of capital, mainly from England, into the state to fund his many projects. He was as generous as he was fearless (during the Civil War he narrowly escaped execution as a captured spy). In the late 1890s, when he sold the Rio Grande for several millions, he distributed an unexpected windfall of $1,000,000 among his railroad employees as a bonus.

79. 1770 Sherman Event Complex (El Jebel Shrine) –

Baerresen Brothers – **1907**		**Score: 4.8**
Meets the Street – 4	Scale – 5	Integrity – 4
Public Spaces – 5	Mass – 5	Imagination – 6

The Shriners moved to North Denver's Willis Case Golf Course in 1924, only 17 years after constructing this exotic Moorish building, boasting a 550-seat auditorium. The first-generation pioneers who had settled on Brown's Bluff were beginning to die off or drift to southeast Denver, further removed from the noise and traffic, as the business core expanded. The hill was still respectable, but less desirable than it had formerly been, as apartment blocks and large structures like this one began to impudently invade the domain of mansions.

Proceed east on 18th Ave. one block to Grant. St., originally known as Grant Avenue or Millionaire's Row. Grant was the "Main Street" of Brown's Bluff, explaining its extra wide roadway. A Grant St. address was a token of added social prestige, akin to a Fifth Avenue address in New York City. Families names like Boettcher, Sheedy, Kountze, and Moffat paraded up and down Grant, but only a minute handful of those homes survive today. Turn north for half a block, where a classical looking high-rise rears its stone-and-stucco head.

80. Portofino – 1827 Grant St. – Davis Partnership –
2003   **Score: 6.2**

| Meets the Street – 7 | Scale – 7 | Integrity - 6 |
| Public Spaces – 6 | Mass – 6 | Imagination – 5 |

Too tall for Tuscany; too open for New York, yet it alludes to both. Portofino takes its cue from the Renaissance Revival **Seton House (1921)**, by Harry J. Manning, located just across the street. Both buildings are quite civilized, exhibiting considerable curb appeal. Seton House, originally the rectory for the Catholic cathedral, was later remodeled into a high school by its eloquent rector, Father Hugh McMenamin. In 1991, Mother Theresa of Calcutta opened Seton House, a hospice for terminal AIDS patients, staffed by her Missionary Sisters of Charity.

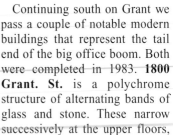

Continuing south on Grant we pass a couple of notable modern buildings that represent the tail end of the big office boom. Both were completed in 1983. **1800 Grant. St.** is a polychrome structure of alternating bands of glass and stone. These narrow successively at the upper floors,

Portofino's colors and entry reflect the charming, old-world Seton House, just across the street, but without any hint of mimicry.

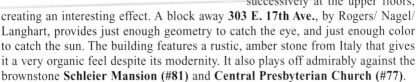

creating an interesting effect. A block away **303 E. 17th Ave.**, by Rogers/ Nagel/ Langhart, provides just enough geometry to catch the eye, and just enough color to catch the sun. The building features a rustic, amber stone from Italy that gives it a very organic feel despite its modernity. It also plays off admirably against the brownstone **Schleier Mansion (#81)** and **Central Presbyterian Church (#77)**.

81. George Schleier Mansion – 1665 Grant St. – Frank Edbrooke –
   1885   **Score: 6.1**

| Meets the Street – 6 | Scale – 6 | Integrity – 7 |
| Public Spaces – 5 | Mass – 7 | Imagination – 6 |

The Queen Anne style that practically defined Brown's Bluff at one time, is still represented by this lone survivor on Grant St. It was built for businessman George Schleier.

Of all the mansions that once populated Capitol Hill, north of Colfax, the George C. Schleier house is a rare survivor. It fairly represents the Queen Anne style that predominated on Grant Avenue. Schleier was another of the many successful, German immigrants, among many like Adolph Coors, Otto Paul Bauer, William and Moritz Barth, and Adolph Zang. Germans represented Denver's largest and most prosperous ethnic contingent before 1900.

The Schleiers were avid art collectors, and today their early efforts are commemorated in the Schleier Art Gallery at the Denver Art Museum. In 1930, Rachel Schleier donated this house to the Archdiocese of Denver for Father Mulroy's Catholic Charities, which that well-known pastor of **Holy Ghost Church (#53)** had initiated three years earlier. Catholic Charities built an addition along 17th Avenue in the 1960s, generally preserving the integrity of the original house, continuing to occupy it well into the 1980s, when the property was sold and completely renovated. Undoubtedly, Catholic Charities' presence was the only reason that this historic place survived the decades of speculation that decimated the vast majority of Grant Street's grand mansions.

82. Capitol Center – 225 E. 16th Ave. – Harry J. Manning –
1924 , 1962
Meets the Street – 7   Scale – 7   **Score: 6.6**
                     Integrity – 6
Public Spaces – 7   Mass – 6   Imagination – 6

Home of Charles B. Kountze, one of the Kountze brothers who founded the Colorado National Bank in 1862. The Kountze estate rambled from Grant St. to Sherman St., anchored by a three-story Queen Anne at the northwest corner of 16th Ave. & Grant. St. Later the family built a substantial addition along Grant that connected it to the stables. The west side of the property remained an open yard, and in the 1920s, that portion along Sherman was developed with the Capitol Life Insurance Bldg. – 1600 Sherman.

The architect was Harry J. Manning who created a petite, marble, Italian Renaissance Revival masterpiece. By the 1950s Capitol Life needed more space and the Kountze family finally decided that the old homestead was expendable, and so the deal was consummated for the remainder of the estate. Interestingly, the family felt so attached to the place that they didn't want to see it turned into the typical Capitol Hill rooming house, so the deed stipulated its demolition. Capitol Life agreed, so when the demand justified a new office tower in the early 1960s, the company razed the extensive house for an 11-story tower that cleverly ties into the older, Harry Manning structure. The white aggregate is not nearly as handsome as Colorado Yule marble, but the new design is classically inspired, if not strictly interpreted. The raised portico links it to the older part and provides a formal sense of entry into the building.

Diagonally across Sherman St., we see the **State Social Services (Farmers Union Bldg.)** at 1575 Sherman St., by S. Arthur Axtens (**1952**). Axtens was one of Denver's more interesting designers – part engineer, part architect. He designed this building to be literally bombproof, during the era of Cold War fears of nuclear annihilation, topping it off with a 100-ft. spire that might have hailed from the 1933 World's Fair. This translucent tower glowed different colors at night, depending on the weather forecast. Eventually the state acquired the property, removing the "Buck Rogers" weather beacon. Later a gray stucco was applied over Axten's buff and pale-green concrete finish that gave the building its distinctive flavor. Now it appears dull and lusterless, although his original stainless steel accents still evoke a smidgen of personality.

One of early Denver's more important citizens, Simon Guggenheim, lived at 1555 Sherman, where the adjoining parking garage now sits. Simon was the sixth son of Meier Guggenheim, scion of the Philadelphia Guggenheims, who amassed a fortune in Colorado mines and smelters. The house was originally built by Chester Morey, the grocery king. After his wife's death in 1900, Morey sold the house to Simon who managed the family's Denver refinery. For the next quarter-century, Simon and Oleg Guggenheim raised their family here (two of their four children were born here) well after his brothers had moved on to New York City.

Denver Public Library, Western History Collection   X-26605
The former home of Chester Morey, and later, Senator Simon Guggenheim at 1555 Sherman St. By 1920 Simon had re-located to New York City where he managed the Guggenheim fortune.

Simon became a U.S. senator in 1907, doling out some $50,000 to buy the necessary votes (At that time the state legislature elected U.S. senators). He also built the Guggenheim Hall that graces the Colorado School of Mines campus in Golden. His most notable achievement in the Senate was to procure funding for several federal buildings in the state, most notably the beautiful **Byron White Courthouse (#51)**, perhaps the city's most distinguished building. The family's businesses were eventually consolidated in New York by 1919. Simon loved Colorado and maintained his connections here until his oldest brother died, and Simon took over the reigns of the Guggenheim empire in the 1920s. Even then he maintained the Denver house for several years, finally selling it in 1925. Simon eventually died in New York in 1941, but he always considered himself a Coloradan, even to the end. The house endured for a number of years until the excavation for the new Farmers Union Building undermined the foundations and it had to be razed.

Frank Edbrooke's distinguished spire draws the eye to stately Central Park Presbyterian Church at 17th & Sherman St.

Backtrack one block to the northeast corner of 16th Ave. and Grant St. **St. Paul Lutheran Church**, completed in 1926 is a plain but handsome example of American Gothic Revival, especially the ornamented carillon tower. It was dubbed the "Glowing Church" because of the effect of sunlight passing through the stained glass windows on the south wall. Continue walking east for one more block where our exploration of Brown's Bluff continues with Tour 5, beginning at 16th Ave. & Logan St.

TOUR 5: CAPITAL HILL TO CIVIC CENTER

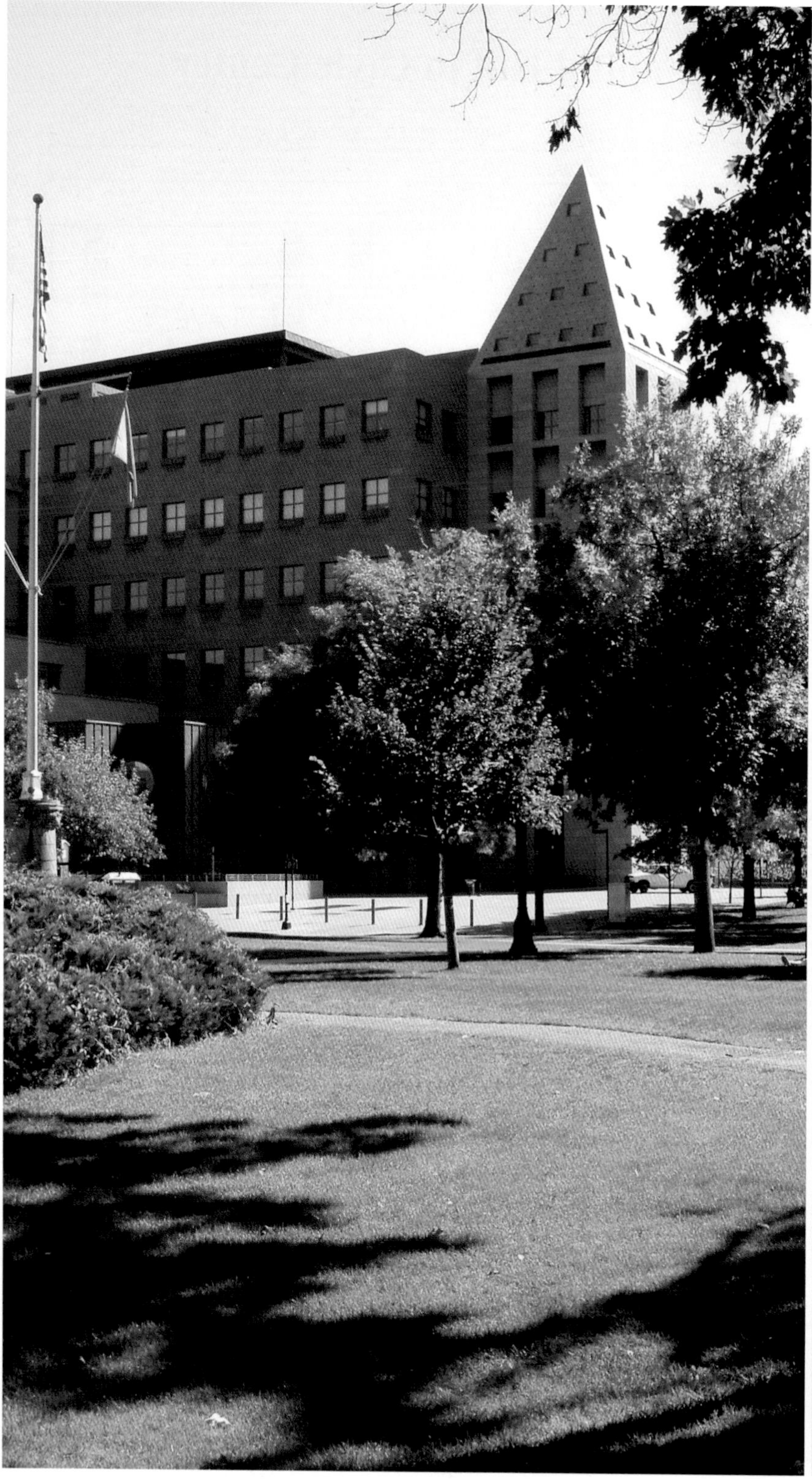

Tour 5. Capitol Hill to Civic Center

Tour 5.   *length 2.2 miles.*   Begins at 16ᵗʰ Ave. & Logan St.

Ends at 11ᵗʰ Ave. & Broadway

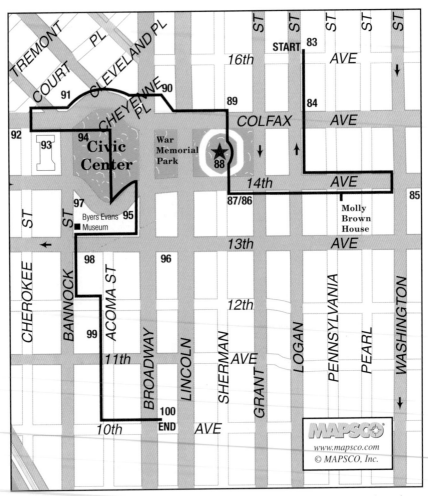

While it may seem that we have exhausted the main downtown area, there is an important district yet to consider, more institutional and civic in character, but still on par with 16ᵗʰ and 17ᵗʰ Sts. The neighborhood stretching along both Colfax Avenue and Broadway is important for its churches and its cultural and government institutions. It boasts downtown's most extensive public open space – the Civic Center – which anchors this "midtown" district. Historically, it was Henry C. Brown's gift of 10 acres for a territorial capitol that defined it and set it on a whole new trajectory. Ever since, Capitol Hill has been a sort of buffer between the commercial downtown and miles of up-scale residential areas that lay south and east.

It was Mayor Robert W. Speer who envisioned a monumental civic park, surrounded by public buildings, just to the west of the Capitol grounds. Speer fought hard to make that vision a reality – carved out of the gritty fabric of streets, alleys, and Victorian tenements. Today this area is a center of political and spiritual power (including two cathedrals). It has become a cultural nexus as well, with a ballet company, two major museums and the state's largest public library. Recent developments around Civic Center – the new "Arts District" – attest to its coming of age. Radiator repairs and tire shops that once defined much of midtown are rapidly disappearing, as the "Golden Triangle" (Speer Blvd., Broadway, and West Colfax Ave.) assumes its proper place in the urban scheme.

83. Fisher Mansion – 1600 Logan St. – Frank Edbrooke / Willis Marean – 1896 **Score: 6.8**

Meets the Street – 6	Scale –7	Integrity – 8
Public Spaces – 6	Mass – 7	Imagination – 6

William G. Fisher, partner in the Daniels & Fisher Store, spurned the more eclectic tastes of his day for a straightforward, Classically-inspired mansion to advertise his millions. The buff, lava stone walls are accented by a simple, hemi-spherical portico, supported by a pair of Ionic columns. When his daughter was married, Fisher constructed a $75,000 ballroom for the wedding reception. The interior woodwork is extensive and opulent, carved from a variety of hardwoods. Notice the stone lions guarding the entry. After the Fishers left, the place served for decades as "International House," before being purchased and restored by the talented architect, David Owen Tryba, as his home and office. Tryba converted the former ballroom into an architectural studio, adding a third floor, without compromising the house's overall integrity.

Immediately across the street sits the **Tudor Revival Grosvenor Arms Apartments**, 333 E. 16th Ave., which opened in 1931. The design by Walter Simon is typical of the imitative forms popular before Modernism seized the day. Over the years Capitol Hill, the haunt of millionaires, gradually drifted from mansions to assorted apartment buildings and rooming houses, as the original owners died off or moved away. Many of the apartment buildings, such as this one and the Olin (in the 1400 block of Logan), were upscale and attractive. After World War II, the quality of new construction declined greatly as speculative buildings proliferated, changing the entire character of the Hill. The city abetted this process by instituting zoning changes in the 1950s, permitting high rises to invade, and the grand old mansions began to disappear altogether, too often replaced by tasteless, shoe-box containers with concrete balconies strapped stiffly to their sides.

84. Cathedral of the Immaculate Conception – 301 E. Colfax Ave.
– Leon Coquard / Gove & Walsh – **1902-12**   **Score: 7.1**

Meets the Street – 5	Scale – 8	Integrity – 7
Public Spaces – 7	Mass – 8	Imagination – 8

Originally dubbed the "Pinnacled Glory of the West," Denver's Catholic cathedral outshines a rather seedy stretch along East Colfax Ave. that, believe it or not, was once a prime residential thoroughfare. This French Gothic Revival edifice dominates the Hill and plays off symbolically against the **State Capitol Building (#88)** only a few

Courtesy, Archdiocese of Denver
Immaculate Conception Cathedral — under construction around 1910.

hundred yards to the west. The cathedral (a minor basilica, or special place of pilgrimage) sits on a very constricted site, considering its size, squeezing Colfax Avenue uncomfortably. Several prominent Catholics like John Campion, Dennis Sheedy, J.K. Mullen, and Molly Brown's husband, J.J. Brown, purchased eight lots about 1900, donating them to the diocese for its construction.

Due to illness, the original architect had to retire from the building project shortly after construction began. This setback was followed by a financial scandal that stalled the project another four years. It seems the rector invested the building funds into several dubious investment schemes. He ended up losing nearly $53,000, and the good will of his donors. Bishop Matz turned in desperation to a spirited young priest who arrived on the scene in 1905, Father Hugh McMenamin. Father "Mac" resurrected the project by enlisting the aid of John Kernan Mullen, Dennis Sheedy,

John Campion, J.J. McGinnity, and William McPhee. The local firm of Gove & Walsh took over as supervising architects. Despite lightning damage to the west spire on August 7, 1912, the cathedral was dedicated on October 27 by Bishop Nicholas Matz. The edifice cost some $500,000 in the end, of which $100,000 came from Mullen.

French Gothic splendor is illuminated by German stained glass. The original interior configuration, prior to a 1970s remodeling, is seen here.
Courtesy, Archdiocese of Denver

The interior is filled with marble from Carrara, Italy, naturally lighted by some of the most extensive stained glass west of the Mississippi. The German stained glass was made in the Zetter Royal Bavarian Art Institute in Munich, which was destroyed during World War II, making these sensational artworks virtually irreplaceable. The main interior nave rises nearly 70' above the floor, endowing it with a tremendous sense of space. The foundation stones, like those in the Capitol, come from Gunnison, Colorado, and the exterior walls are carved from Indiana limestone.

The spires are 212' tall. A carillon consisting of fifteen bells – weighing between 525 and 3,500 pounds apiece – resides in the east spire, which was struck by lightning, on June 23, 1997, necessitating a total reconstruction. The removal of lightning rods for aesthetic reasons, before the pope's visit in 1993, turned out to be a bad idea, after all.

The cathedral was named a minor basilica in 1979, but its greatest moment came in August of 1993 when Pope John Paul II visited Denver for World Youth Day, making the cathedral his headquarters and celebrating Mass here. The cathedral continues as the spiritual center of the Denver Archdiocese, and its rich history belies its relative youth.

Courtesy, Archdiocese of Denver
Lightning damage, east spire - June, 1997

Continue south on Logan St. one block, turning left on 14th Avenue. Continue east for three blocks to St. John's Cathedral. One block east sits the red brick **Pennsylvania Commons**, minus the stone cross that once surmounted it, at 1370 Pennsylvania St. This 1911 building was the new home of St. Mary's Academy, which moved uptown from 15th & California (see #59). It was constructed on land practically adjoining the **Molly Brown House** (by architect William Lang) at 1340 Pennsylvania St. The "Unsinkable" Molly was one of St. Mary's prime benefactors, living here from 1894 until her death in 1932. A year after maneuvering the exclusive girl's academy onto her block, Mrs. Brown booked passage on the Titanic's fateful maiden voyage, and gained immortality as the heroine in its tragic demise.

85. St. John's Episcopal Cathedral – 1313 Clarkson St. – Tracy & Swartwout – **1911**   **Score: 7.2**

Meets the Street – 7   Scale – 8   Integrity – 6
Public Spaces – 8   Mass – 7   Imagination – 7

It started out as St. John's Church in the Wilderness, reflecting conditions in Denver when the first Episcopal church was consecrated in 1862. In 1881, a real cathedral at 20th Ave. & Welton replaced the pioneer church and, despite its grandeur, this edifice survived less than 22 years. A disastrous fire consumed it on May 15, 1903. That fire resulted in two fine buildings being constructed. The cathedral itself relocated to 14th & Clarkson, while its former flock was served by a new parish dedicated to **St. Andrew**. The St. Andrew's congregation commissioned the famous architect, Ralph Adams Cram, responsible for New York's **Cathedral of St. John the Divine**, to design an intimate church, his only work in Colorado. It still exists a short block away from its predecessor, at 20th and Glenarm Pl.

The present cathedral is the result of a national competition won by the New York firm of Tracy & Swartwout. Executed in Indiana limestone, it exudes English Gothic, every bit as much as its Catholic counterpart on East Colfax personifies the French. The few blocks separating them, like the English Channel, demarcate cultures of remarkable variance. The two buildings share similarities and common experience, however. Both cathedrals were in a race to completion, and both were plagued by various financial problems compounded by nature. With St. John's it wasn't lightning, but ground water, that slowed up progress. St. John's sits on a full-block site, with ample space for setbacks and landscaping, giving it a gracious, almost rural, country air.

The long, interior nave is illuminated by over 50 stained glass windows, admitting little real light but creating an ethereal blue cast inside. The choir and chancel are constructed of brick, rather than Indiana limestone, in anticipation of a more permanent apse that was never completed. A proposed transept, topped by a lantern at the crossing, likewise was never finished. The adjoining St. Martin's Chapel and Parish House were designed by Merrill and Burnham Hoyt, and completed in 1928, about the same time that Merrill was assisting on John D. Rockefeller's Riverside Church in New York. Sculptor Arnold Ronnebeck carved a beautiful, wooden reredos in the chapel.

Ronnebeck, a former member of the Kaiser's personal guard in Germany, migrated to the United States in 1925. After dabbling in the New York arts circle that included Gertrude Stein and Georgia O'Keefe, he met his future wife in Taos, finally settling in East Denver, where Hill Middle School now

St. John's English Gothic form features truncated spires. A central lantern and transept were never completed. Nonetheless, the cathedral was an impressive undertaking for the small Episcopal diocese.

sits. With their children and pet goat, Angelica, they existed happily in a house rented from the Denver Public Schools. Ronnebeck became the director of **Chappell House** at 13th and Logan, originally the home of Horace W. Bennett, then David May, before the Chappell family purchased it. The Chappells were early Denver art patrons and their daughter, Mrs. Jean Cramner, willed it to the Denver Art Association in 1922. Thereafter it became the center of Denver's art establishment, and eventually evolved into the Denver Art Museum. Sadly, it was demolished in the 1970s for the tawdry office building that sits there today.

Retrace your steps along 14th Ave., four blocks to Grant St. The impressive Neo-Classical structure at the corner of 14th Ave. & Logan St. is the **First Church of Christ Scientist**. This Frederick J. Sterner design dates back to 1901 and is made from white, Salida lava stone. It provides a sense of solid grounding in its otherwise transient surroundings. The proportions are masterful, but it is the gently-rounded dome covering the interior hall that gives it a unique character.

86. First Baptist Church – 230 E. 14th Ave. – G. Meredith Musick – 1938

Score: 7.3

Meets the Street – 6	Scale – 9	Integrity – 7
Public Spaces – 7	Mass – 8	Imagination – 7

First Baptist Church is one of the most refined structures on Capitol Hill, a colonial New England design along Georgian lines, executed in stone and brick. The

The Georgian steeple identifying First Baptist Church discourses comfortably with the classical Capitol Bldg. and modern office towers.

Corinthian capitals, pediment, and spire are molded from Indiana Oolitic limestone while the imposing columns of hand-polished granite are set with lead and pins, not mortar. The roof is shingled in burnt clay tile. G. Meredith Musick struggled with the trustees over moving the pulpit off-center in the sanctuary, but eventually prevailed. He also used a modified cruciform shape, which he considered to be close to a Roman Catholic basilica. Being the "mother church" for conservative Colorado Baptists, controversy surfaced over the cock-a-top the weather vane, a Protestant symbol of Christ at the Last Supper.

This monumental church rests on a solid foundation, built of sturdy materials to endure for the centuries. That is good news for one of the most beautiful and significant buildings around the historic Capitol. Perhaps the city could be coaxed to relinquish a redundant turn lane and restore the original sidewalk to give this important landmark its proper dignity – and a little breathing space.

87. Old State Museum Bldg. – 14ᵗʰ Ave. at Sherman St. – Frank E. Edbrooke – 1915

Score: 5.8

Meets the Street – 6	Scale – 6	Integrity – 7
Public Spaces – 5	Mass – 6	Imagination – 5

This was Frank E. Edbrooke's last hurrah before retiring, and it reflects the conservatism of his age, 75 at the time. The Neo-Classical proportions are admirable and the white Colorado Yule marble shimmers, but the building seems tame by the architect's earlier standards. Neither was the state in any mood to take chances after 15 years, and considerable political energy was expended finishing the **Capitol Building (#88)** just a decade earlier. Edbrooke had been drafted to complete that important structure during the 1890s. This became the first addition to a state government campus, eventually including ten buildings. It shares the same granite base materials as the Capitol. The State Historical Society and Museum occupied it for several generations, before moving to the "typewriter building" at 1300 Broadway in 1977.

Directly across Sherman, the **State Capitol Annex** by PMGW Affiliated Architects represents a consortium of six independent architects coordinated by G. Meredith Musick. The Annex was a Depression-era project, completed in 1939. The superstructure is faced in white Yule marble from Marble, Colorado. The base is dark, polished Minnesota granite. The building features Moderne touches, like the rounded

corners, but the ordered symmetry feels more Classical. A sloping site provides access on two levels, and the building's base seems to burrow into the terrain.

88. Colorado State Capitol – Colfax Ave.at Sherman St. - Elijah E. Myers / Frank E. Edbrooke – **1886-1900** **Score: 7.4**

Meets the Street – 7	Scale – 7	Integrity – 8
Public Spaces – 8	Mass – 8	Imagination - 6

This is an imposing, though modestly proportioned, capitol building - commanding its prominent site. It proudly overlooks the city of Denver and a 175-mile vista of mountain ranges that reflect the Centennial State's special character. Today, part of that vista has been obliterated by the sky-scraping financial district. The Capitol dome just about aligns with 16th St., allowing us a thin, telescopic glimpse of distant Long's Peak and Rocky Mountain National Park – seen through the thick stand of concrete towers. Few state capitols have such dramatic settings. View ordinances now protect the panorama to the west and southwest, ensuring that mountains will always be a part of the building's backdrop.

Architecturally, the building is a typological, Neo-Classical state-house, common to the 19th century. It almost feels baroque by modern standards. The dome is slender, and relatively tall for the size of its base, giving this capitol a slightly more vertical emphasis than most, including its model, the United States Capitol. What draws the eye, and imagination, is the 24-karat gold leaf glistening in the sunlight, a tangible reminder of what really created Colorado's wealth and prosperity. The polychrome interior is stunning, encrypted with murals and stained glass to commemorate Colorado's colorful history.

As a state, that history began on Aug. 1, 1876, 100 years after the Declaration of Independence was enacted in Philadelphia. President Grant officially proclaimed Colorado as the 38th state, against the howls and protests of Eastern snobs who complained: "there is something repulsive in the idea that a few handfuls of miners and reckless bushwhackers should have the same representation in the Senate as Pennsylvania, Ohio, and New York." New York provincialism sometimes exceeded parochialism on the prairie to be sure, but Coloradans didn't seem to care. There were bigger issues than local prejudice involved in such protests.

Grant's scandal-plagued Republicans desperately needed the three electoral votes

that Colorado provided in the fall elections, allowing Rutherford B. Hayes to squeak into the White House by one vote, 185 to 184, over the Democrat, Samuel Tilden. Hayes actually lost the popular vote, but Colorado gave him the narrow margin of victory he needed in the electoral college – although disputed tallies in other states had to be settled by Congress. The ensuing Compromise of 1877 ended Reconstruction in the South by forcing the removal of any remaining Federal troops. Colorado achieved statehood, the Republicans captured the White House, and the Democrats gained solid control of the South. Thus, Colorado's turbulent territorial days coincided exactly with the Civil War and Reconstruction. The admission of Kansas as a free state, on January 29, 1861, and Colorado's incorporation as a new territory, stimulated the secession of Southern states. Colorado's admission as a state, in 1876, provoked an electoral crisis that finally forced the end of Reconstruction

The last territorial governor was John L. Routt, a Washington insider, friend of President Ulysses S. Grant, neighbor and tenant of Gen. William Tecumsah Sherman. Routt and his wife, Eliza, left the comforts of the East to accept President Grant's appointment of him as governor of the Colorado Territory. The job was not an easy patronage position. After a series of carpetbagger appointees, graft, and corruption

(Routt was the fourth territorial governor in a three-year period), Colorado's political atmosphere was highly charged. The affable Routt not only managed to quell passions, but after strongly endorsing statehood, succeeded himself as first elected governor of the new state in 1876. The Routts, like many transplants, ended up spending the remainder of their lives in Denver. Routt amassed a small fortune by investing in Leadville's Morning Star Mine, served as Denver's mayor from 1883-85, and managed another term as governor from 1891-93. He also planned and helped oversee the eventual construction of a new capitol building. He must have had the wisdom of Solomon and the patience of Job to accomplish what he did in the tumultuous circumstances of the late 19th century. The Capitol building is still his most enduring tribute.

The State Capitol rotunda is a textbook on Neo-Classical symmetry and proportions.

Few buildings claim such a convoluted history of construction as Colorado's seat of government. While the major construction took 14 ½ years, the total elapsed time between Henry C. Brown's initial gift of 10 acres and the final gilding of the golden dome stretched out to 40-some years. Brown, tired of waiting after 11 years of talk and gestures, sued in an attempt to recover the valuable property. The case ended up in the U.S. Supreme Court not once, but twice, under different premises. Brown was a bulldog, if nothing else. The state won the first decision, *Brown vs. Colorado*, in Nov., 1882, and formed a Board of Capitol Managers the following February. This body was appointed to oversee the design and construction of a new capitol building. Former governor John L. Routt, the current governor, and the Capitol Board secretary then set out to get ideas, inspecting capitol buildings in states from Kansas to Michigan – six in all – during a whirlwind two-week trip. After a national competition, Elija E. Myers, who had designed capitols for Michigan and Texas, was chosen. Myers, incidentally, also designed the impressive Arapahoe County Courthouse on Court Pl., between 15th & 16th Sts., constructed in 1880. The troubles were just beginning at this point, however.

The dogged Henry Brown sued again, and once more set back any construction timetable. Again, the U.S. Supreme Court decided in favor of Colorado in 1886, in *Brown vs. Grant*, giving clear and undisputed land title to the state of Colorado. A construction triumvirate of Elijah Myers, Peter Gumry, and contractor William Richardson was selected to supervise actual construction, which began July 6, 1886. As the massive sandstone foundations were prepared, a squabble over the cost of granite caused Richardson to quit the job, stopping work in Oct., 1887. Early in 1889 the state, responding to political pressure, increased funding and agreed to raise the walls, not in white sandstone, but gray Colorado granite. Furthermore, the Board of Capitol Managers was re-organized with former Governor John L. Routt, famed road builder Otto Mears, and Charles Hughes joining the current governor to guide the building's development. Herman Leuders became secretary and Peter Gumry chief superintendent. To further cut costs, the architect Elijah Myers was fired and replaced by Frank E. Edbrooke, a shabby ethical move partly prompted by Myers' history of underestimating actual building costs. By August, 1889, high quality Aberdeen granite from Gunnison County was flowing to the site, and stonemasons were beginning to set the thick walls.

The cornerstone ceremony, witnessed by well over 20,000 people, was held July 4, 1890. The affable Senator Horace Augustus Tabor dedicated a 20-ton cornerstone with a rousing speech. By Oct., 1892, the walls and masonry rotunda were in place, allowing Gumry to move his construction office into the basement of the unfinished edifice. The fabricated cast iron dome was set in place by New Year's, but the interior was far from complete. Despite the Panic of 1893, work continued, although the decision to abandon wood trim in favor of all fireproof materials delayed the moving in. The first officials to occupy the new capitol were the state auditor and state treasurer, in Oct., 1894. Governor David Waite joined them on Nov. 12, and on Jan 2, 1895, the legislature arrived to begin its first session in the new state-house.

This was an auspicious and historic assembly that included three women legislators among its ranks. Colorado was only the second state, after Wyoming, to grant women's suffrage, and these were the first women in American history to serve as members of a state legislative body. Also sitting in that 10th General Assembly was James Brown, the son of Henry C. Brown, who had earlier helped his father bring suit against the state of Colorado, over this very same property!

Building problems were far from solved, however. The interior space was incomplete; the process of installing marble trim and wainscoting proceeded at an agonizing pace. Then tragedy struck, unexpectedly. On August 19, 1895, superintendent Peter Gumry, along with his assistant Robert Greiner, were killed in the disastrous boiler explosion at Gumry's hotel on Lawrence (see#31). Board of

Capitol Managers secretary Herman Leuders narrowly escaped with his life. This untimely disaster nearly derailed the capitol project. In fact, if Leuders had been killed, much of the working knowledge about the project would have been completely lost.

The Capitol Board promoted Frank Edbrooke, who was currently the architect of record, to supervise construction. Edbrooke installed the grand staircase in the rotunda that was not part of Elijah Myers' original design. The project pushed along so that, by the end of 1900, the interior was essentially complete. Leuders estimated its final cost at close to $2,700,000, including furnishings – nearly triple the original $1,000,000 estimate. The dome reached 272' to the top of the lantern. Initially it was sheathed in copper; it was covered in 1908 with 200 ounces of 24-carat gold leaf at Edbrooke's suggestion.

Originally the dome was to be surmounted by a statue, but the plan hit a fatal snag. The proposed figure was not to be just some allegorical Greek hussy. Foolhardy legislators were determined to memorialize the most beautiful woman in the state - forever enshrined for future generations to ogle. You can only imagine the hornet's nest stirred up by this proposal, not only among the lawmakers, but especially among their wives and daughters. Not even Aristotle could resolve such a sensitive question as, "Who is the fairest of them all?" without losing his head over it. In the end, the most beautiful woman had to content herself to gaze in a mirror: a lighted globe ended up gracing her rightful pedestal. The building survived all the turmoil however, to become a fitting symbol that proudly surveys Colorado's purple mountain majesties.

Before Colorado's capitol was completed the state had endured its worst financial crisis ever. The so-called Gilded Age was waning, and the old pioneers were starting to die off. On July 3, 1897, second territorial governor, railroader, educator, and pioneer John Evans died, becoming the first person to lay in state in the still unfinished capitol. A year later, on the east lawn, a moving sculpture called *The Closing Era*, by Preston Powers, was installed over the protests of certain old timers, still chafing over "Sand Creek" and the Indian wars. Of course, it was Governor Evans who had been in office when that terrible massacre had occurred. The political fallout caused his removal from office by President Andrew Johnson. With his passing, the time seemed right to acknowledge the first citizens of this noble land. The moving work was first displayed in 1893 at the Chicago World's Fair, making its way home to Denver. Fittingly, the artist, Preston Powers, taught art at Denver University, an institution founded by none other than John Evans.

The most famous person ever to lay in state in our capitol was William F. Cody, "Buffalo Bill" to the world, and super showman of his day. Buffalo Bill died at his sister's home in Denver, and lay in state here on Jan. 14, 1917, in the great rotunda. More than 18,000 people filed past his bier by day's end, while another 12,000 had to be turned back. Very few politicians or civic leaders ever commanded that kind of respect. Cody was buried on top of Lookout Mountain, right above Golden, in a Denver Mountain Park.

Mention must also be made again of muralist, Allen True, whose set of murals, based on poet Thomas Hornsby Ferril's verse about water in the West, were hung in the rotunda in 1940. True's work adorns numerous Denver buildings including the **Brown Palace Hotel(#68)** and Civic Center. More than a building, the State Capitol could be considered a mini-compendium of Colorado's politics and history from the days of early statehood.

89. Department of Education (State Office Building) – 201 E. Colfax Ave. – William N. Bowman – **1921**   **Score: 7.0**

Meets the Street – 6	Scale – 7	Integrity – 8
Public Spaces – 8	Mass – 7	Imagination – 6

The main foyer in the Department of Education Bldg. matches the grandeur and formal elegance of the State Capitol, just across Colfax Ave.

William N. Byers, founder of the *Rocky Mountain News*, moved uptown and built a house here, high atop Brown's Bluff in 1875. Three years later he sold the paper and retired to another new house at 13th & Bannock St. Byers never sat still for long, however, and in 1879 he became the Denver postmaster. Later, he went on to help organize and serve as vice president of the Denver Tramway Company. Eventually he moved again, to a larger estate built of stone – at 171 S. Washington St. – in the subdivision that bears his name to this day. Byers died in 1902, after witnessing the transformation of Denver from a tent city to the Queen City.

His former residence on Capitol Hill became the site of the third building in the capitol complex. Architect William Bowman designed this Neo-Classical office building, using granite to tie it in with the **Capitol Building**. It is impressive enough from Colfax Ave., but the real beauty is on the inside, filled with polished marble, lots of bronze, and period chandeliers. This is definitely the most dignified and ornate state building, after the Capitol itself, Edbrooke's old **State Museum Bldg.** notwithstanding.

90. 1570 Broadway / Civic Center Station – 1570 Broadway –
Sorco Architects – **1982**

Score: 6.1

Meets the Street – 6	Scale – 6	Integrity – 5
Public Spaces – 7	Mass – 6	Imagination – 6

RTD and the Galbreath Company of Columbus, Ohio, jointly developed this block back in the early 1980s as the southeast terminus of the 16th St. Mall. A bus station sits underneath the large plaza, covering well over half the block; psychologically connecting the Civic Center and State Capitol parks to the 16th St. Mall. A wedge-shaped, 23-story office building hugs the north edge of the block, its form dictated by the 16th St. view corridor. The building actually stair-steps at several levels, nicely breaking up its bulk from Civic Center. Smooth Southwestern style aggregate gives it warmth; the sculpted surface features make it one of the few interesting buildings peering over the north flank of Civic Center. Surrounded by a phalanx of dreary, commercial structures, 1570 Broadway manages to inject a little geometric interest in a barren, competitive city-scape.

Crossing Broadway, we come to a small triangular park which commemorates an important bit of history – the Pioneer Monument and Fountain. The bronze figure pointing the way westward, on his rearing horse, is famous scout Christopher "Kit" Carson. The legendary explorer played a large role in opening this part of the country to settlement. He died and is buried at Ft. Lyons, Colorado, on the Arkansas River, near old Bent's Fort. The monument marks the western terminus of the important Smoky Hill Trail over which settlers migrated from Kansas to the Pikes Peak gold fields. From 1859 until the railroad made that dangerous trek obsolete in the summer of 1870, thousands made the westward pilgrimage.

A few reminders of the trail still exist, such as Four Mile House in southeast Denver, now a living history museum (and, incidentally, one of the oldest structures in the state). After freshening up at Four Mile House, weary travelers were galloped into town by fresh horses. The stages entered Denver City at this point where the Smoky Hill Trail became 15th St. (known as F St. in those earliest days). For many years a firehouse occupied this little triangle, until the Speer administration eyed the site as part of a grandiose civic center. That larger plan faltered initially, but the monumental fountain was pushed forward. By 1910 the world-renowned sculptor, Frederick MacMonnies, was able to unveil this $70,000 monument for the public.

91. Wellington Webb Mun. Office Bldg. – 201 W. Colfax Ave. – Smith, Hegner and Moore / G. Meredith Musick - **1949**
Tower addition, David Owen Tryba – **2002**   Score: **7.2**

Meets the Street – 7	Scale – 7	Integrity – 6
Public Spaces – 7	Mass – 8	Imagination – 8

The convex outline of Wellington Webb City Office Bldg. peers out over Civic Center's geometric symmetry. Unlike the other disjunct office towers, this one molds itself thoughtfully into that formal environment.

The four-story podium facing Civic Center dates to 1949 and was constructed by Denver University for its Business and Architecture schools. The building is an excellent example of the functional International Style, and is listed on the National Register. G. Meredith Musick described it as "...direct, simple, and pleasing, in harmony with the majority of Neo-Classic buildings on Civic Center, but in no way competing with them." The Bedford limestone was meant to match the City & County Bldg. and complement the Voorhies Memorial across Colfax, which it does reasonably well, despite its austere style. The building languished for years as City Hall Annex until the decision was made to construct a new city office building around it in the mid 90s. A design competition was held, won by local architect David Owen Tryba who designed a lens-shaped, Modern Revival structure intersecting a rectangular podium, imitative of the landmark D.U. Business School.

The result was the first major tower north of Civic Center sympathetic to the curves and lines of the existing government architecture. Tryba's 12-story tower is not imitative in any sense, even compared to the former D.U. structure, yet he manages to tie it visually to all that stone and classical alliteration brilliantly. The building truly suggests what it is, a bureaucratic file cabinet, executed in a witty, honest vernacular. It is typological in the sense of stating its function, unlike so many modern government buildings that are indistinguishable from banks and speculative office towers. The main entry plaza at 14ᵗʰ St. & Colfax Ave. is an especially articulate space that clearly identifies its governmental persona. The structure's main aesthetic drawback is the asymmetric placing of an unadorned mechanical tower on the roof, which spoils a nicely curving parapet. Otherwise the form is masterful and generally enhances the architectural environment around Civic Center. If only the garish Denver Newspaper Agency building had followed suit by cladding its new, stark white tower half this well.

92. United States Mint – 320 W. Colfax Ave. – James Knox Taylor / Tracy, Swartwout and Litchfield – **1906**   **Score: 5.6**

Meets the Street – 5   Scale – 6   Integrity – 7
Public Spaces – 5   Mass – 5   Imagination – 6

Nothing captures the imagination like a place where real money gets made, and in fact this block square complex is essentially a factory for the manufacture of coins. It is also the largest gold depository after Fort Knox. The Denver Mint is also a handsome Renaissance Revival structure, seemingly straight from Florence, Italy. All that Pikes Peak granite and ubiquitous carved eagles give it a distinctive American air. A sensational hijacking in 1922 killed one guard and relieved a Federal Reserve truck of $200,000 in bills. One of the robbers was later found dead in a garage on Capitol Hill, but the crime was never completely solved. Mint officials chafe to this day when this theft is referred to as the "Great Mint Robbery." They rightly point out that it was not the mint that was robbed, but a Federal Reserve armored vehicle, parked out on West Colfax.

Actually one inside job occured in 1920, when an employee, Orville Harrington, managed to sneak out some $80,000 worth of gold over a period of months, hiding it inside his wooden leg! Every night Harrington would bury the gold in the back yard of his South Denver home. He was eventually nabbed when suspicious neighbors alerted the authorities.

The building shows only two of its five stories – the remaining three are below the ground. Additions, beginning in 1936, have periodically expanded the mint's capacity, but architecturally they have never matched the standards set by the original segment. The face along West Colfax is still most impressive, although it has not been used as an entrance for decades. The wrought iron security fence, windows and grills add to the sense of impregnability and majesty of this fortress-like structure. It is still Denver's most popular tourist attraction.

93. City and County Bldg. – 1437 Bannock St. - Robt. K. Fuller / Associated Architects – 1932

Score: 5.5

Meets the Street – 4   Scale – 7   Integrity – 5

Public Spaces – 6   Mass – 5   Imagination - 6

Corinthian and Ionic columns don't quite mesh on Denver's City & County Bldg., a Depression-era project. The carillon tower, set atop a Greek pediment, helps distract us from the warring elements to provide a convincing symbol for municipal government.

While its public importance is undeniable and clearly stated, the City & County Building will never take its place among the truly great public buildings, despite the quality of its construction. It seems to emulate Bernini's famous colonnade in front of St. Peter's, but falls far short in conveying a sense of grandeur. Part of the problem stems from the fact that it was designed by a committee of architects, the so-called Allied Architectural Association. Consequently it lacks the purity of vision that we expect from great public buildings. It surely encloses the grand expanse of civic space extending east to the State Capitol. It also creates a visible symbol for the city government.

Certain building elements such as the carillon tower and cupola, adorned by an enormous bronze eagle, are stunning additions, but too many competing ideas seem to be at work here, exemplified by the juxtaposition of the Ionian and Corinthian columns. The scale is monumental, the details cold and impersonal. As a background to Civic Center it succeeds tolerably well; as a foreground statement it has serious flaws. The interior public spaces, layered in travertine, are as sumptuous as any European palace.

The building, like the whole Civic Center itself, was conceived in controversy. Mayor Ben Stapleton pushed the project forward, but funds ran out as the Great Depression deepened. The city had to go back to the voters for another $2.5 million to finish the project. When it opened in 1932, nearly $4.7 million had been expended, $2 million more than the State Capitol had cost. Public art, intended to fill the prominent niches on the front, was never commissioned. The building also cost Stapleton his job as mayor. In time, it was generally accepted by the public as an important civic symbol, no doubt helped along by the longtime tradition of Christmas lighting which has brought the building its greatest fame.

94. City Annex (Old Carnegie Library) – 144 W. Colfax Ave. –
Albert R. Ross - 1910

Score: 5.7

Meets the Street – 6	Scale – 7	Integrity – 6
Public Spaces – 5	Mass – 5	Imagination – 5

This was a pet project of Mayor Robert W. Speer, whose plans to make Denver the "Paris of America" were expressed in buildings like this, well before Civic Center became a reality. Almost half of the money for this library came from Andrew Carnegie, allowing the city to consolidate its library collections for the first time. The classical Greek Revival facade was the work of a New York architect, Albert Ross. The building, three years in construction, served as the main library until Burnham Hoyt's 1956 library was dedicated, across Civic Center.

A sunken garden was created for the entrance after the library facilities were moved, and for years the Denver Water Board occupied the building. Today it houses city offices. Although it is the only functional building located within the Civic Center Park, early plans called for a similar, companion building to be built on the southwest corner of the park, thus creating a symmetry within the center. That idea never came to fruition, leaving this remnant feeling a little bit like a well-heeled straggler.

Civic Center Park at Colfax Ave. & Broadway is probably the crowning achievement of Denver's far-sighted, and effective mayor, Robert W. Speer. "Boss" Speer openly admitted, "I am a boss. I want to be a good one." The former Pennsylvanian came to Colorado in 1878 suffering from tuberculosis shortly after his sister had died of the same lung disease. After spending two years on a ranch where he made a full recovery, the young Democrat moved to Denver and got into real estate and politics. He was successful at both, and by 1885 the 30-year-old Speer was named Denver's Postmaster by President Grover Cleveland.

In 1890 he opened his own real estate firm, R.W. Speer and Company, then was appointed by Gov. John L. Routt as the token Democrat on Denver's three-man Fire and Police Board. The savvy director positioned himself between the two squabbling Republicans on the board, becoming its president. He cultivated a wide range of supporters, from the highest to lowest crusts of Denver society, who became the base of Speer's political machine. In 1901 the big break came when Bob Speer was appointed president of the Denver Board of Public Works, giving him control of half the city's budget.

Denver finally broke away from state control when it became a "home rule" city, with a strong mayoral charter, in 1904. Helped along by his machine and some 10,000 suspect votes, Boss Speer was elected mayor of the new, combined city and county. Speer had visited the 1893 World's Fair in Chicago and subscribed early to the "City Beautiful" movement. He determined to implement that ideal in the adopted city that had given him a new lease on life.

Denver Public Library, Western History Collection   Harry Mellon Rhoads RH-862

Robert W. Speer, a political boss with a sense of vision, became Denver's #1 booster, transforming his adopted city into a place of beauty.

One of Robert Speer's first acts as mayor was the creation of an Art Commission, headed by Henry Read, president of the Denver Art Association, precursor to the Denver Art Museum. Read, known as the artistic power behind the throne, first proposed the idea of a formal civic center that would harmonize with and extend the State Capitol grounds. The plan was grandiose and expensive, sputtering along against the opposition of the Denver newspapers that generally vilified Speer and his cronies (one of the few things *Denver Post* publisher Fred Bonfils and *Rocky Mtn. News* publisher Thomas Patterson actually agreed on). To counteract the negative newspapers, Speer debuted *Denver Municipal Facts* in 1909 to counteract the yellow journalism, the first city ever to publish its own publicity organ.

The Art Commission hired the national "City Beautiful" proponent, Charles Robinson, to produce a plan in 1906. The opposition choked on the $3 million price tag, and Robinson's plan was defeated by a narrow margin. Undaunted, Speer then hired international sculptor Frederick MacMonnies to draft a scaled-down version that shifted the plan south of Colfax, where it currently sits. Despite this plan's also being defeated in 1910, there was progress being made. Speer managed to acquire the land and get a new Carnegie Library constructed on the site before voluntarily leaving office in 1912. The reform government that moved into power proved ineffective, although they did hire the famous park designer, Frederick Law Olmstead, Jr., to review the previous plans and make his own suggestions. They proceeded to fire him, in 1915, after he had constructed the sunken gardens at the heart of the Civic Center.

By 1916, the voters, tired of the ineffective reform government, returned Robert Speer to the mayor's office with a new, "strong mayoral" charter and a squeaky clean election. Speer wasted no time and hired Edward H. Bennett, the successor to the father of the 1893 World's Fair, Daniel Burnham. Bennett immediately re-worked Olmstead's rustic scheme, formalizing it with a pair of colonnades at either end of the axis. One monument became the Voorhies Memorial, with its seal fountain and wading pool, while the southern end was adorned with a Greek Theater, prompting one wag to comment, "What the hell does Denver need a Greek Theater for? We ain't got that many Greeks here."

Court challenges inevitably arose from the opposition. Speer's plan to create an urban oasis had to survive a court challenge, even after it was funded. The state Supreme Court finally cleared the way in 1918, the year of Boss Speer's death. The Greek Theater was designed by Marean & Norton and opened in 1919. The Voorhies Memorial was completed in 1920 to a design by Fisher & Fisher. These two classical forums complement one another with Ionic columns and gently-curving forms that conform to the *Beaux Arts* tradition. Both monuments were decorated by muralist Allen True.

Denver may not have that many Greeks, but it boasts a handsome Greek Theater, set in the verdant confines of Civic Center.

History has treated Robert W. Speer more kindly than his contemporary journalists. He is considered, even today, to be Denver's greatest mayor, showing considerable vision for a machine politician. His achievements after 10 years in office are staggering. Besides Civic Center, Speer paved and lighted over 300 miles of streets: he built storm and sanitary sewers, promoted smoke abatement, channeled the ugly, flood-prone banks of Cherry Creek. He also built municipal bath-houses, championed a system of parkways, doubled urban park space, and created a system of mountain parks unrivaled anywhere.

A grateful city council re-named Cherry Creek Drive, Speer Blvd. in his honor, in 1910. He always considered his greatest accomplishment to be the construction of a **Municipal Auditorium (#44)** that brought music, culture, and fairs to the masses. He was a populist mayor whose first love was his adopted city. Half-way through his third term, Boss Speer suddenly contracted pneumonia and died in May, 1918. His funeral was held in his beloved Auditorium, where thousands turned out to grieve the mayor who vowed to make Denver the "Paris of America." He arrived here in 1878, a "lunger," sick and ready to die. He did in fact die from a lung ailment, but only after his adopted city had given him an extra forty years of life. He used that long reprieve well, and even today Denver benefits from Robert Speer's foresight.

95. Denver Public Library – 10W. 14th Ave. – Burnham Hoyt – **1956**, Michael Graves - **1995**

Score: 7.0

Meets the Street – 6	Scale – 7	Integrity – 7
Public Spaces – 7	Mass – 7	Imagination – 8

The original Burnham Hoyt Library, seen shortly after Gio Ponti's new art museum joined the ranks of Civic Center. Both structures have since been supplemented by major additions, yet each manages to maintain its own character.

Functionally, it is one building, but historically, it's two, hailing from two distinct styles and eras. The original part was Burnham Hoyt's last major project. Sensitive to the scale and *Beaux Arts* configuration of Civic Center, Hoyt skillfully blended classicism with the modern idiom. The most striking feature is a two-story half-rotunda that flows into the open park space like an Arcadian temple. This formal element is supported by inverse columns, outlining large, glassy bays that create a pavilion effect. Beige limestone harmonizes beautifully with the **Greek Theater** and is set in random patterns rather than fixed courses, reinforcing the building's asymmetry.

Despite the fact that virtually every surrounding structure has been replaced since its 1955 opening, the library continues a lively, civil dialogue with its surroundings. Even in today's milieu it feels fresh and vigorous. It has aged well, which is generally the sign of a good building.

Fast forward nearly 40 years to a bond issue, and a competition won by one of the Post-Modernism gurus, Michael Graves. A lot of Denver natives swallowed hard when Graves' new library design was first unveiled. It seemed to be everything that the Hoyt library wasn't: loud, polychrome, and overshadowing. It resembled a sequin-clad chorus girl seated next to a broker in a Brooks Brother's suit. At first the comic-strip penthouse and Pana-vision towers shocked the sensibilities, but time has softened its impact as the once-barren Golden Triangle landscape began to fill in. Now that the

Graves building has more to play off against, it appears less brash, more stately and urbane.

This is not a building meant for an isolated hillside, but for milling around and rubbing its urban shoulders with the neighbors. It possesses warmth and humanity – it's both serious and yet fun to be a part of. The big interior concourse is formal but friendly, as is the folksy Western History reading room on the 5th floor. One practical flaw is the scarcity of direct stair connection between floors, however.

There still remains the question of its relationship with the Hoyt library, to which it is joined like a Siamese twin. If the original building were not quite so forgiving, the pairing might have been disastrous, so the credit there goes to Burnham Hoyt, not Mr. Graves. Michael Graves awakened a hibernating street (13th Ave.) that again feels like a part of the city. As

The central concourse in the new Denver Public Library by Michael Graves.

far as people-magnets around Civic Center area go, the library is still the place that "rocks."

Opposite Broadway, the **Judicial / Heritage Center**, nick-named the "toaster and the typewriter," elicits far less enthusiasm. This Late-Modern pile by Rogers Nagel Langhart (1977) was born of a competition, but one can hardly imagine that the best entry actually won. The larger structure, clad in white granite, houses the state Supreme Court and law library. It is unusual for the fact that it is structurally suspended, like a bridge, from the two end towers, spanning a large vacant plaza. "The bridge to nowhere," aside from being an interesting engineering footnote, boasts little architectural character or value. The plaza is desolate and recently placed security barriers only fortify its forbidding image. The "typewriter" – actually the Colorado Historical Society and Museum – moved out of its stately digs on Sherman St. (#87) to inhabit a root cellar, which is where the museum exhibits, outlining the state's rich history, now reside.

96. ING – Security Life Center – 1290 Broadway – Michael Barber & Assoc. – **1986**

Score: 6.0

Meets the Street – 5	Scale – 6	Integrity – 6
Public Spaces – 6	Mass – 7	Imagination – 6

Built at a time when office construction had screeched to a halt downtown, this glass and stone edifice was a brave undertaking. It was also an important in-fill jump-start for a drifting neighborhood, bringing definition to a bombed out street, 13th Ave. A Post-Modern hybrid of glassy curtain walls set on a traditional, dark granite base, it reflects the azure Colorado sky beautifully while grounding itself firmly in the soil. Mr. Barber creates a prism effect by stair-stepping the corners, thus lightening the building's 15-story mass without sacrificing visibility.

From Civic Center and the State Capitol, the building provides a decent backdrop without imposing itself. It also gives the eye some relief when looking past the regrettable outlines of the Supreme Court Bldg, or the bland, state-owned Centennial Bldg. With the newer neighbors across Broadway, it is starting to feel less forlorn and more interactive. Hooray! Overall, ING is a successful building that uplifts its difficult environs.

Denver Art Museum – two buildings
97. 14ᵗʰ Ave. Wing – 100 W. 14th Ave. – Gio Ponti / James Sudler – 1971

Score: 5.8

Meets the Street – 6	Scale – 5	Integrity – 6
Public Spaces – 5	Mass – 6	Imagination – 7

What is an art museum if not a place to experience the everyday world from a subjective, surreal point of view? Art helps us escape the humdrum confines of daily routine; it is the soul's way of expressing what lies innermost, via the senses. If art momentarily releases us from the mundane, predictable patterns of existence then a building dedicated to art ought to welcome us into that looking glass world with a dash of wit. The Denver Art Museum's two wings, a generation removed in time, are united like an architectural odd couple, producing one of the more intriguing museums around. The original wing's exterior, by Milan's Gio Ponti, buttresses the SW flank of Civic Center: foreboding but not

The former entry to the Denver Art Museum conveys a sense of arrival.

forbidding in its medieval garb.

Funky, irregular crenelations enliven the parapet. Slit-like windows suggest arrow loops, psychologically fortifying this bastion of culture. Thousands of rectangular, glazed tiles give it a smooth, resilient, light-gray skin. The original elliptical entry chamber (60s sci-fi motif) suggesting womb-like intimacy, is much better than its "blah" new counterpart (my vote is to restore the old "sci-fi" entryway to its original purpose). Ponti created a visually engaging structure, which helps define Civic Center, and has avoided the bane of many 60s museums – growing dated. It performs well enough, considering its limited function - the enjoyment of fine art.

98. Fred Hamilton Wing – 100 W. 13th Ave. – Daniel Libeskind – 2005

		Score: 6.0
Meets the Street – 5	Scale – 7	Integrity – 5
Public Spaces – 6	Mass – 6	Imagination – 7

Daniel Libeskind's new Hamilton Wing at the Denver Art Museum plays off amusingly against the surreal towers and turrets of Michael Graves' library. The explosion of colors, forms, and textures can challenge the senses.

Gio Ponti's fortress is but half the story. The new Fred Hamilton wing soars south of 13th Ave. like some giant, mutated origami sculpture. Will Daniel Libeskind's virtuoso work finally establish Denver as an architectural mecca, or is it mere sales gimickry? No doubt his dazzling civic sculpture will become as controversial as the art within. Libeskind's shiny, metal-clad surface is an orgy of geometric planes, angles, and shapes. His type of Deconstructivism abhors the curvilinear, meltdown images of Frank Gehry. Instead of bulging, his buildings jut sharply, like a cubist's house of mirrors, in every conceivable (and perhaps inconceivable) direction. Jagged peaks and valleys abound, suggesting the native Rocky Mountain landscape in profile. Unlike mountains, however, the unconventional forms seem to defy not only gravity but reason.

Closer examination suggests a certain balance and proportion to it, even if it is a bit unnerving. My greatest concern is that some of the wildly angular voids will visually compete with the artwork, thus diminishing appreciation of both. A theater should never upstage the play, which is a distinct possibility here. A more practical concern is that small, irregular galleries spread out over many floors do not make for flexible space.

In the urban sense, this building neither upstages the **Denver Public Library (#95)** nor Civic Center, thanks to its modest scale and background location. Mr. Libeskind describes the building as a "Nexus" – a gateway between downtown and the neighborhood – which it certainly enlivens.

The Hamilton wing actually spans the entire 13th Ave. right-of-way, a dramatic cantilever pointing its titanium finger towards the heart of the pulsating city, signifying that ultimately, art owes its own vitality to the "polis" from which it springs. Libeskind likens it to Michelangelo's *Creation of Adam* in the Sistine Chapel, citing Adam's outstretched finger, though I suspect more hyperbole than symbolism in his metaphor. It's an abstract box for hanging pictures, not an icon. While tiptoeing perilously close to irreverence, Libeskind does seem to understand that no medium can afford to indulge in total reductio ad absurdum if it hopes to convey the aspirations of the human soul.

Byers-Evans House Museum holds its own against overwhelming odds, surrounded by the "avant-garde" art museum. Nowhere else do the "old and new" confront one another so boldly.

Tucked away in the overpowering shadows of the Denver Art Museum, the modest, Italianate **Byers-Evans House Museum** tends to its own business, providing a charming glimpse at Denver's past through the eyes of two early pioneer families. *Rocky Mountain News* founder, William Newton Byers, built this house for himself around 1878, after pioneering the development of Brown's Bluff a few years earlier. He must have been restless because, in 1889, he sold it to William Gray Evans, the son of Gov. John Evans, and moved further out to promote his South Denver real estate venture.

The encroaching city didn't seem to bother the family of William "Tramway Bill"

Evans, who added the south section in 1898. In the 1930s, it was Anne Evans who spearheaded the Central City Summer Opera Festival. Some part of the Evans family continued to live here until it became a museum.

The house itself is modest for a mansion, yet it is fairly typical of the domestic architecture that more well-heeled citizens enjoyed in the late 19th Century. It is undoubtedly representative of the homes that once lined 14th St. before that street's decline and commercialization. Across 14th Ave. there stood a Methodist Church, attached to the little Gothic Revival Evans Chapel that now graces the heart of the Denver University campus, where it was moved to prevent its demolition.

Walk a block south to 12th Ave. and glance one block to the right. **Balustrade** on the north side of 12th was one of the first upscale projects in the Golden Triangle, followed closely by **Century Lofts**, anchoring the south side of the street. Since then numerous buildings have filled in the asphalt-pocked landscape. Further to the west, **The Belvedere** at 475 W. 12th Ave., by Joe Simmons, rises much higher than the neighbors. It is probably the purest of the New York retro-style projects built between 2001 and 2004 by developer Craig Nassi. The Midtown, or Golden Triangle, area continues to fill in with various loft and apartment projects, as formerly gritty garages and auto service businesses give way to a budding, mixed-use arts district.

99. Byers-Evans School – 1125 Acoma St. - David W. Dryden –
1904   Score: 5.0

| Meets the Street – 5 | Scale – 6 | Integrity – 5 |
| Public Spaces – 4 | Mass – 6 | Imagination – 4 |

Named for the neighborhood's two most famous residents, the red brick Georgian structure, surmounted by a charming cupola, sat derelict after educating three generations of West Denver school children. After 100 years, an exterior renovation has finally restored it to its original glory. Today it grounds the so called "Golden Triangle" which is re-establishing itself as a residential neighborhood. Byers-Evans provides historical context as well as architectural stability. Its importance as a landmark is thus enhanced by its ripe old age.

Continue south on Acoma to 10th Ave. and turn left for one block to Broadway.

100. Gart Sports Castle – 1000 Broadway – Jacques J. Benedict -
1928   Score: 7.1

| Meets the Street – 7 | Scale – 7 | Integrity – 7 |
| Public Spaces – 6 | Mass – 8 | Imagination – 8 |

Built for Cullen-Thompson Motor Company by Denver's brilliant and eccentric architect, Jacques J. Benedict, this is absolutely the most ornate auto showroom this city has ever seen. The creamy Gothic / Renaissance facade has dressed up the drab, Broadway habitat since its inception. The detailing, from stained glass to elaborate finials and ogee arches, gives it a church-like aura, regardless of the winged hubcaps that symbolized the Chrysler Motor Corporation. This is Jacques Benedict's only surviving commercial building, although many of his residences, churches, and civic buildings – particularly libraries – are still extant (also see **Holy Ghost Church #53**). Cullen-Thompson was built around the same time as its famous parent structure, the Chrysler Bldg. in New York City. Both buildings exhibit the confident optimism pervading the American economy of the 1920s, shortly before Wall Street's fatal

Gart Sports Castle (see #100, following page) was first an automobile showroom. It is still one of Broadway's more outstanding facades with creamy, gothic finials piercing the azure sky.

crash. This building gives us a little taste of the heady consumerism that gripped Americans during the Jazz Age, only to slip away like a phantom in the 1930s.

Forty years later, car dealerships generally fled to the suburbs, where more land was available. Subsequently, this jewel was purchased by Gart Brothers, a sporting goods store, which glibly re-christened it "The Sports Castle." Since then it has carried that nickname, giving Gart's the kind of unique visibility and identity that no ordinary structure could ever hope to provide. A couple of years ago the exterior was cleaned and restored, and a rooftop tennis court was hidden from ground view, enhancing the building's appearance tremendously.

This is the end of our walking tours, but not the end of the story. The 100 buildings that we have looked at and rated represent the more important milestones in the city's building history, but such a list is hardly comprehensive. In the conclusion we rank the contenders, and perhaps stand them up against a few places in other cities, but for now, keep on walking. It's the best way to explore any great city, and Denver has miles of wonderful neighborhoods that we haven't even touched upon. *Bon Voyage!*

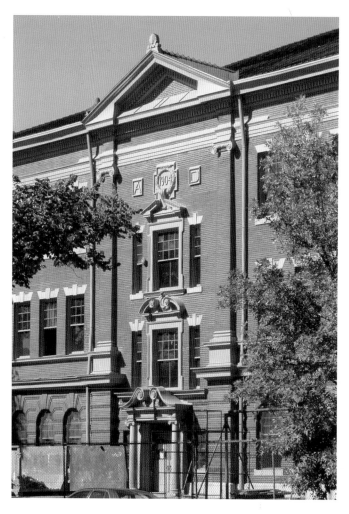

Byers-Evans School at 1125 Acoma Street recalls the Midtown area's history.

Cathedral spires at Colfax & Logan have defined Capitol Hill for nearly a century

Conclusion – Denver's Best Buildings

After all that walking, it's time to find a cozy coffee house and compare our results. What is downtown's best building, at least by our reckoning? It turns out to be the **Byron White Courthouse (#51)** by architects James Knox Taylor and Tracy, Swartwout, and Litchfield. The Courthouse scored 8.7 overall, nailing down one "10" for Integrity. All that beautiful Colorado Yule marble was meticulously restored in 1994 when the Post Office moved away and the entire building was rejuvenated for the courts. This building exemplifies everything we expect from any great public edifice: it is formal, dignified, commanding, yet humanly scaled.

Literally nipping at its heels, in second place, is our dark horse entry, the obscure **Mayer House (#9)** at 1702 Wazee, designed by Olson Sundberg Architects. It scored an 8.6 in spite of its modest dimensions and residential nature. Mayer House feels special because it recalls the great urban brownstone tradition and plays a very public role on its street.

Third place really should be no surprise, the stately **Daniels & Fisher Tower (#28)** at 16th St. & Arapahoe. Ever since its completion in 1911 the D&F Tower has represented Denver to the world. The slender campanile, artfully composed by Frederick J. Sterner, would be a credit to any Italian hill city. It might appear less ornamental than Giotto's 14th century bell tower in Florence (which the D&F Tower tops by 61 feet), but its form is more graceful and sculpted. Our campanile gets an 8.3 score. The city is rightfully proud of this architectural ambassador, but at the same time, we should feel some remorse for allowing its frail profile to be buried among lackluster high rises.

The Federal government also claims fourth place with the new **Alfred A. Arraj Federal Courthouse (#35)** located at 19th St. & Champa. Architects Anderson, Mason, Dale, collaborating with H.O.K., designed a "sustainable" building in a surprisingly fresh manner, contrasting with the Neo-Classical courthouse, diagonally across the street. Their bold, articulate statement reflects Denver's regional importance. Perhaps symbolic Federal architecture is rebounding after some painfully lean years (score: 8.1).

Rounding out the top ten, we have three buildings by the Denver firm of Fisher & Fisher in the fifth, sixth, and eighth slots, an very high success ratio for a single firm. Their **Colorado Business Bank (#37)** at 17th St. & Champa and **University Building (#41)**, one block away at 16th St. & Champa, exemplify the Fishers' creative genius. Seventh place goes to Curtis W. Fentress & Associates for Denver's best Modern skyscraper, **1999 Broadway (#54)**, enfolding J.J. Benedict's lovely **Holy Ghost Church** in its crystalline arms. Close on its heels, in eighth position, is the **Midland Lofts (#65)**, also by Fisher & Fisher.

Ninth place goes to one of Denver's most treasured buildings, the **Brown Palace Hotel (#71)**. The "Brown" finally puts Frank E. Edbrooke on our list, with what has become his signature commission (score: 7.7). It is hard to say whether Edbrooke made Denver a great city, or Denver made Edbrooke a great architect. Either way it was a symbiotic relationship from which both profited greatly. Rounding out our top 10, scoring 7.6, is the **Millenium Building (#8)** by Parkhill – Ivins Architects – another successful Lo-Do in-fill structure. It's at 17th St. & Wazee, just a skip and a hop from the second place Mayer House.

The next ten slots are very close in terms of scores, ranging between 7.5 and 7.1. Several ties are involved, accounting for the inclusion of 11 buildings in this group. Eleventh place, with a 7.5 score, goes to the **U.S. Bank Tower (#40b)**. **Holy Ghost Church (#53)** holds down 12th position at 7.4. Half a point behind this, and tied for 13th place, are the **Colorado State Capitol (#88)** and **Tabor Center (#30)**. (The nominal 7.4 scores are actually 7.35 rounded up.) Fifteenth place is held exclusively by **First Baptist Church (#86)** with a 7.3 score. Sixteenth place is another shared arrangement, at 7.2, among three contenders: **St. John's Episcopal Cathedral (#85)**, **Trinity Methodist Church (#73)**, and the **U.S. Custom House (#52)**. The **Wellington Webb Building (#91)** at Civic Center has a firm grip on 19th place, while **Gart's Sports Castle (#100)** and the **Kittredge Building (#67)** share 20th spot at 7.1.

Immaculate Conception Cathedral (#84), **Colorado Dept. of Education (#89)**, **16 Market Square (#17)**, and the **Denver Public Library (#95)** round out the top 25 buildings in our survey. Are these really downtown Denver's best overall buildings, from a public perspective? Even if you disagree, this book has served its purpose, which is to stimulate thought and discussion. My observations are certainly subjective, but they are also based on a systematic approach. I am not looking for the biggest, loudest, or jazziest statements on the block, but structures that contribute substantially to their urban contexts. Most importantly, they give the downtown area a real sense of place, and relieve the ubiquitous corporate tedium.

This guide makes no claim to be an objective appraisal. Nevertheless, it should sharpen every reader's power of observation. My own personal judgments are based on a systematic approach taken from stated design principles laid down earlier. Those principles are not about the size, visibility, or good press that a building may enjoy. Fame is not the game. A great building is the product of a clear, articulate vision, well organized, and carefully crafted. **Byron White Federal Courthouse** represents just such a vision that has inspired generations of Denverites. It may well be

Courtesy, David Eitemiller
The loggia – Byron White Federal Courthouse

Denver's best urban building to date. Hopefully the future will bring more such successes. Conversely, the least successful building in our survey is an over-sized container that is essentially anti-urban, despite its key location and high profile. The sprawling **Colorado Convention Center** fell below a 3.0 on our scale, suggesting that notoriety and glitzy photos do not a great building make.

The 50 top- ranked buildings are listed below, starting with the Byron White Federal Courthouse and ending with 1700 Broadway. You are free to agree or disagree with the scores. There is, after all, some degree of personal bias involved. There must be some balance however, as indicated by the variety of periods, architectural styles and building types represented on the list. Of the top ranked 50 buildings – 18 are office buildings, 7 are churches, 7 government buildings, 6 hotels, 4 retail stores, and 8 residential and miscellaneous.

Table 1.
Ranking of Downtown's top 50 Buildings

1.	Byron White Courthouse – #51	**8.7**
2.	Mayer House – #9	**8.6**
3.	Daniels & Fisher Tower – #28	**8.3**
4. *tie*	Alfred A. Arraj Courthouse – #35	**8.1**
4. *tie*	Colorado Business Bank – #37	**8.1**
6.	University Building – #41	**8.0**
7.	1999 Broadway Building – #54	**7.8**
8.	Midland Lofts – #65	**7.8**
9.	Brown Palace Hotel – #71	**7.7**
10.	Millenium Building – #8	**7.6**
11.	U.S. Bank (Colo. National) Tower – #40b	**7.5**
12.	Holy Ghost Church – #53	**7.4**
13. *tie*	State Capitol Building – #88	**7.4**
13. *tie*	Tabor Center – #30	**7.4**
15.	First Baptist Church – #86	**7.3**
16. *tie*	St. John's Episcopal Cathedral – #85	**7.2**
16. *tie*	Trinity Methodist Church – #73	**7.2**
16. *tie*	U.S. Custom House – #52	**7.2**
19. *tie*	Wellington Webb Building – #91	**7.2**
20. *tie*	Gart Sports Castle – #100	**7.1**
20. *tie*	Kittredge Building – #67	**7.1**
22.	Immaculate Conception Cathedral – #84	**7.1**
23.	Colorado Dept. of Education – #89	**7.0**
24.	16 Market Square – #17	**7.0**
25. *tie*	Denver Public Library – #95	**7.0**
25. *tie*	Central Presbyterian Church – #77	**7.0**
27. *tie*	Equitable Building – #49	**6.9**
27. *tie*	Blake Street (G.E.) Building – #5	**6.9**
27. *tie*	Palace Lofts – #15	**6.9**
30. *tie*	Mtn. States Telephone (Qwest) – #43	**6.9**
30. *tie*	Coors Field – #6	**6.9**

30. *tie*	Writer Square – #29	6.9
33. *tie*	Sugar Building	6.8
33. *tie*	Buerger Lofts – #36	6.8
33. *tie*	Fisher Mansion – #83	6.8
36. *tie*	Boston Lofts – #38	6.8
36. *tie*	Matrix Capital Bank – #56	6.8
38. *tie*	Larimer Square – #20	6.7
38. *tie*	U.S. Bank (Colo. National) – #40a	6.7
40. *tie*	St. Elizabeth Church – #23	6.7
40. *tie*	Denver Financial Center – #78	6.7
42. *tie*	Trinity Place – #72	6.6
42. *tie*	Adams Mark (Hilton) Hotel – #70	6.6
44. *tie*	Union Station – #2	6.6
44. *tie*	Capitol Life Center – #82	6.6
46. *tie*	Oxford Hotel – #10	6.5
46. *tie*	1670 Broadway – #74	6.5
48. *tie*	Hotel Teatro (Tramway Bldg.) – #24	6.5
48. *tie*	Magnolia Hotel (1st Natl. Bank) – #50	6.5
50.	1700 Broadway (Mile High Center) – #75	6.4

Don't be surprised that there are no actual "10s" (or even "9s") on the list. In fact, the median score for all 100 buildings turns out to be 6.3. Anything better than a 5.0 represents a reasonably good design. The relatively narrow range of scores (one-third fell between 6.0 and 6.9) reflects the composite nature of the scores - and accounts for the inevitable ties as we progress down the list. In order to score much higher than 8.5, a building would have to be an outstanding, world-class landmark. (I wanted a rating system that would work universally, not just locally.) Perhaps Denver is shy on world-class buildings, but then it is only about 150 years old. At that age, New York City hadn't even entered the Revolutionary War, and was considerably behind Philadelphia to boot. Even today, I don't know any New York building that would merit a perfect "10."

Let's rate the **Empire State Building**, possibly Manhattan's purest formal skyscraper, as an example. It soars magnificently with its gleaming Art Deco mast, poised like a centering beacon above the New York skyline. Despite being over-scaled to its neighborhood, the sprawling, plinth-like base and tapered setbacks seem to compensate for its excessive height. Its massing is as skillful as any tall structure ever conceived. It meets the street well, but it also hugs the property line greedily. The interior lobbies are spacious and hum with activity. Its highly stylized motifs exude the 1930s, but fall short of great public buildings like Grand Central Station and St. Patrick's. On our scale it gets – **Score: 8.4**

Meets the Street – 8	Scale – 8	Integrity – 9
Public Spaces – 7	Mass – 10	Imagination – 9

How about a Chicago landmark like the **Auditorium Building** by Adler and Sullivan, 1889. Perhaps the greatest Richardsonian spin-off of its age, the Auditorium influenced a generation of architects, including Denver's own Frank E. Edbrooke. A heavy commercial facade wraps around three sides, concealing a world-class concert hall - one of Louis Sullivan's great masterpieces of fluid form. The building's heavy mass and rugged base is not exactly elegant. Three massive Roman arches on Michigan Ave. psychologically draw the observer in. This building put Chicago into a whole new league as a meeting place when it opened and, in a sense, became the precursor to McCormick Place and the countless conventions which have become synonymous with the City of Big Shoulders. Let's rate the Auditorium on our scale, allowing – **Score: 7.9**

| Meets the Street – 7 | Scale – 7 | Integrity – 9 |
| Public Spaces – 10 | Mass – 6 | Imagination – 8 |

Our quest for the perfect "10" leads us all the way to Boston where few buildings in America could approach the **Boston Public Library** for architectural purity. Resting magnificently on Copley Square, across the way from H.H. Richardson's Trinity Church, this Italian Palazzo landmark was completed in 1895 by the New York firm of McKim, Mead, & White. It is possibly one of the most imposing and refined facades ever devised. A series of 13 rounded arches frames a phenomenal reading room on the second floor, accessed by a grand staircase, and stretching for some 218 feet.

This Renaissance Revival structure is impressively monumental to this day, even resting in the shadow of I.M. Pei's 60-story John Hancock Building. The Paris library that Charles McKim used as his model pales by comparison. This exceedingly sophisticated and urbane building more nearly suggests a "10" than any other I can think of in this country. I think it deserves a lofty – **Score: 9.7**

| Meets the Street – 9 | Scale – 10 | Integrity – 10 |
| Public Spaces – 10 | Mass – 10 | Imagination – 9 |

These three examples from other cities are merely meant as approximate comparisons, because every building, like any person, has its good and bad points. But architecture is to enjoy, and through closer observation we can enhance our enjoyment. If this book does nothing more than to help the reader notice and appreciate the many interesting buildings that become a part of daily life, it will have succeeded. Remember, too, that the best way to see things is, and always will be, on foot, at a leisurely walking pace. Buildings should be enjoyed close up, not from the window of a speeding car, so lace up your favorite walking shoes and go explore the city.

I hope this guide will alert the readers to the wealth of fine architecture in just one locality, downtown Denver, but that is only a start. Many other cities and towns, in Colorado and in every other state, have their story to tell as well. The next time you walk down a street in your town, look around closely and ask yourself, "what story do these buildings have to tell?" Every building is a sentence, every street a chapter, and every town is a book written in sticks, bricks, and mortar.

17th & Broadway highlights three distinct periods of Denver's architecural development.

INDEX

Author / Photographer

Francis J. Pierson, better known as founder of *Pierson Graphics / Maps Unlimited* is also an accomplished writer and photographer. He was born in Denver the same year that Dwight D. Eisenhower was first elected president. Although Pierson had little to do with the electoral outcome, he was proud of the fact that the First Lady, Mamie Doud Eisenhower, was a fellow Denverite. At an early age he began exploring every nook and cranny of his beloved city, save perhaps one, the old county jail.

Studies punctuated his early wanderings as well. By the age of eleven he understood the rudimentary principles of mapping and could rattle off every street name between Sheridan Blvd. and Yosemite St. by heart. A graduate of Denver's George Washington High School, he later studied at the Universities of Colorado, Cincinnati, and Metropolitan State College.

Mr. Pierson has enjoyed an exciting business career, working in architecture / urban planning, oil and gas exploration, publishing, and real estate. In 1979 he began Pierson Graphics Corp., creator of the *Pierson Guides* map and street atlas products, which he later sold to Mapsco, Inc. of Dallas, Texas. The next seven years were spent developing townhomes in Johnstown, Colorado — a project that also included renovating a vintage 1920s bus garage into boutique office and retail space. His most recent exploits, apart from writing this book, include music composition (producing a CD titled *Larkspur Suite*, a musical pictograph of the central Colorado foothills). He has composed various piano, vocal, and ensemble chamber works — and performs on both the piano and trumpet. In his own scratchy voice, he also engages in choral singing.

Love of history rivals his fondness for architecture and music, and it is not surprising that these varied interests would some day manifest themselves in printed form. His avid eclecticism identifies him as a generalist more than a specialist, nor would he have it any other way. His eccentricity is certainly mindful of the famous 19th century crank George Francis Train who made a fortune promoting real estate in Omaha and other Union Pacific railheads, and spent his later years spinning rambling tales to fascinated young listeners on park benches of New York's Madison Square.

Mr Pierson has five grown children: Paul, Katherine, Robert, Daniel, and Elizabeth (and three grandchildren besides). While not quite ready for park benches he remains an active bicyclist and resides in the charming Sunnyside neighborhood of North Denver, where he is the favorite of a little canine spaniel who answers to the call of "Dantee — hound of O'Brien."